D0807107

Joy Road

My Journey from
Addiction to Recovery

Joy Road

My Journey from Addiction to Recovery

♋ Julie Evans ♌

WoodstockArts

Woodstock, New York

The Joy Road sign that appears on the front cover stood at the corner of the author's
Woodstock, New York, property for many years. In 2016 when a snowplow knocked
down the sign the local highways department granted her permission to keep it.

Front Cover Photo: Author with Willi-Belle the goat in Woodstock,
New York, 1996.

Back Cover Photo: Author in ninth grade, Rochester, Minnesota, 1969.

Cataloging-in-Publication data
Evans, Julie, 1956-
    Joy Road : my journey from addiction to recovery / Julie Evans.
    275 pages : illustrations ; 23 cm
    ISBN: 9780967926896
1. Substance abuse—Religious aspects—Christianity. I. Title.
    HV5825.E9 2018
    261.8—dc23
                            2018948952

Book cover design by Melissa Williams Design
Printed in the United States of America

ᘓ Contents ᘔ

❧ Daddy's Baby Girl ❧

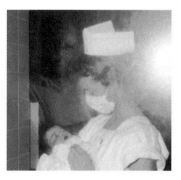

Newborn Julie with nurse. Jack Evans
is reflected in the glass. February 1956.

*I always figured that flash of light
was my spirit.*

In the first photograph ever taken of me I am one hour old, weighing just over five pounds, wrapped in a white blanket. My hair is full and black. In the nursery of St. Mary's Hospital in Rochester, Minnesota, a nurse is holding me. My daddy's reflection appears in the glass that separates us. He is looking at me tenderly. There is a flash of light visible on the glass. These days I have come to believe that light was my spirit waiting to climb into my body once I knew for sure that Daddy really wanted me, his third baby girl.

As I heard it, Jack and Bette Evans thought I was going to be a boy, and they were going to name me Jimmy. Daddy needed a boy he could teach how to build and how to fish, and maybe even how to use a bow and arrow and ride a motorcycle. But I was a girl, and I would be their last baby. My aunt Lois once told me that Mama had already gone through the change but I sneaked in there anyhow. My parents were both forty-three years old when they had me.

෨

I don't know how my parents met or how they navigated the world. I don't know how my dad wooed my mom, or if it was my mom who seduced him. I don't know of a single sexy, romantic, embarrassing, or challenging moment they might have faced as young newlyweds. I don't know if they traveled together or if they danced or if they fought nd I have no idea how they made decisions or how they treated each other. They had their first child twenty years before I was born, so by the time I came along maybe they were just worn out.

I'm not sure why I used to holler for my mama in the middle of the night and wait for her to slip into bed with me. I don't know why they named me Julie. I don't know why Mama got drunk every day. I don't know why Dad had a colostomy bag on when I accidentally went into the bathroom when he was taking a bath.

I do know I was embarrassed to have such old parents.

෨

All the other kids' parents were in their twenties when mine were nearing fifty. My dad had emphysema and coughed all the time, spitting into his handkerchief or slipping open the car door to spit on the ground.

My mom was always with me. If I was downstairs, she was downstairs. If I was upstairs, and she was still awake, she would be with me. We were inseparable for the first eleven years of my life. She would beg me to stay home from school so we could go junking, "on a safari," as she liked to call buying old furniture so I could refinish it. I liked staying home with Mama—until mid-afternoon, when she wasn't herself anymore. She drank too much, and it worried me terribly. I'd hunt for her hidden bottles like buried treasure. When I found them, I'd pour out a few inches and add water so maybe she wouldn't be so drunk when Daddy came home at night.

ॐ

My dad was bald when I was born and used to shave the sides of his head every couple of days. I also saw him shaving his armpits once. He had some scars on his back, where my sister Cyndi told me he'd had to have his arm sewn back on. It had been torn off when he grabbed our neighbor, Marney Brumm, the time the boat they were riding in hit a sandbar and she went flying. Marney said my dad saved her life.

After that boat incident my dad started asking Marney's son, Geordie, to help him do stuff. I hated when Geordie helped my dad do things that I should help him do. I hated being left out just because I was a girl. I would run to my room and lock my door and plot and plan a way to get my dad to notice me. I started to hide important things under my bed, things that Dad would need, like peanut butter and hammers and car keys and the garage door opener, so he would have to come to me to find them.

I made a point of knowing where things were and how they worked. When I heard Dad raising his voice about moldy food or wormy cereal, I started to clean everything so Mama wouldn't get into trouble. It was fun. I rearranged the furniture once a week and organized drawers and cupboards. I vacuumed and raked the shag carpeting just like the man who installed it showed us. When Daddy came home, I'd stand outside each room I'd cleaned and ask him to inspect it, wanting him to notice each drawer or the shine on each piece of furniture. I wanted to be good enough for him, to even be his favorite. I wanted his Surety Waterproofing trucks to say Jack Evans and Daughter, Inc.

ॐ

When I was eight years old Daddy bought me a cute but grumpy little pinto pony named Pogo. It was one of the greatest days of my life. The horse barn where we kept Pogo was near Daddy's warehouse, and I rode there almost every day to visit him. I felt glamorous while riding along the road, people craning their necks to see me.

I took English riding lessons from Mr. Gilbertson, and I loved cleaning the stall and brushing Pogo. I discovered that the secret to training a horse is just to love him. Talking to Pogo helped me through some rough times. Pogo became a champion show pony, but after two years my legs got too long to ride him. Mr. Gilbertson said I had potential but needed a real horse to take me to the next level. I knew he was right, but I also knew how expensive thoroughbreds were. My dad worked hard, sweat streaming down his face every day, but he would never be able to buy me a fancy horse.

Still, I figured out a plan that might work. I saddled up Pogo and rode over to the warehouse to suggest that maybe I could work for him and earn the money to buy the horse myself. Dad told me he'd call his friend Slim.

Oh no, not Slim! I thought to myself. Slim was a hick, a backward cowpoke who wouldn't know a thing about a good horse. I cringed and slunk away, looking ridiculously tall as I rode Pogo to the bowling alley next door, and asked Billy, the waitress, for a bowl of her chicken dumpling soup.

Six months later, on a cold and windy February day while I was taking a riding lesson at the barn, somebody hollered out that my dad had just pulled up in an old guy's beat-up truck that was hitched to a horse trailer. I slid off the horse that I had been working out, stiff-backed, and walked out to meet my father.

As I rounded the corner, Slim spit out a long stream of thick, brown liquid that hit the ground and froze. He lowered the ramp of the trailer, and out backed the manure-stained hind end of a fuzzy-coated white horse. I stood there holding my breath as the rest of the horse appeared. I'd wanted a big brown or black horse, but when this white horse turned his head and looked at me, it was like I was seeing God.

He was perfect. I ran across the icy parking lot to meet him. As I took the lead line, I felt power flow into me.

"His name is Omar," Slim said. I put my hand under Omar's soft muzzle and he licked me. I turned and saw my dad smiling.

∽

Seven years later, when I was sixteen, I held tightly to Daddy's thin hand, praying he would come out of a coma after a twelve-hour brain surgery. Please don't let him die, I cried to myself. I don't know enough about him and I don't know enough to live without him. My mom had died the year before, and I was still devastated over losing her. And now my dad was in a coma, and I didn't even know his parents' real names, only that his dad was called "Butch." His mom had dementia by the time I met her, when I was three years old. All I knew of her was that she insisted on taking away my Betsy Wetsy doll, while Daddy said, "Let her have it, Jubie."

Three weeks later, on the morning of my seventeenth birthday, I walked into the Neuro-Intensive Care Unit of St. Mary's Hospital and found Daddy's bed empty. A nurse who'd seen me arrive pulled me out of the room by my arm. I didn't want to leave but she insisted. Still holding my arm, she led me down a corridor and opened a door to another room. My dad was sitting at a table, with two black eyes and a white turban of gauze on his head from the surgery. A birthday cake with lit candles sat in front of him next to a bouquet of yellow roses. Daddy was smiling and whispering the words to "Happy Birthday." It was the best day of my life.

∽

Only three months later, I sat in another room in the same hospital, but this time in the Oncology Unit. I held Daddy's warm hand in mine and came clean about two important things. I told him the truth about how Mom had died in Greece the previous summer: how my older sister

Julie, Jack, and Kenny on the young couple's wedding day, June 28, 1973.

My daddy lived long enough to give me away.

Cyndi and I had put Mom on a bus in Amsterdam and then hitchhiked to Athens to save money. I told him how Mom had ended up drinking ouzo for three days, then sliding into delirium and alcohol poisoning before being taken to a strange hotel where she was left all alone—until I found her days later.

Daddy also deserved to know the truth about me. I could no longer bear to have secrets. I told him I had met somebody two days before Mom and I had left for our trip to Europe and that we were living together. His name was Kenny Israel and he was helping me survive. Older and more experienced, he'd grown up in New York and had been sent to the Mayo Clinic to get clean.

Later that day, when I told Kenny what I'd done, he went to talk to my dad and asked for my hand in marriage. Kenny told me later that it was the best talk he'd ever had with anyone. He said it made him feel like somebody really believed in him. "I want you to give my baby the kind of life she is accustomed to," Daddy had told him.

We chose Mom's birthday as the day we would marry. It was as if I knew exactly what to do, even though I was seventeen and wasn't one of those girls who dreamt of her wedding day. The invitations were sent out, we had registered for gifts, and we must have rented a place to hold the wedding, but I don't remember that part.

A month before our July 26 wedding date the doctor told me that Daddy's cancer had found its way into his bones. If we wanted to get married in time for him to be with us, we'd have to do it immediately. Kenny and I met with the hospital chaplain, and two days later, on June 28, 1973, we said our vows in the hospital basement in front of nearly every doctor and nurse at St. Mary's Hospital in Rochester, Minnesota— the same place I'd been born.

I remember looking over at my dad when the chaplain asked, "Who gives this young woman to be married?" Dad was wearing a white golf shirt with bold blue and red lines running through it. I had given him that shirt two Father's Days before and he'd never worn it. Weighing ninety pounds and barely able to breathe, he pushed down hard on the arms of the wheelchair, struggled to his feet, and said, "Her daddy does."

❧ I ❧

GRACE

It is unearned love—the love that goes before, that greets us on the way. It's the help you receive when you have no bright ideas left, when you are empty and desperate and have discovered that your best thinking and most charming charm have failed you. Grace is the light or electricity or juice or breeze that takes you from that isolated place and puts you with others who are as startled and embarrassed and eventually grateful as you are to be there.

—Anne Lamott, in *Traveling Mercies*

Chapter 1

❦ Hitchhiking to Key West ❧

Two years later, Kenny and I were living in Phoenix, Arizona. I was a full-time journalism student at Arizona State University and worked part-time at a mall so I could pay to send Kenny through jewelry school. On the weekends, we would climb the mountains and look for semi-precious stones, like turquoise, jasper, and crazy lace agate. We bought our own lapidary equipment.

One day I came home from school to change clothes before work and found Kenny slumped on the couch, unconscious, with a thick, brown leather belt tying off his right arm and a nasty-looking syringe sticking out of a swollen half-inch vein. His lips were white, his face was blue, and he smelled bad; his eyeballs were rolled back in his head. Plus, he wasn't breathing. I braced myself, pulled the needle out, undid the belt, slapped him across the face, and pulled him to the floor to get CPR started. He opened his eyes, took a huge breath, and threw up all over both of us.

He had every excuse in the world, but he couldn't explain this one away. I wanted to get as far away from him as possible. There was no one I could call for help and nothing I could do but move out. I thought that maybe that would jolt him. I moved in with a girl from school, but I didn't fit into her wild life on campus. I moved back home and started packing up the house. The man I had married in the hospital basement, the man who had promised my dad he would take care of me, dove full force into his addiction.

At night I'd lock myself and the dogs in the spare bedroom and try to ignore his ranting and puking and misery. Finally, I got out of our lease, emptied the house, and packed our two desert dogs in the car. I took Kenny to New York to his parents' home and bravely returned to Minneapolis to resume my life. I didn't know until I got there that I had no life in Minneapolis. I had a miserable time. I wanted to get back to college and find a place to live, but nowhere near campus allowed dogs. I had to give my babies away and it broke my heart. Then, I started to drink too much.

My cousin Charlie helped me get a job as a nursing assistant in a cancer hospital. I worked with patients who were both horribly sick and scared, and I went to school at night to prepare for my premed application. My life felt very serious, until I met a girl named Tanya in my public-speaking class. She was everything I wasn't—artistic, lively, and free. We decided to get an apartment together.

After a year of living with Tanya, I got a call from Kenny. He said he was playing his guitar and singing the blues in some bar near the beach in Clearwater, Florida. He claimed he was clean and lonely and couldn't live without me. I had missed him, ached for him, and cried my eyes out over him for two years. It would've taken more nerve *not* to see him, but it was still hard to get up the nerve to go to him.

Tanya helped me find an auto transport company, and I got paid to drive someone else's car to Clearwater. I dropped off the car and took a cab to the address Kenny had given me. When I got there I found only his ugly, empty apartment; his huge, drooling Saint Bernard; a short-sheeted and flea-infested waterbed on the cold, dirty linoleum floor; and no Kenny. I fed the dog and smoked one cigarette after another. I waited a day and a half and then hitchhiked to Key West, not so much because I wanted to but because I could.

In those days, Key West was a place where you could ride an old-fashioned bicycle with foot brakes and no gears. This was Key West before it was utterly gay or totally condo. You could be whoever you wanted to be without anyone giving a damn. I got the first job I asked for.

By nightfall of the first day, I had a bike, a job, and a disgusting little apartment of my own. I didn't call Kenny. On the second day I was straddling the rafters of a new little tennis shop on Duval Street. The owner had hired me the moment he learned I was Jack Evans's daughter. My dad had worked for him back in Minnesota fifteen years before. When I told him my name he asked if I was Jack Evans's daughter. I said, "Yes, my dad taught me everything I know." I didn't mean that I knew a thing about building or painting. Still, he hired me to prepare the shop for business.

As I straddled the rafters to paint the beams, terrified of falling to my death, a heavyset girl appeared beneath me. Barefoot and scantily dressed, with ankle bracelets on her stump-like legs, she had flat, greasy hair with mica-like flakes of dandruff lying on either side of her combed part. She said her name was Peggy. She wanted to show me her artwork, which she would sell me at a discount because she was hungry and broke.

No was not an option. I didn't have the heart to say, no, I don't want to see your art, and no, I don't want you standing there talking to me when the owners walk through the door. She returned ten minutes later holding up pictures of Stone Age-type cartoon characters having sex. I was embarrassed, but I needed to silence this fat, greasy girl, so I climbed down from the rafters and offered to get her some lunch.

We walked across the street to a small Cuban diner. I was fasting at the time, which is much like not eating, only holier, and was completely ignorant of the power of Cuban coffee on the third day of a fast. As I sipped the rich, sweet coffee and watched Peggy dipping smashed Cuban bread into vibrant yellow egg yolk, I felt a little bit the way I had the first time I ever did speed. My mind was clear and I felt renewed, energized, and fortunate, like I could do anything. When Peggy begged me to help her find a ride home, I figured she just needed someone a little less freaky-looking than herself to help her get where she was going. We walked along the road to the water's edge. I looked at her more closely to see if she was both crazy and dangerous. She told me the place was called Mallory Square and that everyone came there to watch the sunset.

That's when a cute long-haired guy she called Love 22 drove up behind us in his school bus. He opened the door and handed me a twenty-two-dollar bill that said, "Twenty-two is the mystical number to the secrets of the universe." It had a picture of a pot leaf and of Love 22 himself. Suddenly it hit me that the next day would be my twenty-second birthday. Meanwhile Peggy was pulling on my arm, trying to get me to walk down the boat ramp into the water. I was high on Cuban coffee, but not that high.

"Where do you live? On that island covered with Christmas trees, or what?"

"Yes," she said, and we stepped into the water at precisely the moment when a powerboat pulled up to the boat ramp. I asked one of the two guys in it if they'd take Peggy to the little island across the way.

"Sure," one of them replied. "If you come along, we'll take her anywhere she wants to go."

Once we were on board the guys each popped open a beer and turned the boat around. Three extremely fast powerboat minutes later, we were arcing to the right around the edge of what really *is* called Christmas Tree Island, and there, basking in the sun, next to the calm sea, were four naked people. I helped Peggy from the boat, and realized midway through my goodbye that the boat guys were not going back to Mallory Square.

I was going to have to get out with her and somehow find myself a ride back home. I leapt barefoot from the boat and landed directly on the sharp spines of a sea urchin. The sting hurt so much it took my breath away and I almost passed out. I was reeling in pain as the boat guys reversed the engine and began to back away. I felt a cold sweat standing in that warm seawater, and when I picked up my throbbing foot to inspect it, I saw a puncture hole but no quill. I took a deep breath and tried to put weight on my foot.

I saw him when I raised my head: dark skin, saggy buttocks, and a thick black braid. He was wearing a headband and a suede medicine bag. A long, limp, suntanned penis hung between his legs.

Chapter 2

❦ Fu Moon on ❧
Christmas Tree Island

He saw me, too. Me with short-cropped black hair and a deep tan. Me with an orange bikini under a now wet and see-through white T-shirt and white cotton painter pants—just me, nervous as hell about being around a bunch of relaxed-looking naked people. Examining my injured foot gave me an excuse not to make eye contact. He stepped into the water and approached me. Just act natural, I told myself. I let my foot slip from my grasp and looked at his naked body and into his chocolate-brown eyes. An eagle feather was tied to his leather headband. His teeth were yellow with nicotine, his black moustache drooped, and his skin was dry and leathery.

"Welcome," he said. "I am Fu Moon."

"Julie," was all I said, with a sort of inner curtsy/spasm/head-nodding kind of thing.

"Welcome to Christmas Tree Island," Fu Moon said, extending his ropey right hand. "Let me show you around." I took his hand and had my first walk with a completely naked total stranger. We approached the others.

"This is Shelter," he said, as we walked up to a small Peter Pan-like man floating on a piece of wood and playing a delicate wooden flute. "Shelter, this is Julie. She's a friend of Peggy's."

I wanted to correct him and say no, no, I'm not a friend of Peggy's, but instead I freed my trembling hand from Fu Moon's shamanic grip and held it out toward Shelter. He was beautiful, with long, flowing hair and an intently caring gaze. (He made no move to shake my hand, so I let my hand float down toward the water and simply nodded, which I hoped portrayed my phenomenal sophistication.) He said nothing.

Fu Moon and I then walked through the calm, warm seawater toward the shore, where Peggy and two other women sunned themselves on a worn rubber mat with a McDonald's logo on it. Fu Moon held my hand tenderly as we approached a hairy-legged woman, clad only in Birkenstocks, with long auburn hair hanging nearly to her waist. I envied her for her large breasts and muscular legs, and she had more pubic hair than any three people combined. She rose from her mat to embrace me.

"This is Prairie Rose," said Fu Moon. "She does much of our cooking. Prairie Rose, this is Julie; I'm hoping she'll like it so much here that she won't want to leave."

Shocked by his words, I forgot about my injured foot and stepped down, causing a searing pain when I tripped on the edge of the mat. I stumbled and Fu Moon lurched forward to catch me, his long, limp penis swinging like a pendulum, nearly hitting me in the face. Prairie Rose reached to catch me as I fell, clutching me to her breasts.

At that moment a gorgeous man emerged from the cluster of pine trees wearing nothing but a long knife strapped to his waist. He had thick, wavy blonde hair framing his chiseled and deeply tanned face.

"They've got Mexican Joe," he said, and the entire tribe began to move.

"What did he do this time?" asked Fu Moon as he picked up three quarter-size stones from the beach.

"I'm not sure," said the man with the body of a Greek god. He noticed me and smiled, adding, "but Joe was here drinking a beer early this morning."

"That's Dreaming Eagle," said Fu Moon in a weird way that made me wonder if he was being possessive. The whole tribe seemed to be set into some sort of we-have-to-save-our-brother mode. I smiled at the one woman I hadn't yet met. She looked Middle Eastern, bookish, and unshaven. She set the book she was reading, *The Lion, the Witch and the Wardrobe*, onto the faded rubber mat and said her name was Julia. I quickly introduced myself, but there was no time to chat, as Fu Moon yanked my hand and we all began to jog away, me on my sore foot wondering how I had landed here in a tropical pine forest with a naked man I didn't know.

We all ran the well-worn paths through the scrub and pine, passing an old man sitting next to a campfire. I found out later his name was Billy. He was fully dressed and drinking what appeared to be coffee. He didn't seem too pleased to have six naked people running through his camp. Fu Moon explained our intrusion in one word—"Joe"—and the old man took a deep breath and went back to his coffee. I thought he looked crazy so I avoided eye contact, relying upon the power of rudeness to keep evil at bay.

As we glided and limped along, Fu Moon pointed out the various dwellings people had built. Shelter had a tree house jutting out over the water, and Julia also lived in a sort of tree house with a long shelf full of books. We passed a hut made of soggy cardboard that belonged to Peggy, and finally we jogged past a geodesic dome covered in hides with primitive pictures of buffalo and bear.

"That's where you will sleep tonight," whispered Fu Moon, my own personal scary guy, "and later I will help you build your own place to sleep, when you are in your moon-time."

Are you out of your mind? I thought. But, as if in a dream, I just kept limp-jogging, listening, and wondering who this overconfident, underdressed maniac actually was. Me? Stay? Here? I didn't think so. These were not my people. This was not my place.

A few minutes later we came upon a beat-up-looking man lying on his side on the shore. Fu Moon let three stones fall to the sand and reached for Joe's hand to pull him to his feet. Everyone gathered around, murmuring and chastising him for stealing beer out of a powerboat over at Mallory Square. Fu Moon put his hands on Joe's shoulders and told him he had to straighten up and be careful. He also asked Joe if we could borrow his canoe later to get over to Mallory for the sunset drum jam.

There's my ride home, I thought. Having found Joe, we returned to the other side of the tiny island, and the girls and I sunned for a while and talked. Prairie Rose and Julia were both Jewish and really smart. Julia had studied at Antioch, and Prairie Rose had gone to the Pratt Institute in New York City. They knew a lot of stuff I didn't know. They said that Fu Moon really liked me and they'd never seen him so attracted to anyone before. I was flattered and tried to imagine what he looked like with clothes on.

I dozed in the sun and when I woke up Fu Moon was sitting next to me. It looked like he had cleaned himself up a bit, and he invited me to see his home. I followed him up the path to his dome. On closer look, what I'd mistaken for hides were actually a heap of regular blankets, though some were painted with buffalo or bear. As we walked through the door flap, I realized the structure was made of little trees all bent and tied with thick cord. The dome was more of an egg shape than round, and the inside was dark and dank, smelly like an old bachelor's unwashed bath towel. Still, Fu Moon had set it up pretty nice. He lit a little gas lantern, and I noticed sheepskin and bear rugs on the floor. More smells of animals and earth . . . and man filled my senses.

As Fu Moon reached for me I felt like he was an old wise man, a teacher, maybe. He seemed so exotic even if he did kind of stink. I hadn't had sex with anybody for almost two years, but it just seemed the right thing to do. We made awkward love on the mildewed, scratchy blankets.

An hour later, I sat staring at the fire wondering why I was here and why I had made love to a man I didn't know. I felt embarrassed and watched the fire to keep from having to look at anybody.

Prairie Rose and Fu Moon prepared an early dinner of kasha (which I'd never tasted), broccoli, and tahini, served in a dried coconut bowl. It was the best food I'd ever eaten. We sat around the fire while Shelter played guitar and Dreaming Eagle sang to us, sounding a bit like James Taylor with laryngitis.

As the girls cleaned up, Fu Moon prepared a large serving of food, and then we walked it over to the old man Billy's place. Fu Moon told me that Billy was a retired shrimper who no longer had a need to do anything more than wake up in the morning and sleep under the stars at night. Billy stood when we approached and shook my hand. He offered me a cup of coffee, cowboy black and strong, and his smile was so real and so toothless that it made me smile. Billy's campsite was simple and clean. I figured all those years living on a boat had helped him condense his life down to the bare essentials. I wondered how all these people had ended up here on Christmas Tree Island.

Leaving Billy with his supper, Fu Moon and I went back to his place to get a few things before we canoed over to the mainland. When he went inside his dome to dress, I waited outside and listened to the water. I inspected my foot, which still hurt terribly when I put weight on it, like a hot needle was stuck in there, but I couldn't see anything to pull out.

It was half past six by the time Fu Moon and I left the others and stepped into Mexican Joe's narrow handmade canoe, me in the front and Fu Moon in the back. We started out on the near side of the island where we could see Mallory Square. People on shore were already beginning to gather for the sunset ceremony.

When Fu Moon put his paddle in the water, the sea seemed rough and splashed up against the sides of the canoe. Being the girl who had said maybe six words all day, I still didn't say much, at least not out loud. Inside I was praying for traveling mercies, wishing myself back to Key West, saying sayonara to my day among the naked. I was also saying goodbye to twenty-one, as I would wake up the next day a twenty-two-year-old. I reached into my bikini top for my Love 22 bill. I hadn't done much with twenty-one and holding that bill I hoped that twenty-two would be a better year.

As I stared at my Love 22 bill, I realized the canoe was rocking like a bucking bronco. Fu Moon was paddling hard but the canoe wasn't moving forward. The sea had become a tempest, the air heavy, and the sky had turned a dark steel gray. How the hell did that happen so fast?

Fu Moon would not be intimidated by choppy water and paddled like a madman, but the canoe didn't budge. When I put my hands down to hold onto the sides, my Love 22 bill fell into the churning sea. I looked back toward Christmas Tree Island and saw we'd nearly washed back up on shore. The others were nowhere in sight. I curled my toes to keep from freaking out.

The canoe remained in one place as if stuck in a vortex. Thick dark clouds filled the sky above and all around us. It looked like the sea wanted to swallow us alive. Fu Moon paddled as hard as a man can paddle, yet we went nowhere. The boat rocked so fiercely I felt queasy. My skin stank like the mildewed blankets in Fu Moon's hut, remorse rising up in me, colliding with the fear of the moment and hitting my stomach with a thud.

I was angry I'd slept with him, angry that I couldn't go home, angry that I'd come to this stupid place at the end of the world, angry that I didn't know how to live a successful life, and most of all angry that Kenny hadn't been where he was supposed to be. Like a pouty teenager, I wanted to get out of the boat, slam the canoe door shut, and stomp off to my room. I wanted to rise from my hand-hewn seat, walk across the water, and strangle Kenny.

All this when out of nowhere a feeling of peace came over me, as if I had fainted and was tingling back to life. I saw it all very clearly. I would build a dome. I would cover my dome with yellow canvas and have a clear thick plastic skylight on top so I could see the stars at night and feel the sun by day. I would live out this adventure and become somebody.

I remembered a little clearing we'd passed on our heroic jog to save Mexican Joe. That's where I'd live, not in Fu Moon's stinky hut, not in my gross little apartment, but here, on this little island in a yellow dome, with Jews who thought they were Indians.

When Fu Moon reached across the canoe and grabbed my arm with his firm grip, the heat of his hand told me I was damp and freezing cold. We didn't need to talk; his grip was language enough to direct me out of the boat. Stepping out of a spinning canoe into warm water that looked like blood felt eerie, but the water ceased to swirl the moment it had me in its salty embrace. I stood beside the canoe knee deep in the now calm water, hearing drum beats in the distance. When I looked at Fu Moon, I felt I was seeing him for the very first time. Without his penis showing and his hair loosened from its braid, he didn't scare me at all.

I had this gut feeling that I was finally on my big adventure, just like my sister Cyndi had her time in Kenya when she was about my age, living in the bush and learning to speak Swahili. Or like my oldest sister, Bevy, when she'd lived in Malibu where baby whales played just beyond her front yard. It was my turn now. I just knew that there on Christmas Tree Island I would figure out who I was.

When Fu Moon stepped back into the boat, I did too. He put his paddle in the water, and again we were caught up in some personalized maelstrom. In this together, we were natives in a dugout canoe in a place of confusing waters. Again, without a word, we took our turn stepping out of the boat. He stood before me and whispered with reverence, "Tell me, what is the water saying? I can't make out the words. It is speaking only to you."

I felt singled out and special, but somehow blank. I figured he was right, but I didn't know what to say. I raised my eyes to answer him in words I didn't know yet, and there behind him was the most gorgeous masterpiece of a sunset that I had ever seen. Stunning colors lit the sky. Tears filled my eyes and I knew what to say: "I'm not supposed to leave."

He stared at me and I summoned my voice.

"I'd like you to show me how to build my house," I said. The words, like humidity, hung in the air. He nodded, turned, and pulled the canoe back to land, where he tied it to a tree.

We sat down. I looked out over the now calm water and felt something let me go.

I had held it together long enough. For the first time in my life I didn't have anybody to take care of or worry about. I was free.

We rose and padded our silent way along the worn trails back to Fu Moon's camp. He started a fire and brought out a bottle of liquor, a flute, and a blanket. He braided his hair, took off his clothes, and laid out a blanket for me to sit on. He then reached deep into the medicine pouch dangling from his waist and brought out tobacco and rolling papers. I watched as his earth-dirty, feminine fingers fashioned the first cigarette of our time together. I watched as he held a strike-anywhere kitchen match, wondering where a naked man would strike. He used his thumbnail to bring the match to life, took a lung-filling drag from his skinny little cigarette, and handed it to me. Even though I had tried to quit smoking, I took it from him and held it, allowing it to cool after he had steamed it. I inhaled and it made me feel dizzy.

He opened the bottle of liquor and passed it to me. As I put my hands on the bottle, the campfire hit a cache of sap and thousands of sparks exploded into the sky around us, turning the dusty campsite into a sort of carnival. In the light of hundreds of little sparks, I looked at Fu Moon and saw an image of myself reflected in his eyes. I looked like a different person, like someone who was interesting and happy and free.

One spark landed on his head, burning his hair and scalp. Another landed on the blanket he'd set down for me, and I stamped it out with my injured right foot. I only just then realized that I must have left my sneakers in the powerboat when the boatmen had dropped Peggy and me off. It seemed a lifetime ago.

The smell of Fu Moon's burning hair mingled with the aromas of tobacco, pinesap, and ocean. We sat for a while under the stars and watched the fire, and when he got up to go inside his buffalo dome, I rose and went with him. He offered me his narrow futon, then settled on the floor next to me on a sheepskin, covering himself with a mildewed blanket.

CHAPTER 3

ଓ TWENTY-TWO ഔ

Jack and Bette Evans
in Oklahoma, 1934.

I wish I knew more stories
about my mom and dad.

When I woke up, it was February 18, 1978—my twenty-second birthday. I had slept in my dirty clothes on a hard futon in a cave of sticks with a man whose real name I didn't know. I was sad. My birthday always made me feel sort of sad. It used to be because nobody understood me, but now it was because there wasn't anybody around who even knew me well enough to not understand me. I wondered if Kenny was thinking of me and feeling awful that he had let me down. I wondered if my mom and dad could see me. I wondered if God had a plan for me.

I got up off the hard futon and pulled back the dome's flap, looking for Fu Moon. There he was, bending over the fire and reaching for a coffee pot. I tried not to notice his butt crack. He handed me a coconut shell filled with coffee. I smiled and asked him to follow me to the little clearing where I wanted to build my new home.

Lowering his tough-skinned naked self to the ground when we arrived, he agreed it was beautiful. He didn't have to tell me that he would prefer I live with him in Buffaloville, the dome of many smells, but I knew it.

Fu Moon motioned for me to sit opposite him. He reached to his right, picked up a long stick, and broke it in half. There was a short log between us, and he began to use it as a drum. Instead of shutting his eyes, he allowed his eyeballs to roll upward in their sockets. His eyelids fluttered, making him look like a Saturday matinée zombie. I tried not to panic and stared at the log.

He continued to drum, and the rhythm became strangely relaxing. I noticed that the small scrub trees around us were moving, even though there was no breeze. Some of these skinny little trees were bending to the ground. His drumming stopped abruptly, and he rose and pulled a Swiss Army knife out of his dangling pouch, opening the tiny saw. He moved swiftly from bowing tree to bowing tree, murmuring and sawing quickly through the animated trees like a skillful surgeon.

He laid the small stack of little trees next to me and told me to pray. I wasn't sure what he meant. When I was young we went to a Methodist church for a very short while, where I would suck on Life Savers until it was time to go. Sometimes I also went to church with my best friend, Libby, but I had no idea what the priest was talking about. The closest I'd ever come to praying was when I was riding my horse and taking care of my mom and dad. Those were the only times I felt really close to God. If I'd truly known how to pray, maybe I could have saved my mom or dad from dying, or rescued my marriage. I wondered if this magical man knew something about me that I didn't know, so I bowed my head and tried to pray while Fu Moon fashioned the little trees into arcs and hoops. When I looked up, he told me to gather nuts and little stones to make a ceremonial circle on the building site.

The vibe was so strange, with the trees bowing and the monotonous drumming, that I jumped at the chance to move around. I headed down a path, my eyes peeled for little objects. I'd spent a good deal of my childhood looking for treasure, so this was right up my alley.

After walking the little island collecting small found objects for my circle and saying hello to the people I'd met the day before, I came upon a campsite that I hadn't seen yet. I saw the body of a small, dark-skinned person lying in a fishnet hammock, snoring. I figured it was Mexican Joe. His camp was like a junk shop: two mismatched kitchen chairs—one wood, one metal—three broken Styrofoam coolers, a big rusty anchor, knotted yellow nylon rope, an awesome pile of sea glass, a stuffed pink elephant with one missing eye, a couple of wooden crates, and a bunch of empty Budweiser cans. I loved the two big shade trees where his hammock was tied.

Turning to leave his campsite, I saw the waking world of Key West across the topaz blue sea. A bunch of fishing boats were already on the water, and a few people stood on balconies. I was standing there, just appreciating the idyllic beauty, when I felt a biting pain on the back of my head. Putting my hand up to the place where I'd been stung, I felt another missile of some sort strike my hand. I turned to see Mexican Joe with a third stone ready to launch from his middle finger and thumb.

"Stop it—that hurts!" I yelled.

"Get outta here!" he yelled back.

I put my finger on my skull, and found there was already a gumball-sized lump forming.

I walked back through the pines feeling awful and scared. I kept touching the little bump on my head, wondering if this was my warning not to live here. I was angry and walked fast, following the path around a large tree, where I ran full force into Billy wearing his green army fatigues. He fell onto his back and lay there like a turtle, waving his arms and legs in a useless attempt to get back on his feet. I reached out my hand to help him, and all the found objects for my ground-blessing ceremony poured onto his chest.

"Here, let me help you," I said, my hand outstretched. He started laughing and so did I and together we gathered my little treasures.

When I got back to my campsite, Fu Moon had already erected the frame of what would soon be known as Julie's house. I let all my little objects fall gently to the ground in front of him and watched with amazement as he formed them into a beautiful mosaic.

"Thank you. I can't believe you did this for me," I said, really meaning it.

His hand hesitated only for a moment as he continued to move the seeds, shells, stones, nuts, twigs, and feathers around until they took on the shape of a heart. Then he silently stood, dusted his hands off on his narrow outer thighs, and walked away.

I was blown away. I love hearts. I love little things. I loved that he did this for me. It felt like the perfect birthday present. Maybe twenty-two really is the mystical number to the secrets of the universe, I thought. I had a fascinating new life and I was going to live in a dome on an island full of naked people. I didn't think I'd ever be comfortable enough to walk around without any clothes on, but I was going to dance like there was no tomorrow at every sunset ceremony, and I'd spend my time making mobiles of feathers and shells and reading Julia's books. I would learn why trees bow and why seas churn. I planned to buy some postcards when I got to town and send them to my sisters, Cyndi and Bevy, telling them about my exciting new life.

About ten minutes later Fu Moon came back into my camp. He said we needed to bless the land with tobacco and must call on the spirit world. He began to sing a song that sounded terrible, kind of like a cat getting run over. He took a pinch of tobacco and pushed it into a long-handled clay pipe. He murmured a prayer to the east, the west, the north, and the south before he inhaled, then spun the pipe around two times and handed it to me. I inhaled and handed it back to him. It seemed like a good ritual, until he took his bony arm and swept it through the beautiful mosaic heart he'd made, scattering all the little objects.

"This is the way it is done," he said.

I don't get it, I thought, confused.

He got up to return to his own camp and prepare for our journey across the water. I didn't like him anymore. I had thought he was holy and kind, but now he just seemed petty and mean.

I was tired and grimy and looked forward to a hot shower. My teeth felt fuzzy and my contacts could have been growing into my corneas for all I knew. No sooner had Fu Moon left than he came back. His hair loosed from its braid, he wore brown corduroys, a plaid flannel shirt and dried-out, dusty red flip-flops on his narrow feet. I followed him to the canoe.

Fu Moon paddled us across the now calm water toward Key West; a trip that took three minutes in a powerboat took twenty minutes in a canoe. I tilted my face to the sun, remembering it was my birthday. We hit shore with a thud, my reverie broken. I stepped out of the canoe boldly, as I thought an expert would, nearly capsizing the boat and my dressed-like-a-lumberjack helmsman.

The learning curve for my new life was daunting, and I was exhausted. My feet felt torn apart as I half ran, half limped up the boat landing of cement and crushed shells. We tied the canoe to a bush. I couldn't wait to shower and change my clothes.

Fu Moon intended to grocery shop for the group, and I'd heard him promise to pick up good, thick cardboard for Peggy to build an addition to her already extensive cardboard home. We left Mallory Square and passed a textile warehouse. Fu Moon led me around back to a dumpster full of scraps and discarded fabric. He said it was where everyone got the material they used for building their homes. He left me there and headed in to town.

I stared at the dumpster. I couldn't do it. I was Jack Evans's daughter and I wasn't about to dig through garbage for what I wanted. The trust fund that Daddy had left for Cyndi and me (Bev had long been managing on her own) afforded us four hundred dollars each month, and with my job at the tennis shop I could walk into that warehouse and buy yellow canvas and clear plastic, even though I was pretty sure that my dad would cringe if he knew what I was doing.

Fu Moon and I had agreed to meet at five o'clock back at the canoe. I'd asked him to stop by my little apartment to take a shower but I doubted he would. For a moment before he left me at the dumpster, I'd felt sorry for him and kissed him goodbye on the cheek, noticing the bags under his eyes. I realized that his whole body seemed kind of deflated.

Back at my awful apartment, I felt relief that I didn't have to live there anymore. Big, ugly palmetto bugs scurried away as I pushed the door open. I made lots of noise before I entered the bathroom, allowing the bugs time to slip under the toilet or behind the tiles. Before I reached into the medicine cabinet to get my contact lens case, I caught a glimpse of the new me in the mirrored door. I looked strong and happy.

My eyeballs were so sore I had to work carefully to get my lenses out of my tired eyes. I tried never to sleep in my contacts but I hadn't had a choice on the island. Now I'd have to wear my thick glasses. When I picked them out I'd hoped they'd make me look like my beautiful older sister Cyndi, but instead they gave me that haunted, I-have-escaped-from-a-mental-hospital look. More disgusting bugs ran for their lives when I let the shower run to steam up the room, a trick I'd learned from my mom. The hot, pounding water washed over me, soothing my aching body.

While I showered, I felt hope rise up in me, realizing I could do whatever I wanted to do. If I decided I didn't like the island, if I found life there too hard or too earthy or too out there, I could just live here if I had to. I turned off the water and reached for a clean, thick white towel. Relaxed after the shower, I felt exhausted, but I had to go to work.

I dressed in a pair of light-blue painter pants and a matching T-shirt, and pulled on my hiking boots so I could climb the ladder and navigate the crossbeams I would be painting. Though I never wanted to be seen in my glasses, I left the apartment with them on, trekking down the two blocks to Duval Street just before ten o'clock, happy to be on time. I rounded the corner and stopped dead in my tracks when I saw Dreaming Eagle peering into the window of the soon-to-be tennis shop, as if he knew I worked there. I had such a crush on him.

Peggy must have told him. I don't think I'd managed to say more than two words to him. I couldn't let him see me with my glasses on, or maybe I should, maybe that would put an end to my fantasy of being Mrs. Dreaming Eagle. I threw back my shoulders and strode across the street and walked directly into a bicyclist. He swerved to miss me but tipped over anyway. He was the small Cuban man I'd seen at the diner the day before. I pulled him up off the pavement and tried my best to quiet him, but he was mad and also drunk. Dreaming Eagle swept in to save the day. He joked with the guy, whose name, I overheard, was Tatato. He picked up his bike for him, made sure it was okay, and helped him get back on the seat. Dreaming Eagle then turned to look at me and winked. I melted and froze.

He was wearing a harem diaper-shorts type of thing, and although his legs were gorgeous, strong and tan, he looked ridiculous. When he smiled I noticed he was missing a bunch of important teeth and I couldn't imagine making love to him. I smiled but then panicked when I saw my employers strolling up the street toward us. I wanted to scream, "Run!" Or, better yet, "Disappear!" Or maybe, "Just don't let them see your missing teeth." And most definitely, "Do not mention anything about me living on the island." Instead, in the tiny nugget of time that I had to prepare myself, I simply turned, smiled, and introduced Ed and Claire Daly to Dreaming Eagle.

Ed was the first to notice Dreamer's attire.

"Hey, those are incredible shorts. Claire, honey, maybe we could sell something like that in the shop. Don't you think it would turn heads?"

Claire hadn't taken her eyes off Dreaming Eagle's aquamarine eyes, but while her thick-waisted husband spoke, she raked her eyes down the front of Dreaming Eagle's body, finally coming to an abrupt halt at his groin. I broke out in a sweat.

"Oh, yeah, sure," she said to her husband, her eyes seeming to invite Dreaming Eagle into her secret garden.

I no longer cared that I had on thick, ugly glasses, and impulsively kissed Dreaming Eagle on his perfect cheek, catching just the faintest smell of rot, and silently adding fresh breath to that list of things that mattered to me. Point made, I looped my arm through Claire's and began to walk across the street to the shop. Ed chattered on about the shorts, Claire whispered questions about Dreaming Eagle, and I became more uptight. We unlocked the double French doors that provided access to the group of boutiques soon to open. Our space was off to the right, but the rafters I was painting were directly above our heads. We all looked up at the same time. Stunned that I had done such a good job, I thought of my dad and wondered if maybe Claire and Ed were thinking of him too.

While they busied themselves with other things, I set up my ladder and got out the paint. Two hours later, after painting two rafters and one set of crossbeams, I climbed down the ladder and walked across Duval to the Cuban diner where I'd had my first strong cup of thick, rich, sweet coffee. Tatato's bike was propped up out front, making me hesitate before pushing open the very light, wooden screen door. I set a little Betty Boop wind chime in motion as I entered the room; everyone turned at the sound. Most of the clientele in the diner were fishermen or shrimpers, and I liked being part of the local scene.

Ten minutes later, buzzing from the caffeine, I went back to the shop and painted for three more hours. I finished all of the beams and was glad to put away my ladder, seal up the paint, and call it a day. I left Ed and Claire a note and headed over to the fabric store that Fu Moon had pointed out.

As I rounded the corner, I saw three people rifling through the fabric-filled dumpster. I wasn't sure if I should say hi to people going through garbage, but as it wasn't exactly garbage-garbage, I said, "Hello." No one said hello back. I walked into the store and right away found the bright-yellow canvas I wanted, running my hand over it like it was mink. It didn't matter what it cost. I had to have it. It was a sign, I thought, to find exactly what I had imagined. I bought the whole bolt. The old couple who owned the place actually gave me, free of charge, the clear, pliable plastic that I planned to use as a skylight. Once I'd told them what I would be doing with it all, they got me needles and thread and some seam sealant.

When I left the cool of the store and hit the hot afternoon pavement of Key West, I felt victorious. Now that I had the makings of my luxury pad safely in hand, I wanted to see about taking the next day off so I could focus on my dome. However, I'd have to put my canvas in the canoe so I wouldn't have to explain what it was to Ed and Claire. As I laid my fabric in the boat under the four narrow, hand-hewn seats, a jolt of fear seized me. Now that I knew more about praying, I said a few magical words over my stuff and headed back to the shop. I told Claire I'd see her in two days and went over to meet Fu Moon.

CHAPTER 4

❧ DANCING AT SUNSET ❧

Approve or disapprove, I wasn't sure what Fu Moon thought of me, but my fabric was nowhere to be found. He was in the process of becoming the island Indian man again—shirt off, hair braided, corduroys rolled up—and he had his knife out. How could I have known him only for one day? Then I remembered it was still my birthday. I felt a little like Dorothy in Oz. This was so not Minnesota anymore.

"Hi, Fu Moon," I said. "Was it okay that I put my fabric in the boat?" It was awkward to have to always call him by two names but I didn't know if I should call him Fu or Moon. He didn't answer. I went from bouncy to self-conscious and then he smiled. What a relief: he wasn't mad. He didn't have laugh lines, so when he smiled his whole face lifted up, giving him the appearance of a wild critter baring his teeth.

"I paddled it over earlier so there would be room for you to sit during the ride home," spoke the man of many lessons, the man who had not forgotten the importance of making a woman comfortable in a canoe, the man whom I had known for little more than thirty hours, the man who, just like every other man I'd slept with, made me realize how quickly I could go from hot to cold.

"Thank you for doing that. What did you think of it? I mean, do you think it will work? Did you see the clear plastic for my skylight? Am

I going to be able to sew that together? How do you keep the rain from getting in the stitch holes?"

He raised his hand to shut me up and smiled again.

"It will be fine," he said softly, motioning me to pick up the end of the canoe as he raised the bow, and we carefully carried it to the water. I gracefully got into the canoe. As we glided along I allowed my hand to touch the water. It was a perfect blue, gentle, warm, and salty.

I have always loved the ocean. The first time I saw one I was a skinny, self-conscious seventeen-year-old Minnesota girl walking toward it, two strides behind Kenny. We were at Jones Beach in New York, and I felt bare-naked in a two-piece swimsuit. We had to step over towels, around boom boxes and picnic blankets. It seemed so ominous, loud and scary, and I slowed down as I approached the surf, while Kenny dove into the frothy sea. When he turned to look for me I was amazed that he was mine—his wet hair slicked back off his face and his lean body all tight muscle. He smiled and I ran into the ocean for the first time. He caught me in his arms when a big wave came.

I looked up and saw Fu Moon with his head tilted to the side, just watching me. Man, I was back there with Kenny. I wondered how I'd ever live without him. I tried to step out of my memories and into the present. My lashes, heavy with tears, dried in the late afternoon sun. I took a breath and looked up to see all the naked folk jumping up and down, so not Gilligan's Island. Breasts bounced and penises swung. I looked back at Key West, afraid that someone might see them, but there wasn't a single person in sight. It seemed this tribe could exist like fairies.

The girls leapt up and down, raising their arms and hollering. When we got closer I could hear them screaming different things:

"Hurry!"

"Come on!"

"Paddle faster!"

"Get out of the boat!"

With the strength and manner of a wrestler, Peggy walked toward us—to grab the boat and drag us in, I figured. I thought Fu Moon might be mad, but he was chuckling. He tossed Peggy the rope and she hauled us in like a pro. Then everyone descended on us. The men helped Fu Moon, the women got me, somebody got the boat, and we were off running again. I was afraid they'd left my little overnight bag behind, but then I saw it hanging from Dreaming Eagle's shoulder.

They all stopped so abruptly that I ran right into Julia. And then they broke into song. They were singing to me. My island mates parted like the Red Sea and there it was in all its magnificence: my home, replete with the heart-shaped mosaic returned to its front yard. My dome was built and was covered with yellow canvas; the roof was clear, allowing light into the structure. I hugged every one of them.

There was a little hinged door made of double-thick canvas and weighted with shells and clever little doodads to close and open it. It was wonderful. A little papaya tree had tiny blossoms on it, and my new friends were all smiling as they sang the final chorus of "Happy Birthday."

Julia pulled back the door and I saw that they had made me a bed and fashioned a nightstand out of driftwood. There was a little rug, an oil lamp, and two books lying on what looked like a feather pillow at the head of my bed.

Masterfully sewn and sealed like shingles on a roof, it must have been created from the bottom up, with overlapping as it went. I thanked everybody and they set about the task of preparing dinner. Awestruck, I just stood there, staring at my little dome. I stepped inside. It was like a holy place. Like a clearing in a forest when a shaft of light beams through, or like entering my parents' bedroom late at night when I was scared of monsters, I let the door fall closed.

It was bigger than it looked. I could easily stand in the center of the room. The bed was almost six feet long and there were still two feet at each end. Even though it was a dirt floor, it was smooth like velvet, and someone had placed a tiny rag rug next to my bed so I could clean my feet. I lay down and looked up through the clear skylight. I could see clouds and a lone bird flying high up in the sky. I closed my eyes and dreamt.

My mom wasn't dead. She was alive and not exactly well, but not dead. Not dead of alcohol poisoning, she was alive and just living a different life, one that didn't include me, her youngest daughter. I needed to find her, to talk to her, and make sure she wasn't mad at me. I checked the mailbox; I tried to figure out the phone. I didn't know what to do. This was the closest I'd gotten to finding her in years. I was both relieved that she wasn't dead and terrified that she thought I'd abandoned her. Where was Dad? I thought I heard him calling my name.

And then, in stages, like a scuba diver coming to the surface, I realized my island mates were calling, trying to wake me for dinner. With much regret I forced myself to leave the search for my mother and woke up.

I padded through the forest toward the sound of voices and the inviting smell of a campfire until I came upon my new friends, my current family. It was dinnertime. Prairie Rose passed around a smooth wooden serving platter covered with pita sandwiches. I'd never had anything like it, made from sprouts, avocado, and cheese. Fu Moon had picked them up at The Rainbow, a health food store in Key West. He said he thought I'd like them. Next they passed around the group's little coconut bowls, heaped with rice, tahini/soy sauce, and perfectly cooked cauliflower. We ate with chopsticks.

Fu Moon instructed everyone to clean up and get ready for sunset at Mallory Square, where the men were going to drum and we girls could dance. I loved dancing to a rhythmic beat; my first boyfriend, Scott, had been a drummer and I started dancing to his drum solos when I was only eleven years old. Since I was ready to go, I offered to clean up and put out the fire while everyone took some time to get ready. Fu Moon walked dinner over to Billy and brought along his bottle and his tobacco. Julia quietly showed me where to scrape, wash, and dry everything and where they kept their kitchen stuff.

Julia had small, delicate fingers, a big bubble of a nose, kinky dark hair, acne, and small, beadlike eyes set in very plump cheeks. She had generous lips and a self-conscious, big-toothed smile, and it seemed as though she had never shaved her armpits or her legs. Julia wore Birkenstocks and usually had a book in her hand. On our few trips to the water's edge to rinse out the two pots and eight coconut bowls, she told me that she was totally crushed out on Shelter. We finished the dishes and headed to the other side of the island where everyone waited for us in the canoes.

Fu Moon paddled the canoe I was in and Dreaming Eagle manned the other. I sat in the front of our boat and had a clear view of the most anatomically stunning set of muscles I'd ever seen. How could any man possibly look that good? Our boat rocked fiercely, and I pulled my eyes from Dreaming Eagle's physique to Fu Moon's dehydrated image behind me.

When we arrived at Mallory Square, a good-sized crowd had already gathered. It was seventy-some degrees and the sun would set in another thirty minutes.

Spackle buckets began appearing, along with drumsticks, dowels, a conga, and a set of bongos; Fu Moon had brought a flute. Key West was the most laid-back place I'd ever been. People wore caftans, moo moos (as we called them back in Minnesota), Indian cotton dresses, Bermuda shorts, and swimsuits with scarves for a bottom. Dreaming Eagle, from whose muscles I'd had yet to calm down, took the cake in his lavender harem diaper-shorts.

Most of the Christmas Tree Island girls wore tai chi shoes, ugly little black canvas numbers that wore out in a minute or two but were still easier to dance in than flip-flops or Birkenstocks. I wore tight yellow overalls and my orange bikini top. Looking out across the water, I was amazed that I couldn't see any indication that people lived there—naked people who built domes for one another, naked people who sang "Happy Birthday," naked people who played spackle buckets very loudly and incredibly well at sunset.

Legend says that when the sun sets in Key West you can actually hear it sizzle as it hits the surface of the water. My Christmas Tree Island clan lit a wand of sage and sweet grass to clear the air of negativity. They offered up thanksgiving to Great Spirit for the day and for the sun and then played their hearts out. Their incredible sound pounded right through my body. My feet moved of their own accord, my hips undulated to the energy of the earth, my face shone like the sun, and all these body parts kept shining and moving and worshipping until the air had gone still and there was no music.

I stopped, reined my body in, and turned to see what the people were staring at. There it was: the huge sun sinking into the ocean, coloring everything in its path magnificently. Prairie Rose passed around a hat and most of the tourists and some of the locals put dollars and coins in it for the musicians and dancers. That's when I learned how the tribe made its grocery and supply money.

After the tourists went back to their swanky hotels, we packed up our things and paddled homeward. Peggy had retrieved a huge garbage bag filled to bursting with fabric parts and pieces from the dumpster near the square. The other boat sported her new addition, which looked to the undiscerning human eye like six large, flattened cardboard boxes from U-Haul. Her uninhibited grin, showing all four of her remaining teeth, got some nourishment from the night sky. Again, I let my hand rest upon the water as Fu Moon paddled us home, but this time when Kenny came to mind it didn't make me sad.

Someone had gone shopping during our drumming ritual, and three spackle buckets overflowed with food and supplies—one with plenty of toilet paper, which we used sparingly. The first time I'd needed a toilet on our little paradise island I'd panicked until Julia showed me our communal bathroom, a driftwood platform over a narrow three-foot hole. After you relieved yourself you'd sprinkle a handful of powdered lime, leaves, and pine needles into the hole.

The girls had told me that Fu Moon was brilliant and could fix anything. He had designed the restroom area, built the fire pits, and helped everyone build their dwellings. Just hearing about it intoxicated me. My dad had been the same. In a way, being on the island was like being at home. I had my own room and, if I got into trouble or needed something fixed, I could just ask Fu Moon.

I was excited to spend my first night in my new dome, in my own bed, on this fantastic island in this faraway place. Fu Moon handed me a gift bundle as I walked back to my camp and asked me to join them all around the fire once I got settled in. He handed me a flashlight and said there were matches in the bundle but not to leave my lamp burning if I came to the fire. Island rules. I went back to my camp, opened my little door and laid the bundle down, letting it fall open. There were matches, a roll of toilet paper, one of those pita sandwiches, an apple, a small pocketknife with an eagle on it, a cup, a canteen of water, bug repellent, and one chocolate Hershey's Kiss. The bundle itself was made of thin hammock net, and Fu Moon had thoughtfully placed ropes needed to tie it to trees on either end. I put everything away, lit my little lamp, and took out my contact lenses, being careful in the dim light to put them safely in their little compartments. After putting on my cumbersome glasses, I picked up one of the books Julia had given me.

I must have fallen asleep within minutes, but I hadn't blown out my lamp. I could have gotten into serious trouble for that. A fire on Christmas Tree Island could be a disaster. I woke up hearing someone outside and seeing a flashlight. I retrieved my glasses from where they'd fallen under my shoulder and put them on. I began to make an earnest apology, but it wasn't Fu Moon. It was Dreaming Eagle, and he smelled delicious—like ocean and coconut and man. His arms felt silky and massive as they wrapped around me. My heart was pounding. I wanted him. I turned my head to the side and reached up to take off my glasses. I opened my mouth and searched for his lips. I ran my hand along his cheek, feeling his face wet with tears and realizing his body was trembling. We fell onto my narrow bed, locked in our embrace, and I held him while he cried. I couldn't help but stroke him after he fell asleep. I must have fallen asleep myself somewhere in the midst of trying to figure everything out. He never told me what was wrong, and by morning he was gone.

As the sun rose I just lay there on my soft, low bed and pondered my day. For the first time in years I didn't have an agenda. I didn't have to go to school or to work or go do something for somebody. Since I'd been a little girl I'd programmed myself to get up and go somewhere or sit down and do something, so this transition into my mellower life was unfamiliar and uncomfortable. With the warm and gorgeous day, heaven really, my discomfort passed. I would still have to go to the mainland six times each week for another week or two, but then, once the tennis shop was open, I would work only four days a week, from ten to eight.

But today I was free. I pulled on my little bikini and a fresh set of clothes, put my contacts in my eyes and toothpaste on my toothbrush, poured myself a cup of water, and went outside to brush my teeth. Butterflies fluttered around the papaya blossoms and the morning light created a rainbow on the dew of a spider web on a pine branch. The heart mosaic had gotten misshapen by my nocturnal visitor, so after putting my stuff away I straightened it up and headed over to Billy's place for a strong cup of coffee.

Billy sat on an old crooked chair wearing faded army fatigues. A canvas cowboy hat hung on his back and his hair was combed into thick roadways. He smiled his semi-toothless grin and nodded for me to pull up a milk crate as he poured me a cup of campfire-brewed coffee. I added sugar, took a long sip, and stared at the fire.

"What do you think so far?" asked Billy, breaking the silence.

"Being here makes me realize how uptight I am. I don't get why nobody wears clothes."

Right then Fu Moon came around the bend, his medicine bag swaying in the morning light.

Billy whispered, "Don't worry none about being uptight; most of these people are wacko."

"Morning," Fu Moon greeted us, with a sharp forward nod of the head. He kept walking, obviously on his way to the toilet.

"What's his story?" I asked.

"All I know is he used to be a big shot for some company, had a family and everything," whispered Billy. "He used to weigh almost three hundred pounds and had a heart attack that got his attention. Probably what turned him into an Indian."

"What do you mean, turned him into an Indian?" I whispered back.

"His name was Simon Gross; he ain't no Indian. He lived in that same town where Dick Van Dyke lived."

"Dick Van Dyke? You mean from *The Dick Van Dyke Show*?"

"Shhh," Billy shushed, "these folks can hear a fish fart."

"Did they all come down here together?" I asked, fascinated.

Fu Moon bounded out of the woods and my question evaporated into the sound of waves washing up on shore. Finished with my coffee, I offered up my milk crate and took my cup to the water's edge to rinse it out.

I put my cleaned cup far up on the shore, took off my pants and shirt, and walked in my bathing suit down the beach and into the chilly salt water. Ribbons of fuchsia and lavender streamed across the sky, though the sun had fully risen. My right foot still felt tender but it was good to walk on the ocean floor.

Even out a ways, the waters were calm and peaceful. I turned underwater to swim back and my hand touched something big, very big, and incredibly smooth. My body tensed but I willed my hand to open and feel what was under it. The instant my hand touched it, it moved quickly, inviting my hand onto its fin. The creature rose in the water and looked right at me. It was a dolphin.

Chapter 5

❧ Extraterrestrials ❧

A circle of magic surrounded me and I barely knew what to do. I loosened my grip on the dolphin's fin but then felt the smooth body of another behind me, six in all. One of them pushed its nose into my hand as another swam under my arm until my hand came to rest on its head. They let me pet them and hug them and I swam with them as if in a dream. They were with me and then they weren't. Within moments of their departure, I saw them far off toward the horizon, swimming and leaping into the air. I swam toward shore and found a shallow spot where my feet could touch solid ground. I was vibrating with excitement. I looked to the shore, hoping that someone had seen my encounter with the water angels, but the worn-out McDonald's mat was empty. Then I saw Mexican Joe peeing on a tree. He was looking right at me. I held his gaze as I slowly rose from the water.

Mexican Joe, wearing blue jeans and a white T-shirt, had zipped up by the time I made it to shore. As I stepped onto the warm sand I lost all desire to talk to anyone about my dolphins. It felt like my secret. I put on my shirt and pants and walked up the beach, staying with my reverie as long as I could.

Mexican Joe had a beer in his hand. It was seven o'clock in the morning.

"Good morning, Joe, I'm Julie, the one you attacked with your stones."

He nodded. He was small and wiry like a boxer, with a beautiful face, his hair a shiny black and his eyes a chocolate brown. I stood a foot taller than he did.

"They l-liked you," he stuttered. "They don't like everyone."

"It was amazing" was all I could find to say.

I combed the beach for shells with holes in them so I could make something. Finding feathers, sea glass, and a shark's tooth, I had the first makings of a mobile, but I needed fishing line, so I went to find Fu Moon. He had the contents of his dome spread out all over his site. I don't know if it was a twist of fate or he if actually realized that all of it stank to high heaven. His blankets, rugs, and clothes were spread over bushes and hung from trees. He was beating dust clouds out of a blanket while I stood nearby waiting for him to see me. He nodded and I walked toward him.

"How long have you been here, I mean, on this island?"

"Not long," he said.

"What made you come?" When he didn't answer I started to leave, but he stopped me when he handed me a tattered picture of a huge, smiling fat man.

"That is me when I was twenty-two."

I handed back the photograph.

"You look pretty happy."

Something softened in Fu Moon.

"I thought I was, but then one day it all changed."

"What happened?"

We sat down on a nearby log.

"I had a heart attack, my wife left me, and I just decided to start over." He picked up a handful of sand and let it sift through his fingers.

"How long ago was that?"

"Ten years. I came here last September."

"How old are you now?"

"I'm forty-two."

It wasn't that different from Kenny and me. All our good times ended when I found him with a needle in his arm.

"Thanks for sharing. I appreciate knowing."

He nodded and I asked him for some fishing line, which he went to fetch.

With everything I needed in hand, I went back to my little dome, sat on my futon, cut several pieces of fishing line, and began threading them through the shells and wrapping them around little pieces of sea glass and feathers. Tying the first fishing knot, I remembered the day I met Kenny. I was sixteen and had just returned home from a year spent in Mamaroneck, New York, as a first-year domestic exchange student.

I wouldn't have met Kenny if my old boyfriend hadn't called and asked me if he could borrow some scaffolding from my dad to build a stage for an outdoor rock concert he was putting together. The concert was held in a cow pasture the following weekend. It was bittersweet to see my old boyfriend, but I had fun. The next day I went back to the cow pasture to check on the scaffolding, and it had already been taken down and loaded onto someone's truck, ready to be returned to my dad's warehouse. That's when I saw a handsome Romeo sitting on an old Rambler drinking a beer. He came over and introduced himself and asked if I'd like to take a ride and see where he was camping.

It was a beautiful spot on the Whitewater River just outside Rochester, Minnesota. Kenny pulled out two fishing poles, handed me one, and taught me how to tie a fishing knot.

Here I was six years later, on my own, using that same knot to make mobiles. Tying line to all my shells and wrapping my feathers, I found them too light to hang properly so I went hunting for something to give them weight. I found little pieces of coral scattered within the tumbled stones and shells on the Key West side of the island. I made two mobiles, one for myself and one for Julia. With that done, it was time to relax somewhere other than at my dome. I headed to the beach to lie in the sun. The hours passed like minutes, the sun pulling me deep into myself as I moved a notch closer to the center of the earth. There was a beautiful breeze on this side of the island, where I swam with the dolphins, where it seemed like I could see forever, where I'd hopped off that speedboat, landed on a sea urchin, and begun my new life.

My skin began to bake. I opened my eyes to look out at the ocean, and there they were, my people: Shelter, floating on his slender log canoe, Prairie Rose and Dreaming Eagle out in the water talking, Fu Moon rolling a cigarette, and Peggy picking at her toes. Julia sat beside me doing some macramé. I imagined that Mexican Joe was taking a siesta in his hammock and Billy was sitting by his campfire.

I pulled myself from the beach and walked into the ocean, slowly lying back into the water and floating. I saw something pink in the sky.

"They're here," I heard Dreaming Eagle say.

"It's always around the new moon," added Prairie Rose.

"We'll build a bonfire tonight after we drum and invite them to join us," said Dreaming Eagle.

I had no clue what they were talking about, but I wanted to seem smarter than I was so I didn't ask. After dinner we paddled across the inlet to Mallory Square, again in two boats, again with Peggy getting out and dragging our canoe up and onto the cement landing dock. I jumped out quickly and made a beeline for my apartment to drop some things off, take a shower, and change my clothes. Scrubbed clean and dressed, I headed over to the tennis shop to check things out before going in to work the next day. Claire and Ed had been busy. They had finished the front display window, creatively dressing a mannequin and a half in upscale tennis wear surrounded by balls and racquets, visors, wristbands, headbands, tennis shoes, tennis bracelets, tennis everything.

The little Cuban diner looked closed but I took a chance on getting a cup of coffee. Something felt very weird when I pulled open the screen door, setting the Betty Boop mobile in motion. Heading to the counter, I stopped in my tracks when I saw the little Cuban guy, Tatato, whom I'd knocked off his bike, holding an ice pack on Mexican Joe's face. Both of them looked sort of sick and hung over.

"What happened?" I asked.

"How did you get in here?" Tatato reacted sharply, springing to his feet as though he was going to fight me. I raised my hands in peace and walked toward Joe as I spoke.

"I just opened the door," I said, feeling annoyed at Tatato and turning to Joe. "What happened to you?" I asked, worried. "It looks like someone's hurt you."

Mexican Joe looked horrible. He spoke in Spanish, quickly telling Tatato to be *simpatico*. Neither of them would tell me what had happened. Feeling powerless, I put a ten-dollar bill on the counter, wishing I could help them.

"Please get yourselves something to eat," I said before leaving.

I headed toward the square, toward the sound of drums, toward the setting sun. I quickened my steps, allowing myself to begin my dance before I even got to Mallory Square. Once I did, I shut my eyes and danced my heart out. It felt so good. The drummers were incredible, and again I could feel the beat in my body. Soon everything stopped while people watched the sun set.

On our way back to our little island I thought about all the times in my life when I had wanted to feel free, to dance with abandon, to sing without my throat clamping shut, and to say exactly what I wanted to say, but sorrow would always catch up with me. Like when I was sixteen and Mom and I had gone to Europe and she had gotten sick from drinking too much. She asked me to promise that I wouldn't leave her alone in that hot, crowded, and filthy hospital room. Holding her soft hand in mine, I had looked into her beautiful blue eyes, the whites yellowed by something gone wrong with her liver, and promised, "I'll never leave you, Mama." A few minutes later, three orderlies came into the room and I was told to leave. I refused, and one of them grabbed me from behind and picked me up. My mom's hand was still in mine, and she tightened her grip. I tried to fight the strong man's hold on me but I couldn't. The other one pried my mother's hand from mine, but she was so sick and swollen and out of it that she didn't say a word. I was carried to the door and pushed so violently across the hall that I collided with the brick wall. The steel door to my mom's hospital room slammed shut just as my head slammed into the wall, and I lost consciousness.

The canoe rocked from side to side as Julia climbed out to pull us onto shore. Lost in my reverie, I recalled the kindhearted stranger who gently patted me on the face in that hospital hallway in Athens, Greece, trying to summon me back to consciousness. She pressed some coins into my hand, telling me what to do to try to save my mother. She told me to get a cab to the American embassy and have them call my father, or, as she'd said in her thick Viennese accent, my mom wouldn't stand a chance.

Shelter reached for my hand and helped me from the boat. I let him. I was so grateful for kindness that I began to cry. Devastated and humbled by how much the memory still hurt, I slowly brought myself back to the present and listened earnestly to the plan. According to Prairie Rose, who seemed extraordinarily intelligent, those pink lights I had seen earlier in the sky were "friends" from another star system. I tried to suppress my skepticism and just listen. She had experience with these things, she said, and she too had thought it was all crazy talk until the day she saw this unexplained phenomenon up close.

In the dark of the new moon, we collected more wood for the signaling bonfire that Dreaming Eagle had already put together. I figured that if these visitors from another star system had already been here once they didn't need a signal, but Prairie Rose seemed to think it was not so much a signaling fire as a celebration to welcome them back.

Fu Moon played a long wooden flute and Shelter beat a hypnotic rhythm on a small drum. It was uncomfortable for me. It seemed crazy, and crazy seemed stupid, and stupid always got me into trouble. When stuff that seemed crazy-strange would come up, I'd try to remember what my dad would think. He'd probably think these people were dangerous and out of their minds, so, with Dad's ideas in my head, I decided to go back to my dome. Billy and Mexican Joe walked down the path toward me. Billy blocked my way.

"You shouldn't miss this. This shit is real."

"What is it?" I asked.

"I've only seen it once. I don't know what to call it."

I hated to miss something important, so I followed them back to the bonfire, where Prairie Rose was telling a story about her first experience with the Golden Star Alliance. The year before, she had met a man who claimed he was a walk-in. A walk-in is supposedly a spirit being from another planet. Or did she say dimension? And, according to Prairie Rose, this spirit is allowed to inhabit the body of a human in order to do some good for mankind. It was pretty far-fetched, but I decided it could be possible. Prairie Rose was smart and educated, and she surely believed what she was saying. I figured she was telling the truth and decided to stay and watch. What harm could it do?

It was dark as we gathered around the bonfire and Fu Moon began to pray. They passed around the peace pipe, and then they walked into the water, the pink water. I looked up and saw three pink neon triangles of light above us. They weren't helium balloons or airplanes or satellites, as far as I could tell. I looked more closely and saw that each was a sort of glossy metallic disk with light around its rim.

Everyone walked into the pink-colored water except for Billy, Mexican Joe, and me. I sat down on the beach and watched the show in the sky. The disks moved through the sky very differently from anything I'd ever seen. They would zip from one place to another and then hover. Everything was bathed in a rose-colored light and a deep vibrating hum filled the air. I kept my eyes on my friends in the water, but I also didn't want to take my eyes off the disks in the sky. I lay back on the beach feeling intoxicated as the light show went on for quite a while.

I must have dozed off or passed out, because when I roused myself the fire was half the size it had been and nobody was in the water. I wasn't sure what had happened to everybody else, but I don't remember being alarmed as I walked back to my camp. I slept well and woke later than usual with the sun high in the sky. I rose and went to the beach just to see what it looked like. Everyone was there already, same as before, just sitting in a sort of stupefied reverence staring out at the water. We just sat there, all of us.

We didn't talk about our "visitors," and nothing really changed. I never really did figure out what that whole thing was, but I did see those lights in the sky. Life just went on after that experience. It became a matter of course, the back and forth between the island and work in Key West woven together by many ritual sunsets at Mallory Square, dancing myself to freedom.

As the days wore on, I hadn't fully realized how weird my island mates were until they were standing in front of me at the newly opened tennis shop when customers were around. Fu Moon looked like an ax murderer from Vermont in his flannel shirt and corduroys, Dreaming Eagle looked like a demented male stripper when he wore his diaper-shorts, and the girls needed to shave their armpits. A glimpse of Prairie Rose's armpit hair made me wonder if she was shoplifting wigs.

After a month in Key West, I got a letter from my best friend, Tanya, in Minneapolis, filled with her artwork and a little note saying her friend Abby was coming to visit me. Meeting Tanya two years before at night school had answered my prayer to have a real friend. Not long after we'd met, she'd invited herself over to the horse farm where I was living. I hesitated, but she kept insisting, and within one hour after finally getting her way and arriving at my place she'd asked me to be her best friend. We hardly even qualified as friends, and there she was asking me to be best friends. We hadn't shared any growing-up stories before she impulsively popped that question. I didn't quite trust her but I found her fascinating. Though I'd acted very cool when she'd mentioned it, inside I was terrified. I hadn't been close with anyone since I'd left Kenny, and the truth was I didn't have any friends at the time. I was just barely alive inside. My spirit had been shattered too often to let my feelings out to play.

And Tanya was all play. She told me she slept a lot, ate whatever she wanted (usually in bed), had sex several times a week, kept a journal (something I'd never even heard of), adored talking on the phone for hours, showered and bathed with a fragrant gel called Vitabath, used Pantene shampoo, and had webbed toes. I could see she had big breasts, blue eyes, and an insatiable curiosity. For Tanya, life was a mystery to explore; for me, it seemed a bittersweet journey to endure.

I had no clue that life could be a juicy adventure and that it didn't matter what people thought of you. I wanted to be her best friend because her concept of reality was so different from mine. Her dreams outreached anything I'd even considered, so I thought for my own sake, for God's sake, for the sake of my dearly departed parents, for the sake of finally catching up to my sisters' phenomenal coolness, I had to latch onto her golden star and truly experience life.

Tanya's friend Abby showed up in Key West only a few days after I'd received Tanya's letter. She moved into my little apartment with her friend Jude. It was fine with me. I lived in my sweet dome on the island and my life had found a nice rhythm.

Two weeks later when I couldn't find anyone to take me over to the mainland, I borrowed Mexican Joe's canoe and paddled myself across the inlet. Paddling his thick-hulled canoe exhausted my upper body. By mid-afternoon at work, I could barely raise my arms and had to rest my elbows on the counter when I slid my customers' purchases into their shopping bags.

It rained for three days before the morning I finally got back to the island. Things were messy and muddy and soggy and everyone was grumpy. Days of unrelenting rain had been hard on our little paradise, but all the vegetation was green and lush. My papaya had four little knobs of fruit on it and my fire pit looked like a little pond. I took everything out of my dome to air dry. I cleaned and straightened but didn't see a soul. By late afternoon I wanted to get over to the square for sunset and, finding no one else on the island, I went looking for Mexican Joe to see if he would paddle me across.

He was sitting in the shade of his tree braiding yellow nylon rope with a skill that spoke of years of practice. When I asked him if he could take me over, he just nodded toward his canoe, threw his glance at the foot of the majestic tree where his paddles rested, and looked away. In Mexican Joe sign language that meant, "Just take it."

I dashed back to my camp, got my things, and hurried back to his place, where with his help I got the canoe in the water. Even paddling around the curve of the island was draining. I thought that maybe I should go back but even the thought of turning around made me nervous, so I stroked and stroked and stroked. As I approached Mallory Square, voices carried out into the water as if I were standing next to them and I could hear and feel the beat of drums. I called on the sounds to strengthen my final pull toward shore, and at the same time looked up at the sky where a perfect rainbow had formed. Having recently learned that the sun must be directly across from a rainbow, I looked back toward the soon-to-set sun and saw a powerboat heading toward Christmas Tree Island.

I wasn't used to landing a boat without Peggy, but she didn't appear. I stepped out into the shallow water and lifted the bow of the canoe and dragged it up to the landing, one awkward tug at a time. I tied it to a bush and put the paddles under the seat. When I stood, my knees buckled and I had to hold onto the side of the boat to steady myself.

Over toward the square something seemed wrong. I didn't see any people I knew. The rainbow had disappeared as quickly as it had come, and dark cloud cover had rolled in, masking the sun. Out of nowhere, a loud clap of thunder dispersed the crowd like a gunshot.

Lightning ripped across the evening sky. Rain fell, soaking everything, and hail pounded down. People panicked and ran. I kept running until I reached my apartment. I pounded on the door until Abby and Jude opened it. Once inside, I leaned against the wall and waited for the terror to leave me. They didn't say a word.

Sopping wet, I needed to change my clothes but couldn't budge. I let myself slide down the wall and just sat there with my eyes closed. When I opened them and straightened my legs, the girls were gone. I got up, went into the bathroom, peeled off my wet clothes, and stood under a hot shower until the numbness washed away.

I heard knocking, so I hurried into a pair of pajamas and went to the door. It was Billy. At first I did a double take. I'd never seen Billy off the island and I couldn't quite place him. It had stopped raining but he was drenched, water streaming down his face. Even his nose was dripping, and then I realized he was crying. I held open the jalousie door and ushered him inside. I grabbed a roll of paper towels and reached out to hug him before he sat down.

The fierceness of his hug squeezed the breath out of me. He held on tight and cried hard. I pushed him back so I could look into his eyes but he just buried his face in my neck and sobbed.

"They killed Joe. Some guys from a powerboat. They hung him from his tree. From his own damn tree. The Coast Guard came and got me and told me we had to leave the island. I couldn't find anybody; I didn't know where to go. He's dead. Joe is dead. The Coast Guard found him an hour ago swinging from his special tree, hung with his own rope. Those motherfucking bastards killed him."

Billy let go of me so suddenly that I lost my balance. "They killed him over a stupid six-pack of beer he took from their boat. They hung him from his tree. Somebody had his canoe so he didn't stand a chance of getting away."

Within the hour almost everyone from the island showed up at my door. We drank coffee and Shelter lit a candle and led us in a prayer, while the girls showered. Dreaming Eagle just sat, stunned, on the couch. Eventually everyone found a place to lie down and we slept until the Coast Guard came pounding on my door the next morning. We were told they would take us to the island to get our belongings.

Together, Shelter, Julia, Prairie Rose, Fu Moon, Billy, Dreaming Eagle, and I all walked in the early morning quiet to Mallory Square, where we were loaded onto a small Coast Guard boat. When we pulled away from Key West I saw Mexican Joe's canoe where I'd tied it the afternoon before, now surrounded by yellow police tape. The boat went fast and dropped us on the same beach where I'd landed my first day on the island. How very different it looked on this sad day. An officer, who probably thought we were all nuts, helped me off the boat. I couldn't blame him. How could he know why we were living as we were, or understand the magic of this place?

I accepted the strength of his arm and stepped into the water off Christmas Tree Island to retrieve what was left of the life I had just started living. They gave us an hour to get our stuff into big, black plastic garbage bags. Peggy wasn't with us and the shell of her cardboard house was all she had left behind.

We walked in silence to our various campsites like mourners at a funeral. Nothing felt the same. My dome had been crushed. When

I lifted up the filthy yellow canvas, I found some of Julia's C. S. Lewis books, Fu Moon's wooden flute, and Billy's .22-caliber rifle. None of my stuff was there. Nothing. But I cared much more about answers than I did about my futon, my oil lamp, or my little pocketknife with the eagle on it.

In the ensuing days I would see a silhouette of Fu Moon or Dreaming Eagle walking rapidly by the shop, but they didn't stop. Billy started drinking too much and moved into a rundown boarding house. When I tracked him down one day he told me that Julia planned on moving to New York City, Prairie Rose had gotten a job as a nanny for some rich people, and Shelter was moving to Paradise Island in the Bahamas to help start a yoga center. No one had seen Peggy and I could never find Fu Moon. Our time together was over. We were remnants cast to the wind. Like bits of tobacco in a loosely rolled cigarette thrown from a car window, we hit the ground and scattered.

Chapter 6

ℭ Jazz Fest, New Orleans, ℬ and R. J.

I thought about calling Kenny but I couldn't. I didn't want him and I didn't want the me I was when I was around him. And I definitely didn't want to live in Key West anymore. I knew what I didn't want but had no clue what I did want.

I needed a juice fast to help me get my head on straight, so I headed over to the health food place for a carrot juice. I ordered my juice and sat down, and right there in the middle of the bulletin board was my answer:

jazz fest – new orleans
need riders to share gas
free place to stay
talk to laura at the counter

I glanced toward the counter to see which one might be Laura and saw Abby's friend Jude sitting at a nearby table. I walked over and sat down with her. She was considering going to the jazz fest too. She knew who Laura was and motioned her over. Laura told us that she, her husband, and their three kids had a place to stay and that we could stay there too. Without thinking about it much, I signed on for the ride.

I needed to quit my job and empty my apartment, but first I wanted to find Love 22. I had lost that twenty-two-dollar bill when Fu

Moon and I had tried to cross the rough water our first time out. I wanted a new one so I could reread what it said about twenty-two being a mystical number and a key to the secrets of the universe. Now that I wasn't doing anything that seemed the right thing to do, I figured if I could just learn one secret about the universe I would know what to do next. I headed over to Mallory Square to look across the water at our little island and to find Love 22's school bus.

I found the folding door of his bus open and peeked inside. Love 22 was asleep on one of the bus seats with his mouth agape. He snored so loudly he woke himself up. He looked like a Hollywood Jesus with his caring brown eyes, long hair, and peaceful ways. His eyes fixed on me and he beckoned me onto the bus. Pulling myself up by the pole at the front, I slid into the first bench seat. Out the window I could see the dumpster at the fabric store, the shell and cement landing dock, Mallory Square, the ocean, and Christmas Tree Island.

"Life is life," he said. "It hurts and can be very hard, but it will amount to something tremendous if you let it." When I went to hug him he handed me a twenty-two-dollar bill, but this time he had written on it. I thanked him, gave him that hug, and left the bus to walk to the square, where I sat down on the edge of the world and let my feet get wet again. On the bill he had written: "No one will have your answers and only you can find your questions, but through it all God loves you." I hoped he was right and that God would show me the way.

Thinking about leaving the little town where Jimmy Buffet lived; the town where a girl could walk into a bar like The Bull or The Monster and dance with all her heart and leave unnoticed; the town where smooth, older guys gave quaaludes to young, unsuspecting girls like me; the town where I could have gotten a boyfriend in ten minutes if I'd wanted one—it made me very sad. What I really wanted I couldn't seem to find. I wanted a second chance, at what I wasn't sure.

&

Two days later Jude and I walked our stuff across town and got into Laura's maroon and white VW bus with its Indian print curtains and carpeted walls. We were off on our adventure with Laura, her husband, Dan, their three little kids, and a guy named Ray who'd shown up at the last minute. Dan drove. He was short and bald with arms thick and rich with muscle. He had a smile that made you look behind you to see if something wonderful was going on. Laura reminded me of Katharine Hepburn if she'd been an earthy, graceful hippie. She held the map, talked incessantly, and smoked one cigarette after another. She would drape her long, elegant arm around her husband's shoulder or wrap it around one of her kids as they sat on her lap. She seemed to be a happy and smart woman. Jacob was eleven, Clarence five, and Dolly three. Dolly spent most of the 1,023-mile trip talking to an uninterested Dachshund named Fred.

Ray looked like a gypsy, with luscious dark hair and long eyelashes. His cool vibe made me a little nervous. Jude, I learned, was nineteen and came from Sacramento.

The trip began at mile marker 0, the southernmost tip of the continental United States. The van chugged across the seven-mile bridge that connects Key West to the mainland. The kids shouted out the names of each key—Sugarloaf, Boot, Grassey, Duck, Ragged, and on and on. We averaged about forty miles before one of us had to pee.

We headed north, cruising along the east coast of Florida next to the shimmering sea. Dan drove the entire twenty-four-hour trip across Florida, through Alabama, Mississippi, and on to Louisiana. Finally we arrived in New Orleans and I nearly let out a cheer.

Our free place to stay felt similar to the van, only bigger—a room with Indian print wall hangings, Indian print bedspreads, fuzzy shag carpeting, lots of windows, and, thank God, a toilet and a tub.

Unfortunately the tub and toilet were in the kitchen and the kitchen was in the living room and the living room was in the bedroom.

I put my stuff in the corner farthest from the door and the toilet before Jude, Ray, and I headed out for a walk. The air hung heavy with humidity and the trees and buildings looked old and spooky. We passed a bar called The Rainbow, which was the name of the health food store that Laura ran in Key West. We thought this was good luck, and Ray suggested we get a drink. Even though Jude was underage she seemed game to try to get served, but I kept walking.

Heading into the French Quarter, I turned onto Bourbon Street. It had an old-world charm to it if you could get past the strip joints and bars. The street stuck to my feet and the air stuck to my skin. A large wooden sign standing in the middle of the sidewalk caught my attention.

Need direction?
Cards read today $10

I opened the door and walked up three flights of stairs to find a heavyset older woman with a deck of tattered playing cards in her hand. She was sitting in the hallway on a folding aluminum chair. A TV table sat in front of her and a half-smoked, unlit cigarette protruded from her lips. No crystal ball or fancy curtains.

"Sit down, honey, there's some things you need to know," she said, motioning me into the aluminum chair across from her.

She stared down at my hand.

"Take that ring off, you shouldn't be wearing that. That's a High Mason's ring. Why are you wearing it? Was it your daddy's?" Reaching her open hand across the table, she commanded, "Take it off now, honey."

My heart thudded in my chest. My fingers wrapped protectively around the one thing I had that had been my father's. Her eyes demanded I hand it over, but when I tried to remove it my finger was too swollen to get the ring over my knuckle. I put my finger in my mouth to wet it and the ring tasted like sulphur.

She started talking like there was someone right there in front of her. "You give me that child's hand, you slimy bastard. Take your filthy grubs off her. Climb back into your damn hole and get the hell out of my hallway."

I looked behind me, wondering what the hell I'd gotten myself in to. Suddenly the ring slipped from my finger as though it was two sizes too large. It clunked onto the TV table and rolled off the edge onto the floor and down the stairs. I pushed my chair back.

"Leave it be, baby, it's got the devil on it."

Pictures of my father flooded my mind: Daddy coming to rescue me when I fell off my horse or got hit by a car or stayed out all night. I remembered how it felt when he carried me to bed when I was a little girl and how much he hated it when I had to carry him from the bed to the couch and back to the bed again when he was dying of cancer. The old woman pushed a box of Kleenex toward me. I blew my nose.

She picked up the deck of playing cards and lit the half-smoked cigarette with an old-fashioned silver lighter. The smell of butane filled the air. She took a long drag and held it in while she put the cigarette out, tapping the end and tucking it behind her ear. I watched her as though she were performing brain surgery.

"Shuffle."

I tried shuffling the way I used to as a kid when Mom would wake me up in the middle of the night. I liked it, since she was sober at that hour, and we would play hostess with the mostest, which meant taking turns making snacks while we played gin rummy. But the old woman's cards were too thick and worn to shuffle as I had back then. These cards were meant for something very different from gin rummy. My mom would have liked this lady, I thought.

"I would have liked your mama too," she said, paralyzing me with excitement.

"Now lay down three cards each in five piles face-down, then go back and lay down a fresh card face-up on every pile."

I did as I was told, but with a newfound respect and fear. First card face-up: Queen of Hearts. Her right eye twitched. Next card face-up: ten of Spades. She moved closer to the table. The next card was the King of Diamonds, followed by the three of Hearts. She went to reach for her cigarette but let her hand instead rest over her heart. The last card face-up: Ace of Clubs.

I wanted to reach across the table and get her cigarette, take a drag, and hold it in a really long time. She didn't say a word. I waited, trying to act relaxed, and leaned back in the chair, which almost tipped over. I lunged forward, grabbing the lightweight TV table. Her hand came forward with speed and strength to stabilize the table, giving me a secure holding place and preserving my army of face-ups.

Her body jerked; her voice deepened; her throat muscles contracted; her eyes stared dead ahead. Then she began to speak.

"You know the secrets of healing because you know love." Her head kind of jerked to the right.

"You will meet a tall, dark stranger with the initials R. J. For a time he will be good for you." She shifted in her chair.

"Avoid the one with so many things and too many problems." With these words her breathing became labored.

"Help is coming." Her whole body trembled slightly.

"You are loved beyond measure," she went on.

I started to cry.

"Do what comes naturally, for that is what you are called to do." Her voice didn't sound like a woman's voice anymore.

There was more but I couldn't keep up with it. Each card represented some aspect of my life—the first, who I was; the second, whom I was to meet; the third, whom I was to avoid; the fourth, who would save me; the fifth, what I came to do. I paid as much attention as I could, taking in each declaration like I was rescuing it from the terrible fate of never being known.

When she stopped talking, her shoulders slumped forward and it was done. She reached for her cigarette and slipped it between her lips. In her trembling hand she held a lighter, but flipping it open was too much. I reached across the table and took it from her, flipping back the rectangular silver lid and moving my shaking thumb on the metal wheel to bring the flame alive. It seemed huge and dangerous when I held it close to her damp face and short cigarette. She held out her hand, raising her lifeless eyes to meet mine, and I reached into my pocket, pulled out a twenty, and put it in her hand. She took a deep drag and sat back, shutting her eyes. I put another twenty on the table and left.

I rushed from the building and headed to the bar where I'd left my friends, but realized I'd forgotten to look for my daddy's ring. I turned around and raced back. I walked up and down a few streets, opened doors, and looked for the stairway. I stood in the middle of each street and looked up to the third story of every building, but I found no folding sign and remembered no landmarks. I sat down on a bench feeling like I had fainted and was just now coming to. All I could think of was smoking cigarettes. It was all too weird, and now I didn't have my daddy's ring. I went and found my friends.

Laura, Jude, Dan, Ray, and the kids all stayed up late and slept in. When they finally woke up we spent the day scoping out Cajun restaurants. They were in search of jambalaya-of-the-gods. I was just looking around. I was the only vegetarian—no one noticed that I ate spicy rice or didn't eat at all. I didn't feel like drinking.

We had come for the greatest jazz festival in the world, the streets filled with music and drunk people. The air felt heavy with humidity and tension. Everywhere I looked, people gorged on food or drink. I realized that my feet stuck to the pavement because people carried their mixed drinks in huge hurricane glasses, then staggered, sloshing their drinks onto the streets. New Orleans was beautiful, but at night the magic turned sick and sexy and twisted.

Two days after our arrival, it was time to get back in the van so we could pay one admission price for everyone. Dan drove and picked up a few hitchhikers on our way to the festival. By the time we drove the van through the gates we totaled fourteen.

We made a plan to meet up at an appointed place and time. I watched old men doing soft-shoe and young girls doing what they do. It was hot and I had dressed in my tight-fitting yellow overalls, my money in my shoe. After a very full day of wandering from stage to stage and listening for a beat I could dance to, I arrived at our appointed meeting place at the appointed time, to no van, no roommates, and no ride.

I went to the exit gate and stood staring at the low-riding cars. There were so many people in each Buick or old Cadillac they looked like they were riding in train cars, facing this way and that. Each vehicle was full to overflowing; each chassis rode close to the ground. When a bicycle zoomed by, I figured that a bike might be my best chance out of there.

"Wait, wait, wait, please give me a buck," I cried out, but the rider either didn't hear me or ignored me. Finally, I stuck my thumb out and smiled at each full car. I waved and carried on, making a big-eyed, pleading face to get some sympathy, but men gawked at me and women glared at me. Before I knew it, a dollar bill turned up in my outstretched hand and I saw the donor bicyclist buzz away.

"No, wait, not that kind of buck—a ride, I need a ride."

The bicycle seemed like an extension of its rider, who artfully leaned to the right as the bike arced gracefully around the clot of traffic. He pulled up beside me. I figured that the heat of the day had caused him to remove his shirt. Beautifully muscled, he was slender and handsome with caramel-colored eyes.

He offered me the seat by simply standing close to his handlebars and looking straight ahead. It wasn't easy for me to get on the seat without kicking him in the butt or using some mounting device. If it had been a horse I would have swung up. He looked back at me like I was wasting time. I gripped his shoulders as if they were a horse's withers and swung my leg over the back of his bike, clearing it entirely. Flushed with embarrassment, I came back to the right side and tried again. The second my fanny hit the seat we were off.

With nowhere to put my feet to secure them, they flapped about, causing me to wobble from side to side. I eyed his strong naked back. How had I missed the thick bike chain crisscrossed over his velvety black skin? He was way too sexy. When he leaned to the right, I was perilously close to falling off, so I thrust my arms around him when he jostled around an opening car door. He smelled of coconut. His skin was like the skin of those dolphins that had surprised me back in the island waters. The chain was big and cold. It was like a chain used to tow a car. I could feel him laughing and let myself relax, pulling my legs in and lowering my heels, pretending I knew what I was doing.

What a way to see New Orleans! He careened through the streets like they were old friends. I held on for dear life, feeling both pumped up and terrified. His body was solid muscle, all strong and able; he was my rescuer and my deliverer.

Suddenly we came to a stop. My head crashed into his back and I almost chipped a tooth on his chain. He kicked his long right leg out in front of him, easily clearing the handlebars, and held the bike like it was a thoroughbred so I could get off. We were parked in front of the same bar I'd passed when we arrived. The Rainbow. His friends owned it.

Finding two stools at the bar, we sat down, each ordering a grapefruit juice. He had big, soft, pillow-like lips and a slight gap between his very white front teeth. I felt drawn to him, wanted to just study him, admire him. Then I heard him say his name: Riley Jefferson.

Oh my God! When the old woman had come to the ten of Spades she had said, "You are going to meet a tall, dark stranger with the initials R. J."

Riley didn't ask me any questions about who I was or where I came from. He just took my hand and quietly told me about his combat tour in Vietnam as if he couldn't go on until I knew these things. He leaned in really close and spoke in short, trembling sentences about parachuting in to villages and having to kill all the people, including the women and children. I was throwing back my grapefruit juice like it was Scotch, finishing three by the time his story reached a resting point. My head was spinning and my heart filled with anguish for him.

As I listened to Riley talk, I tried to remember what the card reader had said about a "tall," he was over six feet tall, "dark," well, that went without saying, "stranger." It felt as if everything that card reader said had been stored in a maze and I couldn't go back to the reading and stay present for Riley as he poured his heart out. He stood to talk to his friend and I went to use the restroom. My butt bones hurt and I walked stiffly when I stood up. When I returned I overheard him say to his buddy, "She's like an angel sent by God." I pulled my shoulders back and walked a little taller.

We stayed glued to our bar stools, taking turns telling short stories about our lives. I told him how I'd ended up on Christmas Tree Island and how far away it all seemed now. While I was telling him what the card reader had said, he slid his hand up my bare arm and leaned in to kiss me. I was swallowed up in the softness of his lips.

His friends came over and met me, but no one intruded on our privacy for long. We nibbled on appetizers and drank water and later some tea. We left the steaming hot bar that we'd entered as strangers and poured out into the velvety night as one. He held my hand in his and gracefully walked his bike alongside us with the other. He seemed so good and upstanding, it was a deep and unforgettable shame that this young man had had to carry razor wire into villages and cut people's heads off. We walked in silence. When he left me at the door, which took a while to find, he asked if he could see me again. He wrapped his arms around me and just held me for a long moment, brushing his lips over mine and then whispering something into my hair. This man charmed me and totally turned me on.

The next night Riley took me to a restaurant that he had helped a friend of his build. They made an incredible vegetarian Cajun dish for me. After dinner we went to his shotgun house on St. Ferdinand Street. Following me through the door, he removed my clothes from behind. By the time he'd picked me up and placed me on his perfectly made bed, I'd lost all inhibitions. His pillowy lips kissed and explored my body, his eyes locking into mine as he found every pleasure spot that my body had. When he mounted me, pushing inside me, I felt filled, complete. I was done.

Afterward, barely able to stand and totally disoriented, I staggered down the hall to pee, figuring there had to be a bathroom somewhere. My heart was still pounding as I gingerly lowered myself to the seat. Relief lasted only a moment, as a mouse ran over my bare foot and I screamed without making a sound, my fairy-tale romance brought back to earth.

The next day Riley woke me early and made love to me again before putting on clean jeans and a fresh white T-shirt to go to his carpenter's job. He had an old truck out front and he dropped me at the apartment. We had a plan to meet in the afternoon for a picnic at the jazz festival. I searched the local hardware stores for a Havahart trap to give Riley so he could capture and release the little mouse.

I felt like I'd been caught in a riptide. The pull toward him was deep and strong. I was hungry to see him again as I headed over to the festival grounds off Esplanade. He met me there and it was a whole different festival from the day before. Riley knew everyone and just being with him made me feel precious. The music, the food, the lovemaking went on for days. He was thoughtful, careful to feed me and look after me, and by far the best lover I'd ever had.

After a week of him I was exhausted and my vagina was sore. I'd begun to have enough. I knew I would miss him but it was just too much. Plus, Laura and Dan were packing the van, ready to head back to Key West.

When Riley came to say goodbye he didn't look at me; he just pulled me into his arms and squeezed me tight. After a few minutes I pushed back from his embrace and raised my face to look at him. Big, fat tears fell from his eyes and rolled down his cheeks.

CHAPTER 7

☙ SEARCHING FOR ANSWERS ❧

I spent the ride back to Key West searching for answers. I didn't know what to do with myself. I had no real reason to stay in Key West. I'd proven that I could do stuff on my own and I was living perfectly well without alcohol or drugs. I'd tried to get back together with Kenny. I'd helped put together a tennis shop. I'd lived in a dome on an island with strange, magical people. I'd met Riley. I was ready to go home but I didn't really have a home to go to. I finally reconciled myself to going back to Minnesota to live with my best friend, Tanya, in Minneapolis, even though being with her could be all-consuming.

I couldn't help but remember the day I'd met Tanya. She'd tapped me on the shoulder one day after class, asking, "Could you put this bird in my hair?" I turned around to take the feathered fake bird from her hand. She leaned toward me as I twisted the little wire feet into her perfumed long blonde hair. The bird was part of her presentation for the public speaking class.

From that moment on, she pestered me at every class to invite her over to Stan and Laura Wisnowski's rundown horse farm, where I lived. I loved the beautiful horses, but Tanya didn't seem the type to like horses, so I brought her upstairs to my tiny, cold bedroom where I had a small television and a coffeepot next to my bed. I hadn't realized how bleak and ugly my reality was until I saw it through Tanya's wide-eyed, vibrant baby blues.

She scanned the room and asked me if I'd like to move and be her roommate. I wished I could, but I couldn't. I'd never been a roommate with a girl and I didn't think it would work. My sisters had both pretty much disowned me after my folks died, and I didn't trust women anymore. She insisted. Then she asked me to be her best friend. I didn't know what to say. She said she'd already found the perfect place, a mansion in St. Paul. The place had a ballroom and was perfect for parties. I hated having to tell her I had no friends and didn't like parties.

Living on a horse farm sounds glamorous, but it was really just a lot of hard work. These particular horses weren't all that bright or interesting, and Stan was no handyman. My father would have detested the shoddy craftsmanship in the house and barn. Seeing it reminded me daily how utterly horrible my life had turned out to be.

One day Tanya was supposed to show me the St. Paul mansion but was late picking me up. She finally arrived driving a bright yellow Pacer. It was all windows. I walked around to the passenger side, got in, and shut the door. The car stank a little.

"Be careful," Tanya said casually. "I threw up on that door last night."

"That is so gross," I said, wiping my hands on my pants. I was uncomfortable and wanted to jump out of the car.

We drove to St. Paul with her rattling off the specifics of the place we were going to see—winding staircase, nine bedrooms, five bathrooms, and a huge ballroom. Then she began recounting her wild escapades of the night before as I stared straight ahead. I tried to remember the last time I'd had wild sex or I'd thrown up on a car door. After our tour of the house we were sitting cross-legged on the mahogany floor in the ballroom, staring up at the gigantic crystal chandelier. "We'll see what happens," she said, as we stood up and I followed her back out to the

Pacer. At her suggestion, she took the vomit side and I drove us back to Minnetonka.

Tanya's being such a free spirit freaked me out. I felt insecure about my body and sex. Before I married Kenny I'd had only one lover ever, and that was Scott. Kenny, on the other hand, had been a regular Don Juan. Everyone had slept with him, and his reputation left me feeling jealous and inadequate. Tanya's being so sexually alive brought up all that insecurity, but I was too embarrassed to tell her that. Instead I told her I'd live with her. I hoped she could loosen me up.

The mansion arrangement fell through but she found us a beautiful house on Dupont Avenue in Minneapolis. She also found another roommate to share the expenses and tend to her needs—Michael, an old boyfriend who adored her.

Tanya was my exact opposite. She'd been an erotic dancer and was now a part-time student—while I worked full-time as a nursing assistant in a cancer hospital and went to night school. My days were spent giving enemas or holding a patient's hand during a spinal tap. I wore ugly white uniforms and tried my best to help people be a little less scared, even though I was pretty scared myself.

Tanya, on the other hand, slept until noon, read books, took long bicycle rides, wrote in a journal, and drew fabulous pictures. She also loved to make love. She had different men coming and going. I remember this hairy Arab lover who she said used to ask her to slap him. He'd spit on the walls while he bathed in our big clawfoot tub. Meanwhile I would be up in my loft room trying to block out sex noises with marijuana and Mary Tyler Moore. I wanted the house clean, with dishes put away and no weird Arabs taking cold baths, smoking cigars, and spitting on the walls. But somehow Tanya's life seemed so much better than mine.

While living with Tanya I realized I had a great big opportunity to change my life. She finagled a trip for us to Paradise Island in the

Bahamas. An old lover of hers, Huntington Hartford, used to own the island and still had pull there. She got us a room at the Ocean Club and took me to her favorite restaurant, Café Martinique. We went dancing with strong, sexy black men and spent our days basking in the sun reading a copy of *Shōgun* we had torn in half. I began to find life fascinating and not just something to get through day after day, so I decided to quit my old life and start another one.

CHAPTER 8

❧ HOPPING A TRAIN WITH ROGER ❧

When I arrived back in Minneapolis from Key West, Tanya decided we should have a party. She told me to invite everyone I knew. The people I felt the closest to were my patients in the cancer hospital where I had worked before leaving for Florida. It made me sad to think how few friends I had. I called Fritz, the farmer whose lap I'd been sitting on when Kenny first came over and kissed me. I also invited two girls from work. Tanya invited all the others.

That evening I met Roger, an old boyfriend of Tanya's. He had a boyish, crooked smile and crazy long hair. His father was a minister. I forget what Roger did during the day, but at night he went by the name Rambo and was the front man in a rock and roll band. Fritz took up with my friend Janice from work, and Tanya flitted around like a hummingbird, charming everyone. Roger and I stood next to each other for hours until it was time to lie down and rest.

Roger reached for me across the waterbed, pulling me into his arms, and slowly removed my clothes. As each article of clothing came off, he licked and caressed me. When he ran his tongue over my elbow I thought I might go out of my mind, but when he brushed his fingers over my kneecap I realized I no longer had a mind. I was pure sensation. He possessed some kind of magic. My body hummed as he stroked it.

We saw each other every day after that. Our lovemaking went deeper than I'd ever gone before, even with Riley. Roger's body was muscular and looked masculine, but he was soft and cried easily. After we had been together for about a month he told me he had written a piano concerto for me. He wanted to play it for me on the pipe organ in his father's church. He called it "La Tua Gioia" and said he had written it so my parents would know in heaven what a beautiful woman their daughter had become.

While I was away one day he let himself into the house on Dupont Avenue and laid out the entire twelve-page concerto on the dining room table. An hour later, when I walked through the door, he popped open a bottle of champagne. With musical notes on paper and bubbles in a glass, he swept me into his arms and told me he loved me. He was crying.

He was shaking but I was the nervous one. The idea of being able to reach my parents terrified and thrilled me. To imagine them listening, leaning over some railing in heaven to hear a little better or to get a peek of their youngest daughter, was too much for me to bear. Unaware of my trepidation, Roger reverently gathered the pages and we headed over to his father's church, where I sat on the crimson-carpeted altar and rested my back against a polished wooden railing. Roger sat at the majestic pipe organ and began to tell his version of my gut-wrenching story on an instrument made for holy moments like this. Tears poured from my eyes. He did it; he captured my life in music. I opened my eyes and thought I saw angels surrounding the two of us.

∞

While Roger had been writing "La Tua Gioia," I had been figuring out the details of a trip we were dreaming up. Even though I wasn't all that keen on the idea, I'd plotted the "hopping a freight train" part with the help of a janitor who had worked on trains and jumped a few trains himself. Roger wanted to hop a freight train to Seattle and then hitchhike to San Francisco, where we would stay with his friends before flying to Hawaii—which might have been my idea. (I hated the thought of getting into trouble on a freight train, hated the idea of asking for things, even a ride in a car, and hated staying in other people's houses.)

We bought Roger some rugged clothes and a backpack, and I bought some almonds, dried fruit, and crackers to eat on the first leg of our journey. We planned on going all the way to Seattle, Washington, from a small town outside of Brainerd, Minnesota. We slept overnight above the department store in town with a friend of our janitor/railroad tutor, who was to be our guide.

We woke up at one o'clock in the morning after sleeping very little, climbed down the creaky stairs of the old building, and scurried out into the black of night. The place had seemed like a ghost town earlier in the day and now it was truly spooky, like something out of *The Twilight Zone*. We followed our guide to the switching station and systematically counted the tracks. They crisscrossed and curved, making it impossible to know which ones we were supposed to follow. Neither of us wanted to get on the wrong train.

I counted the tracks again and when I looked up to ask our guide if I had it right, he was gone. I let my intuition guide me. We set down our backpacks and waited in the most inconspicuous place we could find, next to the track I had chosen. We dozed off and were awakened by what looked like a huge full moon headed directly for us. We jumped to our feet, sure the train was coming.

Its noise was deafening. I ran alongside the train as our guide-to-everything hobo had suggested. He had said to run, so we ran. I looked over my shoulder to make sure Roger was with me, but he was way behind, back where we'd been resting. I saw him trying and failing to put his backpack on over his rain poncho, a poster boy for the uncoordinated. I turned around and ran to help him, yelling over the roar of the train,

"Just carry it," as I grabbed him by the arm and started running again. He resented the tug on his arm and I could feel his pout. I stopped and said, "I'm sorry, but we've got to hurry," kissing him quickly before starting to run again. Like a seven-year-old, he wiped away my kiss.

I was learning fast that running in the dark next to a train is stupid and dangerous. The thing appears to be moving slowly, but as you run you realize it's an impossible situation. You need to find an open boxcar and hoist your body and your belongings up into the thing, all the while hoping beyond hope that the sensitive man you're traveling with is nearby and will do the same. I kept running but got behind Roger so I could see him, which made him want to talk to me and made me want to strangle him. I took his backpack from him and told him to jump into the open car. He screamed, "What?"

I threw both our backpacks into the open boxcar. Its floor was at about chest level when I threw them, but by the time Roger got his butt moving enough to place his large un-calloused hands on the floor of the car, it was at neck level because the tracks were now higher than the slope we were running on. I swung my leg up and caught the edge with my toe, then struggled and got myself in.

There could have been toothless killers in the car, but all I focused on was getting Roger aboard. Herculean adrenaline fueled me and I reached down and pulled his six-foot-two-inch body into the hopefully empty boxcar.

Once Roger was inside, the train accelerated from the modest two miles an hour at which it was traveling when we boarded, to the roaring hundred miles per hour that our guide had told us was normal running speed for such a freighter. I was gasping more than breathing and my muscles burned as though I had torn them. I could barely make out Roger's complaint that I'd hurt his arm.

We had brought some basic survival gear and I knew that somewhere in our backpacks there was a flashlight. I came across a two-pound bag of raw almonds while rummaging through our supplies. I opened that and ate some. I found our small deluxe flashlight but was afraid to turn it on lest a grimy band of hobos was sitting along the back of the boxcar. My hand gripped the flashlight and I shined its light toward the end of the car, empty, toward the front, empty, to the side, empty. We were safe. Roger was still recuperating from the run, the jump, and my pulling him on board.

I made a little nest for us. Being on the train was intoxicating, like riding my horse at a gallop through a cornfield, and cozy, like being in a big, warm Buick beside my dad. Roger and I lay down, wrapped our arms around each other, and fell asleep.

Lying on the boxcar floor zipped into my sleeping bag, I felt the train slowing down in gentle increments and I began to wake up. I figured the train was preparing to do what our guide had described as coupling. It was light out by then so I could see the interior of our car: it was empty of any cargo, all dirty steel. Suddenly, BAM! The train had rammed into something. Roger and I slid down the car and smashed into the end. Our boxcar door slammed shut like the lid of a coffin.

We looked at each other in horror. We were trapped. We spent the next five terrifying minutes blaming each another, and the following five claustrophobic minutes feeling our way around the pitch-black boxcar searching for our flashlight so we could ultimately determine how to pry the door open. I finally found the flashlight, and Roger discovered a piece of wood to serve as our doorman—the security that train-hoppers must have to ensure that they're never sealed to their deaths in a metal boxcar. We desperately needed an abracadabra moment when the door would open enough for us to keep it ajar using the piece of wood.

We waited. We ate almonds. I hated him. He hated me. We had a fight about something that had nothing to do with anything. We tried to pull, pry, force, and will the door open. We waited some more. We weren't moving and hadn't moved for some time.

Soon it felt as though we were low on oxygen. What a movie it would make: the musician and the ex-nursing assistant, the minister's son and the girl who'd lost her father too young, the vagabonds, the nomads, the star-crossed lovers, sealed to their death. No matter how exciting life had become, there would be no director saying, "Quiet on the set" or "That's a wrap." We were in a boxcar in a rail yard we knew not where, at a dead stop. Maybe our car had been decoupled and we were just sitting there, abandoned.

I began pounding on the boxcar door. The sound reverberated. I screamed, and the scream echoed back to me intensified. I pounded on the hard, cold, uncaring door. When Roger covered his ears, I stopped.

Suddenly the train jolted to life, the boxcar door opened about six inches, and we were able to pry it open another foot or so. We jammed our piece of wood in the opening and looked out. My body was trembling. We were somewhere, somewhere alive and well, and we looked at each other and smiled. I loved him again. We had a thin coating of black soot on our faces that made our teeth look really white. Roger's thinning hair stood on end. We were safe. But our reverie was quickly broken by the sound of voices coming toward us.

We pressed ourselves against the farthest, darkest corner and held our breath. The voices got closer; it sounded like two men. I looked down and saw my backpack lying in the shaft of light from the open door. Stretching my leg toward it, trying to loop my foot through the strap, I realized it wasn't my backpack—it was Roger's— but I had no time or desire to lay blame. I decided to be bold, to rein in my hysteria. I walked over and picked the thing up and moved it to the other side of the door. My moment of bravery over, I slunk back into the shadows and watched as two men walked the rails, probably looking for interlopers like us. We waited a good long while, until the coast was clear, before jumping off the train with our stuff and finding a place to relieve ourselves.

I had the worst stomachache of my life. I squatted, hoping I wouldn't die as my bowels exploded with almond-induced diarrhea. After a few quiet moments I would think I was finished but then my belly would cramp and it would start up again. Eventually I limped back to the train, climbed on, and curled up in a ball as the train gained momentum. I fell at last into a deep sleep.

We awoke eight hours later. We sat in stunned silence, watching the world in all its magnificence go by. Trains go places cars cannot, sliding between narrow rock ledges and swooping through glorious forests. Trains have a view of the world that surpasses all others. The spectacular view was of a virgin land.

The next time the train stopped we jumped off with our packs and our little chunk of wood and darted across the tracks, looking for a place to relieve ourselves again. We were surprised at the length of our train. Even though we weren't sure we were headed in the right direction, we were comforted by the awesome feeling of freedom and adventure. Seeing an opportunity for sunshine and fresh air, we climbed up on a car carrying lumber. It resembled a flatbed truck, and the wood on it was warm and soft compared to the steel floor of our boxcar. We could see the sky, and the view made this the perfect choice.

As we sat waiting for the train to move, another one came from the opposite direction, and, since we were in the open air with nowhere to hide, I waved, thinking someone must be looking. The engineer blew his whistle while several cars back a man leaned out an open door and winked, tossing a brown paper bag on the ground directly in front of us. Not sure what to make of it, I decided to find out and jumped off the car to pick it up. Good call. It was sandwiches and milk.

The food and the kindness of a stranger felt incredible, the view of the passing world was incredible, but traveling with Roger twenty-four hours a day was not so incredible. I missed having a toilet, a shower, and a soft bed, plus we were wearing on each other's nerves. We both stank.

My legs were hairy. The way Roger breathed annoyed me. The things he talked about annoyed me. The way he wasn't really fun annoyed me.

కు

On the lumber car we had a seat and a backrest. The smell of fresh-cut, sun-warmed lumber wafted all around us. We could stretch our legs out in front of us, we had sandwiches and milk in our bellies, and the sun shone upon us as we made our way across America. I dozed.

I sensed myself falling from some height, falling through something, from a bridge, it seemed, into smooth silky water. My body plummeted to the bottom, where I came upon a beautiful domed building. I swam inside. It was full of handsome men all clamoring for my attention. I was wanted, hungered for. In a huge, gorgeous room where all these men were after me, I heard the words, "You can breathe." I knew I was under water but I took a breath that woke me up only seconds before we entered an underpass on the train—and my legs were dangling over the edge. I pulled them in as the dream faded, just as the solid brick underpass became a source of shade rather than a weapon of amputation.

Shortly after my underwater dream, we moved from the flatbed car, realizing it was too dangerous: I could have been badly injured. We hoped our new boxcar, red with a pristine white interior, would be our last one before the train pulled into Seattle. The doors on both sides were open, offering us the best views yet, bringing us back to humble, whole, and happy. At one point I stood in the middle of the car to practice my recently learned and barely remembered tai chi movements. On one side of the car we could see the Oregon desert and on the other side the Columbia River. We rode the zipper between these two natural wonders.

Tai chi involves slow movement from one side to the other. It surprised me that I could remember anything of what I'd learned since I'd fallen in love with my tai chi teacher and had chosen to love rather than to learn. But on the train I remembered the movements, transforming into a sort of stork or sea bird, with one leg raised up and moving outward, my body tipping, curving, and balancing. I clicked into a sort of supernatural coordination and it all felt so right. At that exquisite moment, as I looked out onto the tracks, two hobos removed their hats and bowed, saying, "To the Queen." For that single moment, I was the Queen of the Rails, or so said two dusty old men.

Filthy with soot and exhausted, we pulled into the rail yard at last. I jumped from the boxcar on wobbly legs, oh so glad to be walking. I could still feel the train's rhythmic motion in every step. We followed the Seattle skyline and came to a bridge that reminded me of the one in my dream. Walking that bridge to find a hotel, we crossed over a place where a person could have fallen through. Being startled out of my dream had saved me from serious injury and for a time I became a little more careful and kind.

After a long, hot shower and a good night's sleep at a Holiday Inn, we began the next leg of our journey. Being with a man who had never hitchhiked and who breathed loudly wasn't easy, but I bit my tongue. We put out our thumbs, hoping to hitch a ride to the Bay Area. I didn't care much for hitchhiking and Roger hated it after two short awkward rides, so we decided we'd walk to San Francisco.

Not such a great idea, but Roger had a better one. "Let's get a bottle of tequila," he suggested out of the blue. On a mission, we walked in to a little town and bought tequila, lemons, and a little shaker of salt. I sliced the lemons and we walked, licking salt off our wrists, taking swigs from the bottle, and sucking on lemon wedges. Loosening up and laughing at ourselves, we searched for a place to sit down.

Climbing through a patch of rusted barbed wire fence, we headed toward an inviting area of fallen trees surrounded by beautiful green grass. Buzzed from the tequila, we sat down and looked at each other, then burst out laughing. I was laughing because I realized I'd been stupid to take off on this wild adventure with somebody I barely knew. I don't know why he was laughing, but it somehow drew us closer together.

We did some more shots and ate some lemons until a swarm of bees became very interested in one of the lemon wedges I'd thrown overhand some distance from our pastoral living room. I was about to alert Roger and recommend we move when I caught sight of a herd of bulls running toward us through the high grass. I hollered, slipped off the log we were sitting on, and fell into a beehive hidden under it.

We ran, leaving behind the tequila, the lemons, and Roger's hat. We were still laughing even though we were both afraid of the charging bulls and the angry bees. The barbed wire fence seemed very far away; we weren't going to make it. The scout bee shot in front of us, which caused us to veer off course, and Roger lost a shoe. The ground rumbled with the weight and fury of the herd. The fence was in sight, but short of running right into it I couldn't imagine how we could slow down, bend, lift our legs, and climb through in time. Then, all of a sudden, Mr. Uncoordinated, Mr. Couldn't Get On a Train, Mr. Nice and Easy threw his backpack like a javelin and dove through the fence as if he were Mark Spitz. I saw how well it worked and did the same. The bulls kept up their charge, but when they reached the fence they gently loped away. They began to graze as though nothing had happened.

Laughing so hard I could barely breathe, I got out another pair of shoes for Roger and left the deadly almonds that had attempted to lacerate my intestines as an offering for the bulls. Having fun at last, we walked at a good clip but stuck our thumbs out whenever a car passed. Half an hour later a VW van pulled over to pick us up. A man with long hair and wire-rimmed glasses, who introduced himself as John David, was at the wheel. He jumped out and loaded our backpacks into the van. His pretty blonde girlfriend handed us a joint and we settled in.

They had just returned from a spiritual retreat in Hawaii and, feeling benevolent, decided to take us all the way to San Francisco.

Roger and I planned to stay with his friends there and head to Hawaii in three days' time. That was the vision. John David dropped us off at Roger's friends' door. They warmly welcomed us, giving us their living room to make our nest, and left us alone to get settled. Speaking softly, Roger got my attention and solemnly told me that he loved someone else more than he loved me.

I was angry, soon out the door, and down the driveway before he told me who it was. I didn't hear his words until after I'd told him to go to hell. He'd said, "My first love is Jesus Christ." Embarrassed I'd told him to go to hell, I gripped my backpack and held onto my resolve to call it quits. He apologized as though he was wrong instead of me. We both stood in the driveway and cried. God only knows why, but I decided to leave. His friends gave me a lift to the airport and I flew back to Minnesota.

It was the first time I'd ever heard anyone talk about having a relationship with Jesus. Up to that moment, all I knew of Christ was the sight of his stricken body carved out of wood appearing to writhe on the cross in a dark, cold Catholic church.

As the plane sailed through the skies I wondered what, if anything, I'd been missing.

Chapter 9

❧ BEHIND BARS ❧

Following my trip to San Francisco, I had fences to mend with Tanya. I hadn't realized she was angry that I had taken off with Roger. Because I'd had so few close girlfriends in my life, I didn't understand that technically he was still hers. Fortunately, she considered my leaving him in San Francisco as my way of breaking up with him, which helped to soothe her jealous soul.

When I returned to Minneapolis, Tanya was still staying up all night reading, sleeping most of the day, and leading what appeared to be an intriguing and comfortable life. Not knowing quite what to do with myself, I joined another tai chi class and became friends with an old blind woman who needed my help. I moved back into my old room and things proceeded in no particular direction, until the day Tanya suggested we go see the movie *The Deer Hunter*.

The movie was horrible. During it I kept picturing my beautiful Riley parachuting into quaint villages and decapitating mothers and their children, old men and their dreams. As the movie transported me into the horrors of Vietnam, I felt purpose coming to life inside of me. I left the theater knowing my path led back to Riley, to help him heal. I moved to New Orleans within a week.

He loved that I was coming back. He loved me. He had bought me a used car and a small diamond ring, smiling from ear to ear when I walked toward him at the airport. I was all set to help him heal and love him unconditionally.

A movie had inspired my return to New Orleans and to Riley. What had I been thinking? Riley was fine with his life the way it was. He was happy, much happier than I was. He tried hard to fit me into his full life, but I didn't fit very well. Who had I been kidding? I was the one who needed healing and loving, not him. Again, I wasn't at all sure that where I was, was where I needed to be.

Sitting at a desk in the corner of Riley's dreary kitchen, my foot resting atop the Havahart mousetrap I'd bought him, I wondered why I wanted to get out of this whole thing. Why would I want to leave a man whose chocolate brown skin felt like silk, whose lips brought me to heights of passion I'd never known, whose warm, caramel-colored eyes always held a hint of mischief and love?

I could pretend, but I didn't have a clue about how to be with a black man in the South. The other girls in his life brought him Cajun shrimp, dirty rice, fried chicken and greens, even cooked it for him. I didn't know how to do any of that, much less how to be a good woman to a good man. Riley cooked or we ate what the pretty girls brought him. I needed someone to teach me how to be the wife of a rollerskating black carpenter in New Orleans, Louisiana.

When something stirred under my foot, I took it as a sign: one lone mouse had found its way into the Havahart trap and it was my duty to set it free. I picked up the trap and headed out to the used white Camaro that Riley had bought for me. I carefully placed the trap holding my temporary traveling companion on the seat next to me. Setting off to find a good home for the little mouse, without knowing how to get around New Orleans in a car, was a challenge. I wasn't delivering a pie to a housebound neighbor. I had a rodent, a varmint, in my car, but when I looked through the slots on the side of the trap and saw the sorrowful eyes looking back at me I felt sentimental about the little mouse's fate.

I searched for a spot that could give it a long life full of good food and no poison.

I ended up at a cemetery, a place no one had the right to kick me out of, and I carried my buddy past the creepy, raised coffins, stepping over little markers and around the debris of the dead. I wasn't familiar with this below-sea-level burial technique, but I figured that with all these dead people around not many living folk could mess with little mousey. I didn't know what it would find to eat but I thought this place would be safe. I'd grabbed some bread and peanut butter and I laid that down on the path. I thought once I opened the trap it would run for dear life, but it just sat there looking up at me with Disney eyes and total trust.

"It'll be okay; you're safe now," I said, tipping the trap over and turning away. I felt sad the whole way home.

The phone was ringing when I got back to the house on St. Ferdinand Street. I pulled open the door, realizing I hadn't locked it. I ran for the phone. It was Tanya. She had lists of things to tell me. She'd read the entire "C" section at the Minneapolis Library, she had a new beau, and she had been working on the book we planned to write together. As she continued talking, full of her aliveness, I only half-listened. I looked to the front of Riley's shotgun house and could see it from one end to the other. While she rambled on, I thought about how flat my life was and would be and then had the wisdom to ask, "What?" She repeated herself.

She had decided to ride her bike to New York to get our book published—the book I had been trying to start writing for months now, the book based on fact but heavy on fiction, a product of our rich imaginations, the book that had me paralyzed. We would call it "Calls of the Wild: Obscene Phone Callers in America."

We'd started the project a year earlier for a Women's Studies course at the University of Minnesota at Minneapolis. We'd gotten the idea from a phone call Tanya had received from a stranger one night as she was stepping into the bath. "Call me back in an hour," she'd said casually.

"I would like to call you back—you sound nice. What number did I dial?" he'd asked, and that had started a long discussion about his addiction to making obscene phone calls, which led us to find more like him. We wanted to know what motivated people to do such a thing, and to hear their stories. Sometimes the people were creepy, but we heard tender and kind stories too. We interviewed everyone we could find who had received or made an obscene or anonymous phone call.

Tanya rambled on and on. Her mom was giving her a couple of hundred dollars; she "had a good feeling" about this; it was perfect, she'd camp, and I wasn't to worry about her.

"Tanya, are you nuts? I mean, you can't even read a map. How can a person ride a bicycle from Minnesota to New York without knowing how to read a map?"

"It's only fifteen hundred miles. That means if I ride a hundred miles a day I can be there in, like, two weeks. You could meet me there."

While I said the words "I can't meet you there," I knew I wanted to go and I wanted to go where she was, now. I couldn't stand another minute of myself in New Orleans. The place was fine but I wasn't. Riley didn't need me to lick his Vietnam wounds; he was just fine licking his own. He didn't need me here thinking here really sucked; he needed someone who thought here was right and good and perfect. And I needed more adventure. I needed to catch up with how cool Tanya was, how amazing my sisters were, how much they all knew, how much they had all seen.

I heard her groan. And then I finished my sentence with, "I want to go with you." It was decided then and there. I told her I'd send her a check for her to buy me the same bike she had so she would know how to change its flat tires, oil the thingamajigs, and everything else. We became ecstatic with our planning, talking and talking. It was almost as good as lying on the beach on Paradise Island together, the time we tore

Shōgun in half so we could both read it. I felt the warmth of happiness spreading over me like a good tan.

I looked up when I realized I wasn't alone. Riley was standing by the rust-stained sink, his beautiful lips separated in disbelief. His eyes said, "I knew it, I knew you wouldn't stay here," and they didn't say a word about wishing I would. I hung up the phone not sure what I had said, what he had heard, and how I was going to explain this one.

He had heard enough to not even need an explanation. I went to him and put my arms around him, pressing my body into his, and he pressed back. I turned his head toward mine and found his open lips and slipped my tongue into his mouth. As I tightened my grip around his narrow waist, he scooped me up and carried me to his bed.

My bicycle arrived in New Orleans just a little over a week later. It weighed twenty-nine pounds. It was a Motobecane racing bike and had cost me $489 with all the panniers and accessories I would need. I was still receiving four hundred a month from my dad's trust fund, so I could pay for it. It came assembled, but the tires needed air so I proudly walked it to the corner gas station. I felt very white in the all-black neighborhood and extremely self-conscious about the ritzy new bicycle. I carefully lined the valve up with the air hose and pushed the two together. My bike flew up in the air and landed like an old woman falling down the stairs with her knees bent in the wrong direction. Exploded tire, dented body, and twisted frame in the blink of an eye. A kind, drunk older man offered to drive me to the bike shop to get it fixed. I felt too upset to do that and asked if he would just take us home.

I let Riley fix it and practiced riding on his bike. It felt sturdy and dependable, just like him. But I wasn't looking for sturdy and dependable. Maybe I wasn't actually looking for anything, but simply experimenting with what I found.

Looking back, I don't remember Riley and me doing much of anything together except making love and eating. We never went to the movies or read books together. I met his mom once. He wanted to take me rollerskating, but I hated doing things I couldn't do well so I always declined.

The night before I was to leave, Riley came home from work, showered, dressed, and left again. Two of his friends, Janice and John, had made plans to take us out dancing. I loved dancing and Riley could really move, so I thought it would be great, except he couldn't do it, couldn't celebrate my leaving. It hadn't been said that I wouldn't return and I'd had furniture shipped down to New Orleans so one might assume I would, but my decision did have a ring of finality to it. I decided to go out whether he came or not. He knew where we'd be so maybe he would join us.

I didn't have that high, tight butt or those inch-long lashes that Riley's little friend Jackie had. I couldn't cook fried chicken or skate backwards, but I could wear tight jeans and high heels and I could dance, I really could dance. I rolled a perfect joint, stuck it carefully in my sock, and headed to the club. His friends had already arrived and were sipping cocktails, and they were wonderfully warm. They liked me, I liked them, and they both certainly loved Riley. Janice was a California girl through and through, with long blonde hair and bronze skin. Open and delightful, she pushed half of a blue pill toward me when I sat down and said, "Take it, it'll relax you." So I took it. Janice said she knew how I felt, which was a relief, because I didn't know what I was feeling.

With Janice around, I felt liberated from having to understand myself. Her husband also seemed to understand me. He was like Mr. Rogers. He said that Riley didn't know how to handle this kind of thing and that I was right to go. He asked what my favorite drink was. I told him I didn't really have one and he offered me a sip of his. It was delicious—creamy and rich. He ordered me a Black Russian and made sure through the night that I always had one in front of me. For someone who didn't like clubbing, I was in a very sexy and mellow mood. I'd always loved dancing by myself and found the funky rhythm perfect, so I danced to a few songs. As I was finding my way back to our table, a stunning black man motioned me over. Instead I sat down and with a tilt of my head motioned for him to come to me.

As he approached the table he became even more attractive and, realizing my mistake, I got up to stop him. I told my friends I'd be right back and walked toward the front door. The man exited the building directly behind me. I turned toward my car and he walked into me, kissing me deeply and powerfully. I tried to back up but he stuck to me like glue, his kiss moving through me like fire. I felt very drunk and unsteady on my feet, but my car was right there. I needed to sit down to catch my breath. We both got in. I reached in my sock for the joint. He slid his arms under me and lifted me over his lap and sat me next to him on his right side, sliding across to put himself behind the wheel and pulling a lighter from his pocket—all in one very black, very chic, very smooth move.

I was excited, but then he grabbed my head, unzipped his pants, and pressed my mouth onto his cock. I gagged as it hit the back of my throat. I started to vomit and he deftly opened the door on the driver's side, hung my head beyond his lap, and I disposed of my four Black Russians, the half Valium, and most of my dignity. He pulled me back by my hair, pushed me into a sitting position, and started the engine. Appalled at my behavior, I shut my eyes as the car pulled out into Bourbon Street.

I should have told him to pull over and get out, but instead I sat there with the sour taste of vomit in my mouth. The gorgeous man behind the wheel didn't look so gorgeous anymore. He had the joint, half-smoked and unlit, dangling from his smirking lips. I could see through the window behind him that we were leaving the French Quarter. I wanted to jump out, but it was my car. I told him I felt sick again and to pull over. I still remember his tender words: "Puke out the window, bitch."

I was scared and nauseous. I shut my eyes to let the sting of his words and the rise of bile pass. When I opened them, I was in the parking lot of a big housing project. He got out of the car, threw the keys at my face, and told me to rot in hell. I wondered where I had gone wrong. How had I caused a man to say such a thing? I slid into the driver's seat, locked the doors, adjusted my mirror, and backed up. I couldn't wait to get away from there, wherever there was.

I drove around three huge tenement buildings, all very eerie and quiet. I had no idea what time it was, and even if my radio had been working I needed it quiet while I recounted my sins. I needed peace so I could pull myself together. I drove until I came to a major road, stopped at the signal light, and turned the opposite way from my instincts because I have a lousy sense of direction.

I felt better just moving, amazed I hadn't been hurt or robbed, but something was wrong. I looked in my rearview mirror and saw a police car so close I thought it might hit me. I didn't know what to do. I turned on my blinker and suddenly realized I was on the wrong side of the road, with a police car stuck on my behind. I turned on the other blinker to actually pull over. The cop leapt out of his car like he was ready to kill me.

Although he bounded from his vehicle, by the time he got close to me his gait had slowed and become deliberate and precise. My knees knocked together and I felt lightheaded as he ripped open my door.

I held onto the armrest with my weaker left hand, gripping the steering wheel with my right hand until it spun and I almost fell out of the car. When I reached out with my right arm to break my fall, it grazed his gun. Filled with terror, I let my hand drop to the floorboard and caught myself. Somehow I got out of the car, almost stepping on his foot. I stood up; he spun me around, slapped handcuffs on me, and pushed me against his car. When he kicked my legs farther apart, my ankle twisted and my knees buckled. I hit my brow on the car. He frisked me between my legs and patted me down.

Dropping a nickel and a dime on the ground, he said, "Pick those up." I shrugged my shoulders, indicating that I didn't have the use of my hands. He unlocked the cuffs. I rubbed my wrists and bent to the ground to retrieve his coins. I handed them to him but he slapped my hands away. I tried to look into his eyes but his wraparound sunglasses covered them. He took six big steps, turned around, and told me to do the same thing. I did it. It wasn't easy with my knees knocking and the wits scared out of me, but I did it. He told me to lean back against the car. I did. He kicked my legs apart again. This time I was prepared, so I didn't lurch. He stuck his hand between my legs and lingered there. He rubbed and squeezed my inner thigh, first on one side, then the other. He grabbed my arms out from under me and again I took a forward dive into his car. I tasted blood as I bit my lip. Finally, he opened the back door of his squad car and pushed me in headfirst. I yelped and he told me to shut up.

He then called in the location of the arrest, citing that I was driving a stolen vehicle. I protested from the backseat and told him it was my boyfriend's car, that it had been a gift. He ignored me, looking back and forth between the rearview mirror and the speedometer, clocking a hundred and ten miles per hour with no flashers, no siren, just him staring through me.

I had no parents to call, no clue where I was. I couldn't believe this was happening. My boyfriend, whom I was leaving in a few hours, was going to be furious. My mind worked overtime as I tried to figure out how I was going to tell Riley what had happened. What did happen? How had I ended up here?

We got to the station and I saw, from the outside of the building, that we were in Gretna, Louisiana. The clock on his dashboard read two A.M. He pulled me out of the car by wrapping his hand around my neck and pushed me through the front doors of the building without batting an eye.

Officer Daly—according to his nametag—opened a glass-walled cell and shoved me in. I stumbled but managed not to fall onto the filthy, wet floor. The cell reeked of urine. I looked for a place to sit but a slutty-looking woman had already taken the cement bed and a stick-thin woman scratching her arms and looking every bit the junkie sat on the toilet, the only chair in the place. I did the only thing I could do: I made a little chair out of my shoes and sat down at the front of the cell. There was a pay phone on the wall in front of me but I didn't have a dime.

The officer who'd arrested me came over and stood outside the cell, unzipped his pants, and masturbated. I stared straight at the floor while his semen dripped down the glass cell wall. He called the matron to search me. She led me to a private room, told me to undress, and strip-searched me, leaving no place untouched.

I waited while the arresting officer pretended to look for a dime. When I turned my head to the side I saw another glass cell, this one filled mainly with black men, masturbating just as the officer had. I waited, the prostitute sat on the bed laughing to herself, and the junkie scratched her arm so violently that it bled. I waited until another officer came and put me into a little screened-in standing area. Even though he'd seen my driver's license, he asked me my name, where I lived, what I was doing in New Orleans, how much I'd had to drink, and if I wanted to make a phone call.

I waited. I waited as he made me turn around and watch the guys in the cell. They looked like deranged animals, trying to get a better view. I waited as the dime he had given me dropped into the phone.

My first choice would have been to call my dad but I could never have faced him and he'd been dead for five years already. I would rather have called an archangel or Perry Mason, anyone but Riley. The phone picked up on the second ring.

"What's it?" he mumbled.

"It's me, Riley, I got into some trouble and I need your help."

"Why don't you ask the brother you left the club with for help?"

"I'm really sorry about this, honey. I made a terrible mistake."

"Seems like you been making lots of mistakes. I'm a mistake too, aren't I?"

"Riley, they're making it really hard for me here. I'll explain everything. Can you just come and get me, please?" My voice cracked and I began to shake, thinking he might not save me.

"Where are you?"

"I'm in jail." I heard a thump and assumed he had sprung up and hit his head on the loft.

"Shit no, where, what jail? What the hell are you doing in jail? What did you do?"

"He said I had a stolen car."

"Wait a minute, wait a minute. You're in jail because of the car?"

"Well, not exact—" I was saying when a recorded voice came on telling me to deposit five more cents, please. "Riley, I don't have any money. Come get me, please. I'm in a place called Gretna." The phone went dead.

I had no idea if he'd heard me. I had no idea if he'd come for me. I didn't know if I'd get out of there or to the airport or to Minneapolis or onto my bike. I didn't know a thing as I sat back down on my shoes. I hated myself for being there. I put my head in my hands and wept as quietly as I could. The next thing I knew, the hooker was shaking me.

"They won't let your man pick you up, honey. They say they won't take no nigger's money 'less it's the right change. Your man is pissed."

"Where is he? How do you know this?"

"I heard 'em talking out front. He's been here and left. They wouldn't break a hundred."

"A hundred?"

"Yeah, they set your bail at seventy-five. I never heard no bail so short like that. What'd you do, kick a puppy?"

"I didn't do anything except drink too much, throw up, get kidnapped, make the wrong man mad, and end up here. Oh, and I was driving on the wrong side of the road."

She had quit listening as soon as I'd started answering. I figured she didn't have any energy for nonprofit conversations. So, I waited some more. Two hours later the cell door opened. While walking out, I saw the dried semen on the glass cell wall where not only my arresting officer but also the morning shift sergeant had masturbated in front of me. They had stood there on the hour to relieve themselves. I looked down and away, having one of those I-hope-my-dad-can't-see-this-from-heaven moments. The man leading me out squeezed my upper arm, twisting it toward him, and spit more than spoke, "What happened here didn't happen. Do you hear me?" He squeezed harder and twisted farther.

I nodded as he led me through a set of heavy metal gates into a dark, industrial-looking hallway before pushing me against the wall and kissing me roughly. He smelled like ham. I pushed him back and tried to slide out from his forceful embrace. He laughed and led me out into the light.

Riley was glaring at me. They wouldn't even let him enter the building. I grabbed the few things that had been taken from me. The car keys were with the car in an impounded lot, half a county away. I didn't have much to carry, but my sins weighed me down.

I climbed into Riley's work truck and wanted to hug him and thank him but he was in an angry just-been-oppressed-by-the-white-man mood, his hair all nappy and squished, his skin ashy. He had sleep crystals in his eyes and wore ripped sweatpants and a paint-splattered T-shirt. I felt twelve years old when I lifted up on the old truck door to shut it. He broke the silence with a question.

"So what was the dude's name who you left with?"

"I don't know."

"You don't know?"

"I don't know."

"Why don't you know?"

"I don't know, I just didn't ask."

"You let a guy whose name you don't know kiss you?"

"How did you know he kissed me?"

"He kissed you?"

"What do you mean?"

"You just said he kissed you," he said, his voice rising as he punched the heel of his hand into the hard black steering wheel.

"I don't know his name. He did kiss me but that's all."

"Yeah, right."

"Really."

I screamed, "Riley, look out!" as he swerved, just missing a car going twenty miles an hour in the left lane. I slumped back in the seat. It felt good to be sitting on something other than my shoes on a slimy, stinking cement floor in a disgusting jail cell. My butt muscles relaxed, I shut my eyes, and I felt myself go airborne.

Riley had pulled me onto his lap and was kissing me. It wasn't affection; it was territorial. There were three men's kisses in my mouth, plus germs from a penis, alcohol, vomit, and burning unspoken words. I turned my head and gave him the warmest hug I could, slipped off his lap, and looked at the clock on the dash.

"What time is it really?" I was too spent to remember if he'd set this one ahead a half hour or ten minutes or if it really worked. He looked at his watch and told me it was a quarter to nine. I shut my eyes again, feeling the grit of slept-in contact lenses on my sore eyeballs. The truck came to a stop. I looked up and we were home. I thought we were a million miles from St. Ferdinand Street and I'd have time for a quick nap. It turned out Gretna was only six humiliating miles from our front door. We were already home and my flight was leaving in less than an hour.

Pumped up by adrenaline that appeared like a gift from God, I opened the door and jumped out of the truck. I leaned back in to kiss Riley goodbye and told him how sorry I was. He put on those sweetheart eyes and told me to get my stuff: he would take me to the airport. I wished I had time to shower but I just grabbed my packed bag, thankful I'd already shipped the bike, and ran back to the truck.

It was a relief to know I'd get out of this town. The mean, slick man from the club probably lived very close and those cops were more than creepy. Plus, I'd disgraced myself. I didn't remove my contacts, because Riley had never seen me in my thick, ugly glasses and I didn't want to arrive in Minneapolis looking like a halfwit. I reached into my bag for some artificial tears, squirted them in my eyes, and laid my head back against the broken headrest. Riley was saying something but it had all caught up with me and I couldn't hear a thing.

When I opened my eyes, he was crying. The sleep crystals, loosened from his eyes, rode the waterfall down his cheeks. I wished he looked a little bit more like I was used to, but I looked awful too. I put my hand on his chest and said, "I love you so much."

It took less than twenty minutes to get to the airport. He didn't park. We both got out of the truck and did what we did best. We held each other so close we were one. I pulled back and reached for my suitcase as he slid his arm around my waist and escorted me to the curb and into the check-in line.

"I'll see you really soon and I am so sorry about last night and today," I cried. "I'm just sorry about everything." I pulled the little diamond engagement ring from my finger and put it in his hand. "I don't think I deserve to have this or to expect you to wait for me. If you want to give it to me when I come back, you can."

I kissed him goodbye and saw his shoulders relax as he put the little ring on the tip of his pinkie. That ring would probably fit Jackie a lot better than it fit me—Jackie, the rollerskating, ultra-slim, stunningly beautiful, sweet black eighteen-year-old who had loved Riley since she was a little girl.

I checked my bag and headed to the restroom to clean up. I did the best I could—brushing my teeth, combing my hair, washing the bottom of my shoes—and sat on the toilet for a good long while to just have some privacy.

They announced my flight as I sat there. On my way to the gate I bought a cup of coffee, and that's when I realized I hadn't gotten to the bank. I had only a twenty-dollar bill in my sock. It didn't matter. For now I just needed to board my flight and watch New Orleans disappear behind me.

I thought I'd sleep like a stone and eat like a horse, but I picked at my food and stared out the window like a zombie. Sitting on a plane for several hours in clothes that I'd had on when I drank too much, passed out, and sat on the floor in a jail cell was horrible. I stank and ached and regretted everything. I desperately needed to sleep, but before I knew it a voice asked us to fasten our seat belts for landing.

ೞ II ೞ

STARTING OVER

For what it's worth: it's never too late or, in my case, too early to be whoever you want to be. There's no time limit, stop whenever you want. You can change or stay the same, there are no rules to this thing. We can make the best or the worst of it. I hope you make the best of it. And I hope you see things that startle you. I hope you feel things you never felt before. I hope you meet people with a different point of view. I hope you live a life you're proud of. If you find that you're not, I hope you have the courage to start all over again.

—Eric Roth, from the screenplay for
The Curious Case of Benjamin Button

CHAPTER 10

❧ BICYCLING TO NEW YORK CITY ❧

When I got off the plane, I walked the long corridor to where friends and family stand, and there was Tanya, my best friend in the whole world. She would understand everything. As I got closer, I saw her jumping up and down, holding three big helium balloons and wearing a propeller beanie. I looked her in the eye and whispered, "I just got out of jail." She released the helium balloons as though we'd rehearsed the scene a thousand times.

We got into her bright yellow Pacer and drove to her mother's house, where she'd been staying in preparation for our journey. It was a great house in a good neighborhood; her father had been in the cigar business.

I called my bank and had them wire money to Western Union, which was only open for another two hours. I called my old friend Marty, who sold pot, and arranged to meet him. I called Riley to thank him and to tell him again that I was sorry. At last I peeled off my jail-wear and slipped into the gorgeous bubble bath that Tanya had drawn for me, the most luxurious bath I'd ever taken.

I decided not to wash or dry clean the things I'd worn during my nightmare. I would never wear them again. They would have always reminded me of a night that would've broken my father's heart:

me sitting on the edge of my high heels in a urine-soaked cell in the company of unkind women and men who would do anything to relieve their misery. I lowered my filthy hair into the bubbles as I watched the whole scene again, this time from a distance—the warm water touching my very soul.

After my bath and a change of clothes, I mounted my bike and headed over to Western Union with Tanya. Minneapolis is an extraordinary city, connected by a series of lakes. We were riding around one of the lakes on this spectacular summer day, off to secure my money for our trip and have a nice lunch, when I looked up and saw a bicyclist headed toward Tanya. She was looking at the lake and didn't see this crazy kid. I yelled, "Watch out!" and she looked up just in time, veering out of his way, but the distraction caused me to take my eyes off the road and my front wheel dropped off the five-inch lip of tarmac. My bike fell down hard on the pavement, sending me down too, headfirst.

The next thing I knew I was in the back of somebody's car. I didn't recognize the driver, didn't know where I was, and started yelling at him. I must have scared him, because he veered off the road. Tanya, sitting in the seat in front of me, reached her hand over and told me I had hit my head and needed to go to the hospital. I shut up. My head really hurt.

Some hours later, the doctor told me I had a severe concussion and certainly could not leave on a long bike trip. In fact, he instructed Tanya to wake me up every hour or two for the next twenty-four hours. I needed to take it easy, he said, and allow at least a week to recuperate.

We left on our journey thirty-six hours later. Wobbly but relieved to be on the road, I set out on a trip that, in retrospect, we were not prepared to take, to publicize a book that hadn't even been written yet. My head kept pounding and pounding. Tanya's old boyfriend Michael had been commandeered to drive us to County Route 12, one of the many county roads that we would travel. Less than two hours after leaving, we pulled into the parking lot of a funky-looking bar outside Menomonie, Wisconsin, and Michael finessed the bikes from their carrier. He wanted to send us off with a toast. We left our bikes propped against the building, went inside, and ordered big frosty mugs of beer. It was August of 1979. We had three rounds. Exuberant and daring, we then mounted our metal steeds and headed toward New York City.

Wrenched from the comfort of dreaming and talking about our cross-country bicycle trip into the hard, dusty reality of pedaling, I could barely stay upright on the narrow seat due to the unequal weight of the panniers on the back of my bike. Plus, I wore stupid bike shoes that were nearly impossible to slip into the narrow metal brackets on my bike pedals, and I carried a full pack on the front of my handlebars. Tanya and I each had a sleeping bag and a bedroll, and I brought a tent bungee-tied on top of the panniers. Dressed in skin-tight bike pants, bike gloves, and bike shirts, we pedaled about ten miles that first day before pulling into the Muddy Creek campground. We set up camp, ate peanut butter sandwiches and apples, and tried to sleep.

My head hurt. I hated riding a bike uphill. It was more work than I was cut out for, and I couldn't operate the stupid gears. There was one lever on either side of my handlebars and, if I got it wrong, my feet would suddenly spin out of control, forcing me to pedal ultrafast or tip over. With so much weight on the back wheel, I lurched from side to side. I decided to keep it in the one firm gear, which required me to work feverishly to get up hills, but I preferred that to tipping, panicking, or veering onto the deadly curbed shoulder.

Tanya seemed fine; she was always out ahead. I struggled without her knowing it. When she'd look back I would smile and nod. We stopped often for snacks. I'd nearly killed myself trying to loosen my water bottle from its wire holder and had to stop if I wanted to quench my thirst. Tanya couldn't wait to try out all the dehydrated food she'd bought. We'd brought Pemmican Bars that were supposedly all the rage but we were in big trouble if that was all we had to eat. I spit mine out. She tried hers, pretending to enjoy it, chewing and nodding her head, but then spit hers out too.

On our second day out we stopped at a little park to have lunch. We sat at a picnic table and ate nuts and raisins and drank all the water we wanted while resting and looking at our map. We had ridden nonstop for four hours. It was hot with no breeze to cool us down. Still, it was awesome, this thing we were doing.

To our surprise, when we stood up after our lunch, our legs had gone crazy numb, and they didn't want to straighten. Our quadriceps had cleverly shortened by at least two inches. We hobbled like old women back to our bicycles. Lifting my leg high enough to mount my bicycle took every ounce of muscle power I had. In absolute agony, we rode on, our pain easing eventually, and we cycled like kids for four more hours.

On our third day riding, I finally knocked my gears around until I felt the chain grip and the pedaling became easier. After that, I knew the sequence of gears to help me up the hills and keep me safe going down them.

At night we camped in our dome tent at campsites or near streams, but once in a while we'd pedal into a small town and find a boarding house or a motel so we could take a shower and sleep in a bed with sheets. Day after day we'd wake up, stretch, and get back in the saddle.

◌

I didn't grow up riding a bike, and my muscles burned when we pumped up hills, even with the right gears in place. My shoulders ached from the awkward position that the handlebars required, my neck was so stiff I couldn't turn my head to see the traffic behind me, and my head still hurt. But the scenery was beautiful, at least what I saw of it. I could scarcely afford the risk of looking around, with potholes, gravel, and

Julie on the bike trip from Minneapolis to New York City, 1979.

Once I'd mastered the gears, the riding became easier.

cars whizzing by threatening to knock me off my bike. I spent one day trying not to run over caterpillars and the next day butterflies seemed to surround me. I got very good at setting up camp and felt quite the countrywoman, gathering wood, starting the fire, and cooking oatmeal or macaroni and cheese over a campfire. I liked anything and everything that didn't ask me to sit on a hard narrow seat bent forward working my ass off.

In Wisconsin the August weather had been hot and dry, but when we crossed the state line into Michigan rain fell in sheets. We pulled on our specially designed bicycle rain ponchos that covered our entire bodies, our handlebars, and our panniers, but then we could see only the road directly in front of us and nothing else. After three days of squishy riding and soggy camping, I rejoiced when I spied a riot of color, speeding up and actually getting in front of Tanya.

I hollered over the pelting rain, "Let's stop, I want to take pictures and go meet those people."

She followed me down a gravel drive. We had apparently come upon an outdoor museum of old farm equipment painted delightfully bright colors: one was a rusted saw blade painted red with a yellow rubber glove for a hat with the title "Whatchamacallit" written beneath it. Hundreds of sculptures later, we arrived at the farmhouse door and a heavyset woman named Bertha ushered us in out of the rain. Her slender husband, Al, dressed in a flannel shirt and overalls, sat at the kitchen table eating a grilled cheese sandwich, and before we knew it so were we. They invited us to spend the night and we gratefully accepted. It was nice to dry off and just relax. We took the tour and heard all about Al's life work, creating the sculpture garden.

"A fella from Nestlé's came out here once and ended up naming a candy bar after that rooster saw blade piece," he told us with pride—his Whatchamacallit.

We had a few more close encounters with townsfolk, but mostly we just rode and rode and rode some more. Many times along the way we wanted to quit, but there comes a time when all you can do is keep moving. We headed north a bit into Canada and I developed a high fever, nearly bent in half with horrible cramps. We checked into a motel run by a chiropractor and his family. He helped relieve my cramps a bit, but we didn't have the money to linger, and thankfully the fever had subsided, even if we both were running low on energy.

Tanya and I just wanted to get where we were going, to New York City. I especially wanted the ride to be over. Neither the pounding in my head nor my cramps had fully subsided when we crossed the border at Niagara Falls. We agreed it was truly a wonder of the world. We wanted to dawdle, but we had a book to write so we could make good on the purpose of this adventure.

CHAPTER 11

❧ CALLS OF THE WILD ❧

In Niagara Falls, when we were three hundred miles from New York City, we thought the end was in sight. I'd felt perpetually weak with stomach pain, but Tanya, as always, had been fine and we pressed on for at least five more days. Here we were, on our unpublicized publicity tour to get a book published that wasn't written yet.

When we came within sight of the city, we'd been on the road for almost three weeks and had traveled over fifteen hundred miles atop our thin-wheeled bicycles. I don't remember what bridge we crossed in to New York (I had to focus hard on the road to forget about my pain) but the sight of the skyline mesmerized me. Awestruck, I hadn't been paying full attention to the road, and suddenly I was on my own.

As Tanya rode out ahead of me I watched in horror as her front wheel dropped into a pothole the size of a bathtub. She righted her bike but I nearly drove into an open car door in the process. My heart thumped in my chest but I couldn't stop. I didn't know where I was going, and I knew that if I lost sight of Tanya I would be screwed.

I had to super-pedal to avoid colliding with pedestrians and cars and to keep up with Tanya. I was sharing the road with flying ninjas that turned out to be rollerskaters, skateboarders, scooter riders and bike messengers. We were in more danger within ten minutes of reaching the Big Apple than we had been while traveling the fifteen hundred miles to get there.

After what seemed like hours, at least to me, we arrived at The Franconia, a well-veneered but worn-out residence for the well-veneered but worn-out residents who had almost made it. It was located directly across the street from The Dakota, the success of whose occupants is defined by the mention of its name. We had made it to the Upper West Side of the city that never sleeps, and that was good enough for us.

Like Riley, I had become one with my bike; my ride and I were one, or maybe more like one-point-one. I could be riding it, and then the next minute whipping it out from under me to walk alongside it. And that's what I did when we approached the awning of The Franconia. We were stars! Two remarkable women who'd set out to do something spectacular and brought it all the way home.

The doorman yelled at us about bringing our bikes inside to reception. No problem: he just didn't realize who we were, because who we were hadn't yet been established. I figured I just needed to explain myself, which is what prompted me to introduce the two of us to the people in the elevator.

"Hi, I'm Julie and this is Tanya and these are our bikes. We just rode all the way from Minnesota."

No one responded. There was complete silence. My forced smile began to dry my teeth out. I repeated myself and still no one said a word. We all watched the numbers light one after the other above our heads, my sentence hovering in the air over us.

Tanya had sublet an apartment for us for a few weeks, which certainly seemed enough time to write our smash bestseller and get it published. We rolled our bikes into the apartment. We had figured that, being so close to Central Park, it would be marvelous, but everything about the place seemed used and stuck in the Sixties. The sheets, the pillows, the tub, and the toilet seat all had a grimy overtone.

The next day I woke up early and went downstairs to the also frozen-in-time diner, and had the largest and most delicious bran muffin in the world. They grilled it in butter. I sat self-consciously watching all the people not notice me until I came up with a plan and immediately went up to tell Tanya. Together we decided that we would call a few newspapers and news shows to tell them we would soon be arriving in the city after our fifteen-hundred-mile bike ride from Minnesota. We were on our way, almost there, and they could catch a glimpse of history if they wanted to. Surely it was newsworthy, two young women, one blonde and blue-eyed, the other brunette and green-eyed, both vibrantly interesting, arriving in New York to publish their book about the impact of obscene phone callers. Who wouldn't want to meet us, photograph us, and interview us? Tanya immediately called the *New York Post,* which agreed to pick up our story.

Tanya was used to writing. She could perch anywhere and draw or write. I wasn't sure how to write. I had to prepare. I took up drinking coffee and started smoking again and found my ritual: grilled muffin, coffee with cream, and a cigarette. Now all I needed was some talent.

Tanya's bike was stolen on our second day when she had run in to a health food store for vitamins. I, on the other hand, continued to lug my two-wheeled mate around. For me waking up every morning in the city that never sleeps was like putting on a wet, cold swimsuit. It was dreadful and hard for me to get used to.

I would suddenly wake at five in the morning to the sound of garbage trucks, look out the window and see people scurrying around in the new day, or finishing off the old one. I would sit and stare at the typewriter, but the words wouldn't come. I was uneasy sitting in front of a typewriter. I would carry a journal with me. Tanya constantly wrote in a journal but I didn't have that flair. I couldn't find my muse. I felt like a fraud, an impostor.

Tanya wrote or drew all the time—though she wasn't writing the book; she was doing something much more creative, like painting portraits of every single person she saw. The writing of "Calls of the Wild" seemed to be up to me. She would delicately eat cookies in bed while she wrote in one of her tremendously large journals. It seemed the journey from chair to bed was enough to inspire hours of writing. She pored over newspapers and magazines and read a book every few days. I was sure our fate was safe in her hands.

As the days passed, I finally felt stories building in me. We had decided to embellish the stories we had and to find more people whose lives had been changed, ruined, or at least touched by obscene phone callers. At a loss for how to proceed, I called Bell Telephone and set up an interview with the Aggravated Harassment Bureau's chief, Gene McManus. He was wonderful and helpful. Stories about people who had suffered at the hands of obscene phone callers began to fill my notebook. He set up an interview for me with the New York Police Department. Obscene phone calls were epidemic, and they often led to homicide. It was arranged that I would meet with six undercover detectives at the Midtown North Precinct. My research produced great data for the book that was impossible to write.

It was terrifying and erotic to sit around a table upstairs at the precinct house as six detectives spilled out story after story about obscene callers, sexual deviants, and homicides that had started with a simple call. These were men who spent their lives pretending to be someone else so that they could penetrate crime rings. They were slightly off the beam. I kept looking at my little tape recorder, its red light glowing, as their stories got bigger, braver, and more bizarre. Unfortunately, someone stole my recorder before the night was over. I'm pretty sure the sergeant took it. His detectives had said too much.

Tanya had been working the press end for us. The *Washington Post* reprinted the piece from the *New York Post,* and from that we landed

Publicity shot of Julie for
"Calls of the Wild," 1979.

*We thought we were ready
to take on the world.*

an agent, Marianne Strong. Amazingly quickly, we had dates for photo shoots and press parties. Our agent set up radio interviews, and even got us invited to appear on *Tomorrow with Tom Snyder* in November. We were so excited. Now we had to really apply ourselves to writing the book. Three chapters and an introduction were mandatory, but we both had writer's block.

Our agent suggested we hire a publicist and an editor who would work on spec, which meant that they would do the work first and get paid if and when our book got published. The publicist was a thick-fleshed woman with a mustache, right out of the pages of our imagination. She answered her door, wheezing from the effort, surrounded by six oily-skinned little dogs, each with its own colored rubber band holding bangs out of its face. We sat with her and described ourselves while she spun press-worthy characters out of our words.

With the publicist's flair for the sensational, the meager funds left to me after my father's horrific death from colon cancer transformed me into a twenty-three-year-old jet-set heiress. Tanya's six months in a questionable school of communications became a scintillating short career in broadcast journalism. We entered that apartment as two kind of crazy and pretty girls, and left her dank domain transformed into fascinating celebrities.

Caught up in the spell her words had woven, we decided to take some of my jet-set heiress inheritance ($1,250 every three months) and get ourselves a makeover and outfits befitting our new station in life.

This is something Tanya and I did well. First we got facials at a Christine Valmy salon, and right next door was Vidal Sassoon, where we both got our hair shampooed and styled. Within a few short blocks, we found boutiques enough to land me a stunning cobalt-blue jumpsuit and Tanya a chic leopard chiffon dress and new high heels.

After our sublet at The Franconia ended, we lived at a few different addresses. If it was a place Tanya found, it was a luxury suite or a Central Park penthouse. If it was a place I found, it was within our budget and in a questionable neighborhood.

I hadn't been feeling well, very tender in my middle and a little lightheaded, as I'd been on the bike trip. Tanya insisted I go to a doctor. She took me to Beth Israel, where we sat in the waiting room with a young boy who had dropped acid by putting it in his eyes and blinding himself. Watching how the staff handled people made me feel even worse.

By the time my turn came up, I felt really terrible; everything hurt. A nurse led me into a small examining room where I undressed and waited, wearing nothing but suspicion and a paper dress. The doctor didn't introduce himself and didn't mince words. He told me to lie back and then proceeded to poke my belly. I wanted to scream, punch him, and run, but instead I tried to bear the pain of his touch. He called in a nurse and had me put my feet in the metal stirrups. As he inserted the cold speculum into my red, hot vagina I thought I would die. From far off I heard him say he would have to "yank out" my Copper Seven IUD and that I had a terrible case of pelvic inflammatory disease.

The removal of the IUD, coupled with the painful inflammation, left my body devastated. I wasn't supposed to stand upright because the condition could spread, so we had to get me to a place where I could lie down and start to heal.

With Tanya supporting me, we walked to the Hotel Nassau and with the last of our dwindling funds we got a room. Once I was in bed, Tanya put on her most flattering blue dress and her expensive high heels and went out to get money, have my prescription filled, and buy groceries. I lay there, relieved to have her take care of me. I hurt all over, feeling swollen, lacerated, and feverish. When I rolled onto my side I found myself staring into the face of a gigantic cockroach resting on the pillow beside me. I screamed and tried to flick it away but its sticky feet held onto the back of my hand. I wasn't allowed to stand, but that didn't stop me from springing to my feet and then falling to my knees in absolute agony.

The nasty bug remained stuck on my hand as I lay prostrate on the filthy worn carpet. The bed frame was covered in a thick, gummy grime, and the box spring was rust-stained where it met the metal frame; the mattress sagged, and the sheets, both flat, had untucked themselves. Leaning on my elbows, I looked deliberately at my hitchhiker and positioned my other hand directly in front of its obstinate body before flicking it hard enough to send it flying into the faux-paneled wall.

I tried to get up without allowing my body to be completely upright, which is what the doctor had warned me could cause the pelvic inflammatory disease to spread. Neither the shabby armchair nor the straight-backed chair would do, so I decided to lie on top of the covers and rest until Tanya returned.

I dozed off, miraculously sleeping through the night. Thinking I was dreaming, I woke to the sound of a relentlessly honking horn and someone yelling that she'd found Jesus. I heard this at least three times before I realized it was Tanya's voice coming from the street two floors below. I slid my body sideways to the window and saw her waving and jumping up and down next to a shiny black limousine. Standing beside her was a short Hispanic man. I waved back as they both squinted up at me. I looked at the cheap clock on the veneered desk; it was six o'clock in the morning.

A few minutes later Tanya slid her key into the lock and pushed the door open. Grinning like a five-year-old, she presented me with a vial of cocaine, a bag of groceries, and a stack of money.

"That's Jesus. He's from Caracas. It's in Venezuela. His name really is Jesus but it's pronounced Hay Seuss. I met him at Régine's. He's rich and wonderful. He wants to give us a place to finish our book," she said, hugging me. "I have to go but I'll call you later." And she was gone. She had bought me everything she liked to eat and the one thing that she knew I used to love. My nightmare *had* become a dream. I laid out three thick lines, rolled up a bill, and filled my body with the illusion of peace.

In a much better mood, I looked out the window again, the cocaine mixing with my blood like we were family, and I saw Jesus looking up at me. He was short and plump, not at all the Tab Hunter version of Jesus. He wore a tight black suit and his dark hair was long and slightly greasy. He smoked like a girl. He had been generous, that I could attest to. He waved to me. I was so grateful, so high, so grateful and so high. I felt myself sailing into his arms. He looked away when beautiful, blonde Tanya headed toward him. There was no final glance in my direction. Maybe he didn't even see me, maybe the windows prevented him from seeing how extraordinary I also was.

The next day, with Tanya's ingenuity and Jesus's money, we moved to a nicer hotel, where we made plans to fly to Caracas to write. I met Jesus again later that day when he came to our room to pick up Tanya. He was fidgety, with darting eyes and a sort of dark energy, but he had really good cocaine and gave me a film canister full of it before he took Tanya out to dinner. I wondered who the hell this guy was. No one gives that much cocaine away without wanting something in return.

I had to lie low for a few days as my body healed, so I stayed high all day long and would force myself to sleep. I didn't see a lot of Tanya.

She was staying with Jesus at The Plaza. I tried to write; I could feel the stories trying to come together. My interview with the detectives at Midtown North had been brilliant and I had excellent notes even though my tape recorder had been stolen. But I couldn't concentrate well enough to write. Tanya thought this would all be remedied by flying to Venezuela. As soon as I had finished my antibiotics and was feeling better, we flew to Caracas.

What a dismal place. Jesus set us up in what must have been his sex pad—a small studio apartment with a round king-sized bed. The ceiling over the bed was a big mirror. The refrigerator was stocked with Dom Perignon and caviar. There was only one set of towels in the bathroom but there were two thick white bathrobes in the closet.

I found a pound of marijuana and several ounces of mediocre cocaine on a shelf in the closet. On our first day in Caracas, Tanya drank a bottle of champagne, I did way too much coke, and we both got sick. Finding a spa menu in the nightstand, Tanya made appointments for two detoxifying paraffin treatments at a spa across from the apartment building, which helped us spring back.

On our second day we read and spent time recuperating, and on the third day Jesus came over and told Tanya he wanted to watch us make love. We weren't lovers and he had no business asking such a thing, but I had lived long enough to know there's no such thing as a free lunch or a free apartment. He brought out a box of sex toys. I'd never seen so many rubbery, funky-looking objects in my life, and to think other people had used them was disgusting, demeaning, and downright scary. Tanya gave me a pleading look and we tried to fake it. When Jesus unzipped his pants Tanya got mad at him and insisted he leave the apartment and buy us tickets back to New York. I watched all this unfold feeling cheap and stupid and not at all like an author who was going to be on national television, and not a bit like Jack Evans's baby daughter.

Jesus sent us back to New York and we moved into an apartment belonging to Tanya's friend Huntington, but Tanya and I were mad at each other.

We attended press parties for our book, which I guess was also on spec, where people tried to figure out who was important or influential, and I was neither. I enjoyed the photo shoots that our agent had put together and did well with the radio interviews, but I just wasn't into writing a book. When Tanya met another millionaire whose name I don't recall, I got tired of trying to keep up with her.

Riley called and told me I should come "home," and that sounded much better than my life in New York. I got on a plane and went back to Riley. I figured I could work on the book just as easily there as anywhere, and I'd come back for *Tomorrow with Tom Snyder*.

Chapter 12

❧ Truth Serum ❧

I hated New Orleans even more this time. Riley was moody, and the mice had multiplied in my absence. I struggled with my writing and found it intolerable to live in a hostile neighborhood with a man who couldn't, or wouldn't, forgive me. I endured each day. Frustrated with writing one paragraph and then deleting it, I called Tanya, desperate for inspiration, and found her in heaven. A guy named Tony had taken her shopping for some new clothes and shoes.

Knowing our national debut was only two weeks away and looking for a reason to leave New Orleans, I flew back to New York. Even though Tanya seemed perfectly content, I wanted to loosen Tony's grip on her—and in my own mind, keep her out of harm's way. And then I met him. He was elegant, educated, and dressed impeccably. She certainly didn't need my help.

Tanya was staying in a penthouse near Central Park at the time, so I moved back in with her. But I felt confused and lonely. I didn't like subletting other people's apartments, and staying in hotels didn't feel real. I had to learn how to survive a life that I hated living, because I didn't know what else to do. I began to study my notes for our television debut. I called my kinfolk in Oklahoma for the first time in a year and told them to watch.

Tanya was having a ball. When she wasn't with Tony or reading or exploring, she would sit in hotel lobbies and draw pictures of people or write in one of her big journals. I could just see her smiling, crinkling her nose and showing off her near-perfect teeth. She infatuated everyone she met. Dancing in clubs was the one thing we still did together. I didn't want to banter. I didn't want to flirt. I just wanted to dance. I also wanted to sleep alone. I wanted to figure out who I was. I wanted to be free and to feel comfortable in my own skin.

The day finally came to appear on Tom Snyder's show. I loved the whole experience—the green room, the makeup artists, and the fuss. I loved being on camera. It was fabulous and exciting. I did most of the talking because Tanya hadn't slept the night before and I had to cover for her. I came across as free and open and I said all the right things. At the end of our taping Tom Snyder opened his arms and I jumped onto his lap. He said I had done a wonderful job.

After the show we went out dancing and watched ourselves on a big television at the club. It was a remarkable feeling—plus our makeup was perfect and we both looked beautiful.

Based on my performance on *Tomorrow with Tom Snyder*, I booked some minor morning talk shows and flew to both Cincinnati and Cleveland. It turned out to be a bit of a nightmare because I'd had a one-night stand the night before, which threw me off track. I still have the only videotape of those TV interviews about the obscene phone caller book. We also did eighty-four radio interviews, talking about who made obscene calls and what a victim could do to stop them. It may have looked and sounded like we were making progress, but we weren't.

Finally, Tanya quit seeing Tony. Riley started living with Jackie and changed his phone number. Tanya and I got a street-level apartment that we didn't like, next to a taxi garage and a police station. I never could catch up with the pace of the city. New York overwhelmed me with choices. I thought I would pass out just thinking about what to do next. The *Village Voice* intimidated me and the *New Yorker* sent me over the edge because I felt so unsophisticated. Tanya, on the other hand, read everything with glee and enjoyed overwhelming circumstances. She carved out a life for herself that any creative person would envy.

I spent my time in acting classes and on the street talking to bums and homeless people. I fed the pigeons and Tanya drank champagne with millionaires. She was the mighty oak and I was a funky wooden swing hanging from one of her branches.

I met a nice guy named Dale one day. He had picked me up in his cab. He was sexy and funny but had no money whatsoever though he lived in Brooklyn Heights. I didn't know exactly how to feel. I mostly felt envy or admiration, but something shook loose on the night of Tanya's twenty-sixth birthday in April 1979.

I had aimed high to celebrate, starting with hiring a Rolls-Royce from a garage in the lower West Village. I picked out a yellow tulip to place in the crystal vase in its back seat. I reserved a table at a private club called La Mouge off Bank Street, where seven guests sipped Tanya's favorite champagne. Tanya had asked for a quaalude for her birthday, and I got a few from a dentist friend. It was all going well at first, glamorous and stylish, and her current beau, a sophisticated Frenchman, seemed to approve. We excused ourselves and went to the bathroom, where I gave her the quaalude. She begged me to take one, said she was sure I would love it. I didn't want to because I don't like anything that deadens my energy, but I obliged her. Back at the table, we listened to the singer, drank, and ate, and then poof—the situation formally known as my life exploded.

Unbeknownst to me, the quaalude worked as a truth serum, and according to Tanya I completely destroyed our relationship by telling her what I thought of her. That's it. That's all she would tell me. Our friend Danny was with us and he backed up her story, but to this day

I have no memory whatsoever of even having a conversation, not a word of it.

I woke up the next morning in Brooklyn Heights in Dale's apartment. He explained how Tanya had left in tears without seeing the Rolls-Royce, and didn't even know another party awaited her at Régine's nightclub, along with a sleek twelve-speed bicycle with twenty-six helium balloons tied to its handlebars. Dale said that Tanya's Parisian boyfriend had stomped off in a fury, leaving Tanya at La Mouge. Danny had comforted Tanya while I did coke in the bathroom to counteract the quaalude. I don't remember any of it.

When I woke up the next day it felt like the end of the world, the streets in Brooklyn Heights hostile and bleak. Everything had gone flat, and Tanya refused to talk to me. She ran after the Parisian man who'd offered to fly her to San Francisco. She went, just like that, gone. Best friend gone; purpose for being in New York, gone; any shred of self-esteem, gone.

I broke up with Dale, packed up the apartment, and rented a studio on Jane Street. I was devastated. It was a beautiful building but a tiny apartment. The day I moved in, my nosy neighbor came by to tell me that she had found the previous tenant dead with cockroaches crawling in and out of her gaping mouth. I could never shake the image.

I kept up with the acting classes, which gave me something to say I was doing, but it all scared me to death. The acting classes brought up a lot of feelings, and the teacher insisted that all her students were in therapy to deal with just such stuff. The people in my class were meant to be in show business. I wasn't sure what I was meant to do.

When Gina joined my acting class, my world brightened. She was everything I would have liked to be. She'd gone to Bennington, came from a sophisticated family, knew and loved theater, had a luscious singing voice, and knew how to flawlessly apply eyeliner and how to make tuna salad with yogurt. Sleek and wholesome. After class one day she invited me to an actor's party—an actor named Herbert, an actor named Herbert who dealt cocaine.

I had no clue how to select a therapist, so my teacher recommended Oscar Frick, a man who had made staring at a clock into an art form, a man who wore thin nylon socks and who claimed that our best sessions were those when I used the bathroom first to do an inordinate amount of cocaine before I started talking and he started staring.

I had received a chunk of money from my dad's trust fund, so at least I could afford the therapist I didn't like and the acting class that filled me with dread. I would leave Oscar and walk home from Union Square. On Thirteenth Street I met a man named Mike who had hundreds of LPs and no top teeth. Like a psychic or a prophet, he could see into me and light my path. He'd give me three dollars and I'd go buy him a bottle of Thunderbird and we'd really talk, about the hard stuff. That became my Tuesdays—Oscar in the morning, Mike on the way home.

Mike would say, "What's wrong, girl?" And I'd start talking. He'd tip back his head with the bottle deep inside his mouth and drink the whole thing. I'd watch his Adam's apple bob up and down, usually six times, pouring down his poison, his eyes softening with anticipation of relief.

Mike had been with the Merchant Marine and had nearly died rescuing a fellow officer who'd gotten too close to a propeller while fixing a boat. He came up with the guy in his arms and misjudged the boat bottom and hit his face hard against the steel. He'd smashed his face in and lost his teeth, but he'd saved the guy. Mike had started drinking heavily, and that's not what those "few proud men" are supposed to do. The Merchant Marine asked him to leave, and he did. Too proud to take his pension, he was soon homeless. He was a kind man who would listen to me without my having to pay him.

CHAPTER 13

❧ MY SISTER CYNDI ❧

Out of the blue I got a letter from my sister Cyndi. She was coming in from Africa and wanted to see me. This was very big and scary news. We'd spent very little time together since Dad died. It had been five or six years since I'd seen her.

Cyndi had led an amazing life. Her intelligence and savvy intimidated me. Thinking I needed a buffer, I called Katherine, an old friend of hers who lived in the city, and asked her to come along for the ride. Cyndi had led a glamorous life and people were intrigued by what had happened to her. I hired another Rolls-Royce and in a moment of weakness took a cab uptown the evening before to score a quarter ounce of coke from Herbert.

When Cyndi walked through the security gate I hardly recognized her. She looked frumpy. She wore a cheap dress and her once beautiful hair was thin and lifeless. I was flabbergasted. Her years of living in Greece, England, and Africa had knitted her voice into a bizarre affect. We slid into the gorgeous two-toned Rolls, with Cyndi in the middle.

I reached for her hand and held it. It was good to touch her. With a lump in my throat, I asked if she ever thought about what happened to Mom. Cyndi was the sister who'd hitchhiked with me through Europe, teaching me how to fashion a magazine into a tampon and how to make

The Evans family, Rochester, Minnesota, 1960. From left: Bette, Cyndi, Beverly, Julie, and Jack.

There aren't nearly enough pictures of my family all together.

my hand into a chillum to smoke hash. She was also the sister who'd run out of the filthy hospital in Greece to buy Mommy a nightgown, leaving me alone to care for our dying mother. That same sister dropped my hand and told me to "let go of that family shit."

Her friend just sat there. I flinched and went cold as if I'd been slapped. I reached into my backpack and wrapped my shaking hand around my apartment keys, gripping them, before putting them into her hand. I told the driver where she was going and held it together long enough to explain to Cyndi where everything was and that I was going to take a walk. I asked the driver to pull over and I got out. I managed to leave her, but not what she'd said in the Rolls-Royce.

I couldn't stop shaking. I hadn't noticed where we were when I got out of the car, but it looked like somewhere in the Bowery. To make matters worse, it was four-thirty in the morning. It was dark and I was soul-scared, feeling disconnected from everything. I knew I was walking but I wasn't there. I wasn't anywhere. I was a zombie girl. I walked by bums in boxes and bums in bags; I walked by bums who were talking to themselves; I walked by bums who lashed out at me as though they were snakes.

I walked until I saw a sign for Mulberry Street. Julia, the bookish girl from Key West, lived here. We were sort of friends. I went to her building. Thankfully the outer door was unlocked and I walked up the three flights to her apartment. By then it was five or six in the morning. I must have knocked, and I must have woken Julia up, but I don't remember.

All of a sudden I was inside her door. I couldn't move my mouth. She sensed I was in real trouble and offered to sweep my aura. Julia waved her hands over me and I jerked and moaned. Still I couldn't rest, couldn't get comfortable; the world was black and I was dying. I had no words for this edge; nothing helped and I didn't even know what had happened.

At eight o'clock I called Oscar Frick. He told me to come right over. Julia got me into a cab. He greeted me at his office door, something he always did. He told me to sit down, but I couldn't sit. I held onto the back of the chair. My body jerked this way and that and my breath came in huge gulps; I couldn't get a grip. Oscar put a twenty-dollar bill in my hand.

"Take a cab to St. Vincent's Hospital, go to the psychiatric wing, and ask to see a doctor. They'll give you something to calm you down."

I did exactly what I was told. I told the woman sitting behind a counter at the entrance to the wing that I needed help. Help came in seconds: three men in white coats. I felt like roadkill. They more carried than guided me, putting me in a small room where everything was bolted down. The intensity of my anxiety and upset made me seem crazy. A woman entered the room during my meltdown.

"Does the television talk to you?" she asked, her pen poised. I didn't know why she had asked me that.

"I'm sorry, what did you say?" I asked, wanting to say the right thing.

"Does the television talk to you?" she said again.

"Why are you asking me that?"

"Don't raise your voice to me." With those words my fate was sealed.

She had papers for me to sign. She wanted to commit me to the psych ward.

Sitting in that cold room, terrified, stripped of my clothes, fighting an internal war that I didn't understand, I searched my mind for someone to blame. I wanted to say it was my sister's fault for being so cold, or my mom's fault for drinking herself to death, but I didn't think it would matter. I didn't have the heart to try to blame it on my dad, because he was always sick. He had suffered enough without adding blame to emphysema, regret, an aneurysm, and cancer.

I wanted to figure out how I'd gotten here, but this would take too many steps. Kenny had introduced me to cocaine but I had courted the killer. Gina introduced me to Herbert, and Herbert knew vigilantes from Peru who would swallow three or four condoms full of pure rock mother-of-pearl cocaine, but it wasn't their fault. I just sat there in the bare room barely holding on.

The intake lady handed me a pen, three pieces of paper, and no choice. Sign here, here, and here. I wanted to say, "I'm not me. I can't sign these. The real me is upset with this me. She is somewhere else getting a new life ready for us. I can't sign these because I am not crazy or dangerous; I am just broken and scared. I can't sign these because I don't like you and I don't think you can help me. I can't sign these."

"I can't sign these," was all I could muster. She said I had to. I told her I didn't believe that and would like to see her supervisor. Magic words that would open the door to possibility.

"Let me see your supervisor," I said again, with more confidence. An option arose. Angrily she spit some words at me. "If you call a friend, and that person will take responsibility for you, then you can go home."

I called Gina, but I don't remember what I said. Finally, after who knows how long I'd waited in absolute terror, Gina showed up. She looked like Katharine Hepburn, all in black and wearing expensive sunglasses.

She appeared with two guys from acting class; I was ashamed to have them see me like this. Gina was laughing and casual and glamorous and I was beyond ugly and freaked out and disgusting. We got me a prescription for an anti-anxiety drug that takes three weeks to have an effect, even when you take ten of them, as I did, hoping it would take effect immediately.

Gina and her friends from class deposited me at my apartment, where Gina entertained the young gentlemen with her good looks, charm, and sense of humor. I couldn't yet reach the "isn't this hysterical" point and I didn't have much to say. My sister had come and gone and was staying in our cousin Ronny's apartment. I didn't want her to know about my ordeal but I felt her presence in my apartment. She had left me a very brief note thanking me for the apartment and for picking her up, but not a word about love.

When Tanya left New York, I thought I had stayed because she was so irresponsible and had left tons of unpaid bills and unfinished business, but the truth is I stayed because I had become addicted to cocaine, really addicted. It's pretty easy to hide in a big city, and I needed to hide. I'd learned that it isn't easy to hide in an acting class that forces you to deal with yourself, but somehow I thought I hid my cocaine problem. Only a coke addict would think that she looked normal. Nostrils filled with caked white powder isn't normal; neither are chronic sniffling, jaw grinding, or an inability to be still.

I wouldn't eat for a week and then suddenly I'd need fresh carrot juice. I'd walk to a health food store on Seventh Avenue, and get twenty-five pounds of carrots and juice them until I felt my blood sugar return to something like normal. I'd run long distances on the abandoned West Side Highway, back and forth, as many times as it took to feel less scared. I'd stay up all night doing coke, and then I'd use Triscuits and mozzarella cheese washed down with cranberry juice to re-enter the earth's orbit.

I'd watch Mary Tyler Moore reruns and pray that I could have her life. I'd see demons clinging to the outside of my barred windows, and I'd be kept awake by my own fear. I'd ride my bike to the Bowery to talk with homeless people and give them money. I'd do too much coke and then write. I'd write until my heart began to leap or fail or jump or whatever it's called when your body convulses and your hand jerks. I have those journals and only one person has read them, and it isn't me.

CHAPTER 14

❧ MEETING ANDREW ❧

Three weeks later I met Andrew in one of those precious moments when I wasn't out of my mind completely. He just happened to me. He was from Scotland, and on his way back to Canterbury, England, where he was working toward his doctorate in psychology. He had been in Indiana for some sort of teaching program and was staying in New York with my friend Phyllis from acting class. I don't know how he knew her, but that is how we met. He had chiseled features, deep brown eyes, and long hair, and he was sexy and dynamic and fascinating.

I used the restroom a few times to keep my cocaine equilibrium on, but I didn't drink or go schizy. I had my glow on that night. He liked me. I liked him too.

I had a hard time standing still to have a conversation when my mind could focus only on getting more cocaine up my nose, but somehow I stayed present enough for him not to notice. He was everything I'd ever dreamed of and I hung on his every word. It was as if there were just the two of us in Phyllis's loft full of actors and dreamers. I was so turned on that I could hardly swallow. I didn't need cocaine now. I just wanted this amazing man to love me, sweep me up and take me in his arms.

As the night wore on, we found ourselves alone. My body was on high alert. My mouth craved his lips and my hands wanted to trace the outline of his jaw. I don't remember if we made love that night or if I went home and he courted me (I guess I was too coked up to know), but I do remember that he told me he had to leave the States in only three weeks. I wanted to spend that time doing whatever his itinerary dictated. We went to lots of museums, where I followed Andrew around and acted like I knew art or history. We made love a lot. I felt pulled into him, like in that old song about having somebody under your skin. Jagged on the inside from the coke, I figured I could hold it together for a few weeks.

One night when we got together, his face was white and drawn. I thought he was going to tell me that he'd met someone else or wanted to stop seeing so much of me. He spoke so softly I had trouble hearing him when he told me that he might have some sort of sexually transmitted disease. I hadn't figured on that. Thank God we found a free clinic, where they tested us, and everything was fine.

Three weeks of trying to manage my addiction and my attraction, three weeks with a highly charged man who put his sexual needs before everything else, three weeks was all we had, so I could do this, I kept telling myself, I could keep up this pace and later I would collapse and rest. Then Andrew asked me to marry him.

He wanted to get married on June 28, just as Kenny and I had. With Kenny it had been a hospital basement with Dad wheeled in weighing ninety pounds. That was holy. I wondered if this was holy. He seemed to think it was clever or funny or poetic. I thought it could be wonderful, so I said yes before I thought about it or reasoned through it. I said yes because it was perfect. Andrew was fascinating and knew all I would ever need to know. He would guide me in all things brilliant and extraordinary; he would usher me into the world of interesting people.

We had only two days before he would be leaving for Canterbury, and school. I would stay in New York and get my act together. It seemed like a plan. I really loved him so much. I made some phone calls and found out that the only way we could get married in time was to go to the free clinic and get a blood test, take the results to a judge's chamber in Brooklyn, and plead for the court to have mercy in this case and allow us to wed.

The atmosphere in the courthouse felt strained; many diverse people seemed to have urgent needs with no clue how to impress a judge. In contrast, sharp, crisply dressed attorneys seemed to be at home in this alternate reality. The judge heard our case and granted us a marriage license for the day before Andrew's departure.

Now I had to find someone to marry us. I called Julia, who suggested I phone a palm reader named Rashi Gupta whom I'd met before. He was a pretend holy guy who would lie on top of his female clients to get a sense of their vibration; he was forty to my twenty-four. He had dark, East Indian skin, a slim body, and a sort of wispy goatee and mustache. He smelled like cloves and mildew, and he somehow convinced women that he was spiritual and that his spirituality could rub off on them if they let him lie on top of them so he could read their energy. He hooked me up with a minister friend of his and I called her. We talked; she sounded sincere and we arranged for the wedding. It would take place later that night in Central Park.

I needed cocaine and came up with some excuse to stop at Herb's place on the way to the park. I ran in, jumped into the elevator, hurried through the purchase of a little over three grams, jumped back into the elevator, and snorted a good half a gram before I got back into the cab. How I had money to spend on anything besides rent is a mystery to me. But now I was ready to get married to this man who enchanted and terrified me.

We got out of the cab on the edge of Central Park near The Dakota and Strawberry Fields and walked briskly to the designated meeting place at the north end of Sheep Meadow. There they were: a plump, short, black reverend and her unusual-looking teenage daughter. I handed her the marriage license and a hundred-dollar bill and reached for Andrew's hand. He was staring at the teenager, who was rocking back and forth on her heels. She had a big red Christmas bow stuck to the side of her head and was drooling foamy, thick saliva, and with each breath it was as if she were blowing little bubbles.

The moon was full. Andrew and I stared straight ahead as the reverend wove our lives together with a few thoughtfully chosen words. I wish I could remember what they were.

We were married. It cost more to get high than to get married. I began to second-guess myself. It bothered me that Andrew was going back to England and I was going to stay here and continue writing the elusive book. I don't remember him ever trying to talk me into going with him. He might have tried, but we weren't close enough to plan our future together. We were only brave enough to get married. I kept thinking about Kenny as I held Andrew's hand.

We went back to Phyllis's loft on Avenue B for our very short honeymoon. Both of us had on hideous overalls sporting a large pocket on each thigh, from a company called Parachute; mine were orange and his brown. They must have been the rage or why would we have worn such ugly, ugly clothes? I normally didn't wear anything so baggy.

Having never liked sleeping at other people's places, I lay awake and watched Andrew breathe. He was so different on the inside from the men I'd known, smarter and more creative. He had a boyish look to him, with chiseled features and a welcoming mouth, sexy dark eyes, and thick lashes. His hair was dark and wavy, just long enough to look a little wild. He was fit and muscular, from good genes and a lifetime of soccer. He had it all. His hands were those of an intelligent young scholar; his mind was sharp and contemporary but steeped in ancient wisdom. His heart was unknown to me, but his arm weighed a ton and made it impossible for me to move or, better yet, get up and find some coffee.

I felt uncomfortable as hell. I lay beside him for a few hours, but as soon as the sun began to peek through the unshaded windows I patted the floor beside our futon and found a pair of those wedding overalls. I dreaded waking him, facing him, and dealing with my own feelings about marrying him. I felt shy and embarrassed, tired and scared and dumb. I didn't make a sound. His arm lay across my chest and just getting out from under him took at least half an hour. The room was still in shadow as I slipped on the overalls, deciding to forego my contact lenses, and floated my way to the door. It was five in the morning but I had to find a cup of coffee and a moment to think.

As the heavy metal apartment door shut behind me, I stuck my hand in the pocket of my voluminous overalls to make sure the key was there. Where the key should have been, there was a thick wad of money and I realized I had grabbed the wrong pair of overalls. It was Andrew's traveling cash, maybe five hundred dollars, but there was no key to get back in. I told myself I'd figure it out later; I wanted coffee and time to think.

Out on Avenue B between First and Second Streets, I couldn't see a thing without my contacts. I felt shaky from the coke, the wedding, and no sleep; I just wanted a cup of coffee. Crossing the street without my lenses in, I thought I saw a homeless man huddled under a thick blanket. He was sitting up, but I couldn't see until I was right next to him if his eyes were open. He winked and I gasped, quickly stepping backward, when I felt something sharp and cool across my throat. Somebody yanked my hair back and a knife dug into my flesh. I tried to pull the knife away but a hand came up to rip my little diamond necklace off. I grabbed the hand and said, "You can't have that." Then I felt another hand reach into the pocket where Andrew's traveling money was.

I couldn't see anyone, since they were behind me—or whether the knife bearer was alone—but I think three people were mugging me. Andrew hadn't given me a diamond, so they naturally ignored the pale green plastic thing on my finger.

Hands searched the pocket where my apartment key would have been if I'd had on my own overalls. I could see the building where Andrew slept, but I couldn't see it clearly. I figured I was still somewhere near the man under the blanket. With the knife pressed against my throat, I couldn't squirm or scream, and then it was over. They ran off and I only saw their blurry backs. My hand went to my throat. There was blood. The little diamond cross my dad had given me when I was in sixth grade and the money were both gone. I turned to the man who had watched this whole thing and on shaking legs approached him.

All I could say was, "Where?" His eyes looked to the corner and I began to run.

Possessed by a deep need to lash out, I ran until I couldn't run any more. Winded, then slowing to a walk, I intuited my way to the muggers to get back my necklace and Andrew's money. Turning in at a seedy building, I stepped around two people propping one another up on the staircase. I seemed to know exactly where I was going and walked up three flights of grimy stairs. When I got to their door, I knew it, and tried the knob. It wasn't locked.

I went in. The smell of rats, dirty diapers, and rotten food hit me all at once. Despair hung in the air like humidity. Something was causing a pizza box on the table to move. I stepped away and the carcasses of cockroaches crunched beneath my feet. I couldn't see well enough to know exactly how terrifying the place was, but I was scared.

I headed into what could have been a bedroom. The bed wasn't made; the mattress was stained; empty bottles and plates full of cigarette butts rested on the nightstand. The dresser was next to the door and was covered with used syringes. I picked them up one at a time and stabbed them into the wooden dresser. My heart was racing when I heard footsteps and voices, maybe even laughter. I swept my arm across the plastic tubes, breaking all the needles. I ran out the door and down the stairs.

I passed people coming up.

Oh God, help me, I prayed. What was I thinking? How did I get so messed up? Why did you let them take my cross and Andrew's money? How can they live like that? I am not like that; my addiction is not like that. I don't sneak up on people early in the morning and take their money or something their dad gave them when they were little. I don't have rats in a pizza box on my table. I don't live in a place that stinks. I am trying to get better. Thank you for not letting them kill me or hurt me worse than they did.

I had these thoughts as I ran down the stairs of the crack house, stunned at the number of people now littering the stairway. By twos and threes they filled every other step.

The air on the street hit me like cold water. I was out. I'd made it, but I was still afraid, still locked out of Phyllis's apartment, and still married to a man I didn't exactly know. And now I had to figure out how to come up with a replacement five hundred dollars before he left for England that night. I ran to the corner and skidded to a stop when I reached the homeless guy with the watchful eyes and dirty blanket. I asked him for a dime, a dime to call my new husband to ask him to let me in, to accept my apology, to run around with me as I attempted to replace his cash, to be worth being married to, to hope with me, and to understand me. My hand went to my throat; it stung where the knife had been. I looked down at my hand and it had fresh blood on it. How long had I been out there?

Sitting Bull of Alphabet City eased his blackened hand through the front of his blanket with a withered dollar. My heart sank; there was no place open to get change. I gently shook my head and walked across the street. I'd decided to throw little stones at Phyllis's window to wake up Andrew.

I had never done what I was about to do. I had to bend down close to the ground to look for pebbles to throw at what I hoped would be the right window. It wasn't safe out on the street. Plus, I had just broken into someone's apartment and wrecked his stuff so I was vulnerable and nervous. I found some pebbles and changed my choice of window to aim at. On about the tenth throw, I hit the right window and Andrew opened it and leaned out. I hollered for him to let me in; he got to the door after a few minutes, and I rushed in.

Andrew listened while slowly waking up, hair all messy, wearing the other pair of overalls and no shirt. He apparently had not heard a word I said as he scooped me up, carried me to the loft, and began to nibble my neck. My neck, the raw bleeding neck of a mugged person, I was thinking. He tossed me down on the bed and began to take my clothes off. I was hurt that he didn't care about what I'd just gone through and I tried to push him away. I felt he didn't care about me. I let him finish, told him what had happened, and probably focused on the money more than I should have.

I went into the bathroom and let the water run hot, filling the room with steam. At that moment I decided to stop doing coke. I could see it was the root of all my problems. I was tired of all this shit, all these problems, and always having to undo or redo stuff because I had bungled it. I took a shower and tried to figure out how I was going to replace the cash that had been stolen. It never dawned on me to call the police.

When I put on my own overalls, I found the vials of coke. I postponed my vow, to make it easier to carry my burdens and get through this day. I would quit later. We began our day together and again I fell in love with Andrew for his charm and vibrancy, his obliviousness to anxiety, his self-confidence and good looks, his breathtaking accent, and his playful character. I couldn't understand myself. One minute I was turned off and the next minute turned on. My heart wasn't at peace, my mind wasn't mine, and my body was numb.

I had to ask Gina for money, even though I realized I might have already borrowed money from her and not paid it back. She was the only person I could ask.

I called Gina. She lived on Elizabeth Street. Andrew waited in a bodega while I climbed the four flights of stairs to Gina's. She had been in the bathtub, which was in the kitchen, where you entered the apartment. She answered the door dripping from underneath a worn light-blue chenille robe. Her head was cocked at a perturbed angle. She wasn't wearing her contacts and squinted at me as if scrutinizing every word I said. She was more beautiful than ever when she was angry, and it was hard to concentrate on how mad she was and how much she was against the marriage.

It dawned on me that she had been the one who lent me the money I needed to get married. Where was all that money? I stuck my hand in my pocket to hide its shaking. My fingers instinctively curled around one of two glass vials of cocaine that rested in my pocket. That's where my money had gone. I felt sick. Gina left little wet footprints when she padded across the old wooden floor. When she found the money she turned to me and said, "This is it, I can't give you any more and I can't be your friend any longer."

It was a horrible day. I was undone inside, certain only of my mistakes. I couldn't ask Gina if I could use the bathroom and secretly fill my nose and the hole in my heart with the stuff in my pocket, because there was no hiding place, no sanctuary to lay out a thick, long line. I took the money and ran down the stairs. I couldn't cry, because I'd never stop. I couldn't think of anything except needing to shove a gram of cocaine up my nose. I had to kill this pain, this ache, this itch, this craving that demanded more and more all the time, more of me, more of it to temper me, more money to pay for it, more sanity to burn up in its craziness.

As I remember it, Andrew and I found a little diner, and before we sat down I carefully reached out for Andrew's hand and placed five one-hundred-dollar bills in it. He smiled and put the money away, just like that, my friendship with Gina sliding into his pocket and out of my reach. Then I was on my way to the ladies' room. New York is used to dealing with drug addicts and maniacs, so even the toilets don't accommodate a coke addict. There was no cistern or other flat surface to pour out the rock-filled white powder and chop it into clean thick lines to then suck up my nose with a rolled-up bill. It's wasteful to stick a rolled-up bill into the vial and suck up those rocks, because they don't enter the bloodstream smoothly, but I did it anyway.

I returned to the table, having finished one vial, which contained maybe half a gram of very pure coke. My throat was numb, my heart ecstatic, and my nose running. I realized I had to hold my sinuses open by pressing on my cheeks and sucking in really hard after a few minutes, when the rocks had melted in my nostrils. I tried not to grind my jaws. My body was overjoyed, overwhelmed, over-amped, but now I could function. I ordered orange juice and coffee and a toasted bran muffin. I excused myself under the guise of calling the train station and got a chance to snort what was stuck in my upper nostrils. What a rush! What a thrill! What a mess.

We had planned for Andrew to take the train to the airport at about three in the afternoon. Our honeymoon was nearly over, with no outpouring of emotion, no deep and penetrating moment of truth, no thanks, and no real understanding. I had set a precedent long before in a place far away that hid how hard I worked to correct my mistakes. Andrew wasn't the first guy, or the last, who didn't thank me much. I wrapped my bran muffin to go.

We must have discussed my going to England with him, but his staying in New York was not an option, not now. He had to complete his doctorate and he was student-teaching in Canterbury.

After a midnight marriage ceremony in Central Park, an early morning mugging, and the loss of my friend, we headed to the Metropolitan Museum of Art. While Andrew had grown up with art and culture, I had grown up with a horse and a sick mom and dad. I didn't know anything about the great masters and had little or no understanding of abstract art, but it felt good to be with someone who did.

Watching him pack, I became so sad that I decided to go with him to the airport. With each moment he became more beautiful and tenderhearted. We said goodbye for a long time and then I left, taking the train back to my humble abode on Horatio Street.

I had recently agreed to let a friend from Minneapolis share my apartment for a while, until he figured out what he wanted to do. I had met Andrew the day after my friend moved in, and had spent almost all my time with Andrew at Phyllis's place. When I got back to my apartment I was upset to find that Jake had invited his new girlfriend to stay there. Feeling claustrophobic in my own apartment, I turned on a little fan for some white noise, found an episode of *The Mary Tyler Moore Show*, and nibbled on my bran muffin, but I couldn't shake my uneasiness. I hadn't done any more coke and didn't want to do any more. I decided to get dressed and head over to the park to buy a doobie, something to take the edge off. The minute my feet hit the sidewalk I felt better, like I was a part of something. I took a deep breath of the evening air, a deep breath as a married woman on the evening of June 28, 1981, with a faraway new husband.

❧ III ❧

FORGIVENESS

to love life, to love it even
when you have no stomach for it
and everything you've held dear
crumbles like burnt paper in your hands,
your throat filled with the silt of it.
When grief sits with you, its tropical heat
thickening the air, heavy as water
more fit for gills than lungs;
when grief weights you like your own flesh
only more of it, an obesity of grief,
you think, How can a body withstand this?
Then you hold life like a face
between your palms, a plain face,
no charming smile, no violet eyes,
and you say, yes, I will take you
I will love you, again.

—Ellen Bass, "The Thing Is," from *Mules of Love*

CHAPTER 15

☙ MY SVENGALI ❧

New York is a funny place. When you're inside you think about meeting people, but when you get outside you try to avoid them. I walked Horatio to Greenwich to Seventh Avenue, taking the long strides of someone determined to get somewhere. I just kept walking. I crossed to Sixth Avenue and when I saw the Avenue of the Americas street sign I remembered the first time I'd seen it. I was ten years old and stuffing stories and memories into my cheeks like a little chipmunk. I was visiting my sister Beverly and her husband, Allyn. They were savvy and powerful New Yorkers. She worked with the handicapped and he wrote for the *Village Voice*. They lived on Mott Street and led intriguing lives. I couldn't wait to tell my friends all about New York City.

Now I didn't know who my friends were or how to explain anything. Lost in my own memories, but not slack enough to drop my guard, I saw the floor sweeper from the health food store. He was walking toward me kind of bent over; the sole of his right shoe had come loose; his hair was wispy, long, and uncut; and his wire-rimmed glasses were slipping down his nose. He walked right by me. When he passed he must have recognized me, because he spun around, straightened up, pushed his glasses up his nose, and stood right next to me. He was thin and tall with piercing blue eyes.

"Can I walk with you?" he asked. I nodded and we both headed in my direction.

Because he was a floor sweeper and wasn't talking, I began telling him what had happened to me—not just in the last three days, but kind of in my whole life. I told him all sorts of colorful stories, like about working the Minnesota State Fair with Tanya and hanging out with the people who worked in the freak show. I told him about my mom's death, my dad's death, my sisters' unwillingness to include me in their lives. And I told him about Kenny and Andrew. By the time we got to the park, I was pumped up on all my stories.

I hadn't really looked at the guy since we started walking, because we'd been side by side, and now we were sitting side by side on a bench in Washington Square Park. I wanted to turn and look at him but I felt shy. I'd poured too many ingredients into this unknown bowl.

I laid my hand on his leg to thank him for listening to me rant and felt something hard. I froze as the ropey muscles in his right leg tensed, and the gun he carried pushed up even higher into my palm. I kept my hand in place so as not to appear frightened and asked him why he had a gun in his pocket. He picked up my hand and pulled it toward his other thigh and laid it on top of that pocket, which seemed to contain a thick stack of money.

"Well, if you didn't have a pocketful of money you probably wouldn't need the gun," I said, and gently removed my hand, turning to face him and looking into his eyes.

"What's your name?" I asked.

I figured he thought I was scintillating and cool. I mean, he was a floor sweeper. Granted, he was a floor sweeper with a gun and money, but the summer breeze and the night air had confused me into thinking I was the hip one. But Norman, that was his name, wasn't a floor sweeper, and he wasn't wowed by my stories. He was studying me, as he had been for several months. He said that he'd instructed his employees to buzz his office every time I came into the health food store so he could grab his broom and watch me.

Embarrassed by my miscalculations, I suggested we go for coffee. He chose the place but wouldn't even drink the water in the diner. He was a purist, a macrobiotic, and he didn't drink coffee, or apparently water. He spun his glass slowly around in circles, the limp lemon hanging on for dear life while I rambled on and on and on. Everything I did, ate, drank, and craved was anti-macrobiotic. Grapes, oranges, and almost every fruit were, to him, stimulant food—frivolous at best, dangerous at their worst.

As I brought my cup of coffee to my lips he quietly discussed the damaging effects of caffeine, and I was guessing that cocaine was just plain evil. After the coffee and the pouring forth of way too much information, I was drained. Exhausted and sad about the whole Andrew thing, I bade this Norman guy goodnight and rose to leave the diner. He handed me a piece of paper with his number on it. He said to call him if I needed anything, anything at all. He said he'd be happy to lend me some money, but I told him I was starting a new job the next day in Macy's toy department, where I would be demonstrating monkey puppets.

"I should be fine," I told him, "but thank you."

It was good to be back on the street. I needed time to collect myself. I had had a rough day, a rough few days. The joint I'd bought wasn't pot and didn't take the edge off, yet as I walked the streets of the Village I felt stronger knowing I'd shared something about my life with someone. Norman seemed to be a good person. I could tell he was smart.

I let myself into the apartment. Jake was there; it sounded like he had company and it felt like someone had been in my room. I looked for my stash of coke that I wasn't going to use anymore. The first hiding place had been disturbed and the second place hadn't been detected yet. I was too tired to confront him but had suspected all along that he had something to do with the excessive amount of coke I went through.

I flipped on the fan and the television and locked my door. I was determined to sleep even if it took me all night to do it—and it did. By morning I was exhausted from trying to fall asleep. I showered and dressed and took a cab to Macy's, which probably cost the equivalent of a day's pay. I was nervous, and I forgot that sometimes it's quicker to walk slowly than to take a cab through Midtown. I never shopped at Macy's, the prices were too high, but I had fallen in love with the idea of Macy's when I saw *Miracle on 34th Street* as a little girl.

I found the toy department and my multilingual Russian manager. I soon had the legs of a big, beautiful, soft brown monkey puppet securely fastened around my waist and his long, luscious arms fastened with Velcro around my neck. I had my right hand up his back and in his head with my pointer, middle, and ring fingers in his upper lip and my thumb in his lower. Almost immediately my puppet friend came to life and children from all over the world surrounded us, toys our common language. I sold over a hundred puppets in the first hour and a half. Each puppet gave me someone to hold onto and something to do while sorting through my life. Too bad I didn't work on commission.

At midday my manager paged me to come to the customer service desk. She seemed irritated with me, which was not at all what I expected, having made such tremendous sales in her department on a slow day in retail.

"Employees do not get personal phone calls," was all she said. I told her I didn't know who would be calling me and that I was really sorry. I took the call. "Get over here now, now, hurry," said the strained voice on the other end. "Hurry," was how he ended it. It sounded like Norman, but I wasn't sure who it was, or where it was that I was supposed to go.

"Norman? Is that you? Are you okay?" I asked as quietly as I could, with my manager glaring at me and my heart pounding in my chest. "What's wrong?"

"Just get here, now."

I jotted down the address. Seventeenth and Seventh was nearly twenty blocks away. I placed the phone back on the cradle and quickly explained to my manager that there was an emergency and I had to leave. I speed-walked out of the store. Once on the street, I ran like hell, purpose streaming through my body like adrenaline. Someone needed me. The need to help overwhelmed any reason I could find not to go to this man.

He lived in an older building on Seventeenth Street on the West Side. The outer door was ajar and the inner door was locked. I stared at the names on the wall of buzzers but Norman's wasn't listed. I pushed my hand over a row of them and someone buzzed me in. He had said the fourth floor, so I ran up four flights of stairs two at a time. I whirled around the landings. On the second floor I began to smell smoke, the air becoming acrid. My eyes were watering, my lungs were straining after my full-force run, and now the ascent into a cloud of smoke was more than I could handle.

I stopped three steps short of the top landing. The door was slightly open. I heard whimpering and could see into the room: a man curled up into a ball, lying on the floor, whimpering and whining. Smoke billowed into the hallway and I pushed the door open.

"Take off your clothes," he said. I started to move toward him and he repeated himself. "Stop. Take all your clothes off. Leave them at the door. There's a bath for you. Just get in it; we've got to get the evil out of you." He was rolling in a ball on the floor, snot dripping from his nose, in a kind of pain that seemed to worsen with each passing moment. I racked my brain for some idea of what this was, and all I could figure was it was some kind of ritual or ceremony. Smoke came from a smudge stick made of sage, sweet grass, and cedar, which I knew Native Americans use to remove evil spirits. The room felt toxic with fumes of release and healing.

I stood transfixed by the weirdness of everything. Norman was in pain, that was obvious, but why, and what did I have to do with it?

He wasn't looking at me, so I started to undress. He didn't seem able to get up, and I wanted to believe he really could help me. Did I have an evil spirit in me? If I did, I desperately wanted to be well and good and pure again.

I took off my clothes and piled them on top of my shoes at the door as he'd instructed. Norman's apartment was crammed with stuff and there was only a narrow path clear enough to walk through. He never looked at my nervous nakedness as I carefully navigated his hallway. The bathroom was easy to find, first door on the left, faucet dripping, smelling of Clorox, and filled with the glow of twenty candles. These weren't the candles of romance; mismatched candles of every size, shape, and color were stuck onto jar lids and in odd candelabras. And this wasn't the smell of seductive bath salts or sexy bubble bath; this was hardcore chlorine.

"Get in the tub, NOW!" he yelled.

You've got to be kidding me, I thought. But the curled-up man was dead serious. I did what he said. I slid my foot into a bath that felt oily with chlorine. I hesitated, and from the other room I heard him gasp and sputter, and then I heard what sounded like the voice of my decades-dead grandfather, Paw Paw. He had been kind to me as a child. He had a tender heart and let me pet the kittens out back in his barn. He seemed to genuinely enjoy my company.

"Get them potatoes outta your ears, Julie Elizabeth, and get in that there tub." Confused, I stared at the door, hopeful that something good would come from this. With my heart thumping hard, I forced my body into the bath and lay back. As I submerged my chest, I felt a sharp pain inside like something being pulled on. I wanted to get out, but the pain was too great; my whole body went rigid and something pushed out through my rib cage, feeling as though it could break my bones. Just as the dark thing left me, all twenty mismatched candles went dark.

It got quiet, my chest ached, the faucet dripped, and I could hear

Norman moaning. I felt better but not good. I lay there a few minutes and then I heard his strained voice.

"Take off the rings." I looked at my right ring finger and there was my little diamond band made by Tiffany's to fit perfectly under the opal engagement ring that had been stolen out of the desk drawer at the gym where I worked after Kenny and I were separated. I looked at my left hand, fourth finger, and there was the light green plastic ring that Andrew had placed there just three nights before.

"Take them off," demanded the voice. I pulled the right one off and then the left, and held them in the palm of my hand until I heard the order to throw them. I threw them against a closed door, but they didn't make a sound. They disappeared. There was no sound of them striking the door or the floor. My hand collapsed into the water and I felt relief. I lay back, heart pounding, and took a very deep breath.

I didn't hear anything after that. No orders or reprimands, just the gentle sound of my breathing and the faucet dripping. It was peaceful in a way, and then I sat up straight as if I'd been poked by a pin and turned my ear toward the door. Nothing. No sound. The bath was cold now, the room dank and dark; my skin felt like a cheap vinyl purse. Something was wrong. I didn't know much about what a person goes through after spirit healing, but I knew I had to get up. I could hardly move.

I used a small worn YMCA towel to dry off and wasn't sure what to put on, but when I opened the door there was a pair of hideous orange drawstring pants and a matching hideous T-shirt folded atop a pair of unused bamboo flip-flops. I put it all on and went to find my exorcist.

I could barely walk in the flip-flops. I had to raise each foot several inches to get anywhere, as though I were walking on the moon. But I wasn't weightless and I had no idea whether I had taken a giant step, a baby step, or just a step closer to the edge.

Norman lay in a fetal position, clamped tightly like a clenched fist, his face covered with tears and sweat and snot. Nearly tripping in the clumsy flip-flops, I did my best to rush to his side. I put my hand on his shoulder; his body was rigid and unresponsive. I got a cool cloth to clean him up. Passing my pile of clothes near the door where I'd left them, I imagined a tentacle spiraling out from them. I swept them out the door with a broom waiting there for the job and firmly, very firmly, shut the door.

I searched for my rings as soon as I got back to the bathroom. I turned on the lights and got down on my orange knees and searched. No sign of them. I got a cool cloth and a good look around before I headed back to the man who might have just delivered me from evil.

Norman was like an autistic child stuck in his own strange, rocking position. I sat him up and began the slow and gentle process of unclenching him, wrapping a blanket around his cold, stiff body. I sat behind him and pulled his tight body into mine, gently massaging his neck and shoulders. It took him nearly an hour to emerge from his bizarre state. When he did return he asked me a question I didn't know how to answer: "What happened?"

"I hoped you could tell me," I said, gently touching his face. I began at the beginning, at Macy's, when I'd gotten the call. Oh God, Macy's! I wondered what time it was as I recounted step by step, drip by drip, horror by horror, ghost by ghost, inch by inch, word by word, the story of our first séance. He didn't seem to remember a thing.

I'm not sure if his not knowing what happened made it more real and more important, but it seemed crucial that I tell it all and consider it thoroughly. At his suggestion I made him a cup of burdock root tea, which was made from the weirdest thing in the world, a long root that looked like an opossum's tail.

I asked him what he wanted in it and he didn't want anything. Scanning the kitchen counter, I didn't even know what rice syrup or red miso were. In any case, I didn't dare add anything to the burdock root; Norman seemed very clear about what he needed.

He still had trouble straightening his legs, but his upper body had eased. I handed him the tea and he cupped it between his beautiful long fingers. I pushed his wire-rimmed glasses up on his nose. Noticing the lenses were smudged, I took off his glasses and washed them in the sink. Looking around his kitchen again, I realized it was a mess: old stainless steel pots dented with age and books about health, finance, and healing were everywhere. Survivalist magazines and piles of articles and mail were all over his kitchen counter. I put his glasses back on him, but he didn't smile.

We were quiet, and I realized how noisy I was on the inside. I just watched him drink his opossum tail tea while my eyes strained to study the apartment filled with what appeared to be intelligent disarray. Cardboard boxes, stacked at least three high, lined every wall in every room. The coffee table, end tables, and night tables were all made from cardboard boxes. So were the shelves. The beige linoleum floor needed a mop but wasn't filthy. The ugly bathroom, no longer a church for the chemically insane, was just a normal bathroom with a broken towel rack and a toilet that ran. I had peeked into Norman's bedroom on my way back to the living room and saw only a mattress on the floor. His gun and his money lay next to the bed.

Nothing looked new except the television and the books. His shoes, too, were worn—the sole of one them had come undone from the leather upper. I'd heard it flapping the day before when we were walking to the park. His black jeans hung loosely from the waist and the inseam was too short. He wore a hideous orange T-shirt. He had unkempt gray hair but a shaven face. All in all Norman was a handsome man.

When he returned to himself, he jerked away and told me to go back to my apartment, get all my clothes, and take them to a certain laundry. He gave me a roll of money to do this. He also gave me my first lesson in underground living by telling me not to give my real name and address when I dropped them off. It seemed stupid but I liked having a mission. I went to my apartment and got all of my clothes and took them to the Chinese laundry he'd specified.

When I got back to his place later he wouldn't look at me or talk to me. He was upset about something. After what seemed a very long time he told me I needed to see a psychic named Maya Perez.

"She's very good," he said. "It's very hard to get an appointment but I know her and got you in. I talked to her while you were gone and she said it's critical you get to her."

After the exorcism in the bathtub I wasn't feeling all that enthusiastic for more psychic stuff; my skin had practically grown a life of its own and my hair was stiff as straw. I had lost two rings (or they had dematerialized), and I could still hear Paw Paw's voice. Actually, I felt like leaving. I said good night and headed toward the door, reaching into my pocket to give him back his money.

"I'll be able to cover the laundry," I said, "but thanks."

Back at Horatio Street, my door was locked and I didn't have a key. I knocked, waited, heard voices shush, and knocked again. I pounded. I waited. I walked to the corner and called. No answer.

I walked all the way to Julia's and crashed on her couch. I lay awake all night worrying about everything. I went out early to buy an outfit to wear to work, since all my clothes were at the Chinese laundry and I couldn't get into my place anyway to get the rest of my stuff. I didn't have much, but without it I didn't have anything.

My supervisor gave me the cold shoulder when I got to work. I picked out one of the large monkey puppets, un-Velcroed its arms and legs, and put it on. Sliding my right arm into the cavity of its body and, finally, into its mouth, I felt a rush of joy knowing that for a little while I didn't have to figure anything out. No Jake or Andrew or Norman or Kenny or Tanya or Gina. Any minute now, little kids would be making eye contact with the one real thing in the room, a large monkey.

On my break I wanted to call somebody, especially Norman. I liked having a job but I hated time clocks and I didn't like the supervisor. I loved monkeys but I didn't like being in a big department store. I gave in and called Norman. He must have been sitting by the phone waiting for me to call. He picked up on the first ring. He had told me the day before that he never answered his phone; he always let the machine pick up, monitoring everything, so I figured he must be feeling okay about me. I told him I'd stop by after work and prayed I wouldn't have to do anything weird.

I just wanted to do something normal like have dinner or see a movie. I was even ready to help him rearrange his apartment. I felt drawn to him, like he was some extension of my dad or some gift from God. I liked him, which made me think about why I'd married Andrew. I replayed our time together. Thinking about how everything had happened with Andrew and the marriage and the mugging and all that stuff, I got to Norman's street before I knew it and he was standing on the corner. He had on ugly new shoes and had gotten a horrible haircut.

I was a hugger; he wasn't. I let him decide how we would greet one another, which was a short moment of eye contact, a brief smile, and a rather somber nod and bowing of the head. With my copying him, we both ended up looking at our shoes, as if eye contact would be excruciating. When we finally looked up into each other's eyes, I found it painfully exciting.

I had no clue as to why this strange man affected me so, until he smiled at me. I let out a little gasp. He was gorgeous when he smiled. He had perfect white teeth, wonderful bone structure, and incredible blue eyes that twinkled, and his face was so unaccustomed to grinning that it quivered slightly. I tried to straighten up and be more than I thought I was.

We started walking. I think we were in love, but that made no sense. The guy had pretended to be a poor floor sweeper for a whole year; he spied on me, followed me, had his employees summon him when I appeared in the store; he channeled on my behalf, and soaked me in a tub of Clorox to rid me of what was killing me. But he lived in a world of cardboard boxes, didn't seem to believe in comfort, and probably thought I was crazy. If I'd known we would become close I would have been more careful about what I told him, but it was too late for that; I'd already spilled all my beans.

We walked for twenty minutes, passing every kind of store, a bunch of restaurants, and hundreds of people doing a thousand different things. Norman just walked, keeping his focus straight ahead. He didn't comment on anything.

He took me to a busy macrobiotic restaurant for a bowl of miso soup with flaccid pieces of tofu and slimy pieces of fishy-tasting seaweed. This was accompanied by a small cabbage salad with carrot/sesame dressing and a bowl of brown rice and adzuki beans (allegedly the healthiest beans a person can eat). I personally thanked God for the modest condiments in the center of our table: a fabulous sesame seed and sea salt combo in a shaker and, of course, tamari. I made a mental note to breathe quietly, chew more, eat slowly, and improve my handling of chopsticks.

Norman sat silent; I could see his discomfort by the set of his brow. It wasn't only worry that held him prisoner; it was something else too. He spun his drink of water as he had before, rubbing his finger along the rim of the glass. He chewed each bite more times than I chewed an entire meal. He ate his icky-looking fish, root vegetables, and pile of hideous seaweed. I felt awkward and messy.

His deliberate, meticulous movements made him look as though he were in pain. I wasn't sure if he even liked me. After he finished eating he returned to the annoying spinning of his glass.

"You married a warlock," he said. My mind flashed to the few *Bewitched* episodes I'd seen where Samantha's father showed up.

"What the hell does that mean?" I gasped.

Norman explained that he had talked to the psychic, Maya Perez, and she had told him that I'd married a warlock and that it was imperative I dissolve this union before I turned twenty-six. I was twenty-five and five months at the time. Marrying Andrew had been confusing enough, and now the thought of divorcing him confused me more.

Norman was very uncomfortable. He must be deeply concerned for my safety, I thought, if he would set up an appointment for me with Maya for the following day. He said that Maya knew it was a very complicated situation, but that it could be done.

How could Andrew be a warlock? That was ridiculous. I thought hard about Andrew, looking for anything that seemed weird or wrong, and I agreed to go with Norman to meet Maya in Mahwah, New Jersey. I asked him to walk with me to the cleaners and help me carry everything to my apartment, but instead I moved into Norman's spare room.

It made more sense to stay at Norman's. Being around him made me want to be smart, and I couldn't do that if I was getting high. It would be good for me, and much easier than figuring out how to get rid of Jake or finding a new apartment. So I just took over a little room in Norman's crowded reality, a little room with a twin mattress on the floor, a box for a night table, and a narrow closet.

The next day we walked uptown to Norman's warehouse to get a van to drive to see Maya. A young Irish musician had pulled it up to the front of the building and was tuning it up for us. Norman let this guy and his band live in one of his buildings somewhere and they did stuff for him. He had met them in the subway, where they were playing their music. Norman thought they had a lot of potential. I think Norman thought I had potential. I think Norman thought a lot about potential.

I hadn't been on a road trip for some time and enjoyed the chance to get out of the city, but I felt apprehensive about the day. I found

Maya's house dreary. When we knocked, Maya didn't answer the door. Norman took the lead, opened the door with reverence, and walked quietly into a dark room where a woman sat on a wooden chair. He laid down a bag of health food items that he'd brought along for her. I was uneasy. She looked me over without a smile.

Norman nodded toward the other wooden chair. I sat down. He put a small tape recorder on the table and pressed Start. I looked at the back of his head as he walked away. Maya reached across the table and snatched my hand like a crow picking at roadkill. She asked me questions about Andrew that I never would have thought about. What did he smell like? When he looked at me did his eyes vibrate? Did he talk about his father? I thought carefully and answered the best I could, but nothing fazed her. It was as if she wasn't really listening to me.

Once she'd put the idea into my head it was hard to get rid of it. I kept picturing Andrew's face, and then every time I did, I saw his eyeballs vibrating. This whole thing felt wrong and stupid. Not just the Maya Perez thing, but also the Norman thing and the Andrew thing, but mostly the Julie thing. What was I doing, looking everywhere trying to find me? On the drive home I decided I had to figure this whole thing out. When we got back to Norman's place I retreated into my monastic cell of a room and listened to the tape.

As I pulled the stiff white sheets up and over my head and fell asleep, I burrowed into myself and tried to think rationally about this whole thing. I woke up a few hours later filled with what I hoped was common sense. There had to be a way through all of this confusion and chaos. I couldn't be married to a warlock, because warlocks don't exist. But wait just a minute, I thought: I don't know anything about warlocks, only that a warlock is a male witch. I'd met people who said they were witches, or thought they were, but none of them were men. How could Andrew be a warlock?

I didn't know how to figure this out and asked Norman to help me. I looked through his books on the occult, metaphysics, and paranormal phenomena. If anyone could guide me through this, it was Norman. From what I understood, the best people to ask about witches and warlocks are witches and warlocks, channels and mediums, and people who operate in the supernatural realm.

Norman, however, was fully educated in these matters. After making many phone calls, he located an East Indian psychic in Florida and put me on the phone. The guy asked me questions for an hour and spoke very proper and convincing English, mentioning an entity on the third plane. I had no idea what the third plane was and even the word "entity" had me puzzled. He said that I was in a dangerous situation and had to get out of it, thus corroborating Maya's assertion.

Norman explained everything to me. An entity, he said, is a spiritual being or presence, and the third plane refers to a level of reality. I just had to take Norman at his word, because I couldn't understand it. I was learning things I had wanted to know all my life.

He took me to see Maya quite a few more times. I hadn't realized that she was deaf and had asked me all those questions to read my energy and enter my psyche. We always recorded the sessions so I could study them, which I did. Norman believed that Maya was very wise, but to me she seemed weird and unfriendly.

Norman took me to see Donald Lepore, a famous naturopath. Don muscle-tested me to determine which supplements I needed. Two hours later we left with thirty-six bottles of medicine. Norman's younger and less successful brother gave me polarity treatments to balance my energy, but instead they irritated me. I wrote long love letters to Andrew when no one was looking. Even though all the information pouring in from Norman's sources made Andrew out to be a bad guy, I still felt close to him.

Every second spent with Norman taught me something. I'd never met such an intelligent person in my life, not even my father. Norman knew everything about everything. He had the spiritual knowledge that Dad didn't have, or at least had never shared with me. Norman understood politics and researched every product he sold in his stores. He had gone to Pratt Institute, so he must have been drawn to express his creativity, but I experienced him first as a businessman and appreciated how he figured things out.

As the weeks passed Norman became very sick. He began throwing up what looked like chunks of his organs. I'd seen things like that at the hospital. He told me to collect some of it from the toilet and we'd take it to his friend Dr. Michael Smith who specialized in detoxing heroin addicts. It seemed to intrigue Norman that he was in the midst of a healing crisis. It made sense to approach the body's ills this way. We took the mason jars of gunk to his doctor friend, but I never heard his diagnosis. Norman thought it was due to working with resins and other toxic art materials when he was younger, and he believed his body was strong enough to heal after years on his macrobiotic diet.

Norman's condition got much worse and he became frail. He had horrible migraines that pinned him to the bed. This was right up my alley. My mom had the gift of healing and countless times she'd taught me the value of touch. I could get closer to him when he was this vulnerable. I'd lay my hands on his hot and hurting head and massage his rigid shoulders and stiff neck. I liked being able to help him. I felt like his protector during this time. He called it "hitting the wall" and believed he was making tremendous progress.

I quit my job at Macy's and became Norman's full-time caregiver. I was right at home taking care of someone other than myself. I'd run his errands and check in on the stores. I'd escort him to the bank and to certain meetings to make sure he got there. This didn't sit too well with Kate, the girl who managed his largest health food store. She didn't like the fact that Norman liked me and that I'd moved into his apartment. At first I thought it was her concern for a friend, but soon

I realized that she was bitterly jealous. This became another reason to doubt myself.

I devoted myself to helping Norman. I learned to cook and eat the way he ate. I cleaned and organized his apartment. I bought softer sheets and a big comforter for his bed. After a few months, Norman got sweeter. He would write me little notes on tiny pieces of paper. He was exact and precise, but when he lightened up he could be fun and funny. Our life together became an adventure. I still lived in my little room and honored my marriage vows, but Norman began to whittle away at my resolve.

Norman owned and co-owned property all over the place, besides health food stores, restaurants, and buildings in New York City. He had helped a friend buy a house in Woodstock, New York, and owned a big farmhouse in Vermont. I enjoyed getting out of the city and going on the road with him. We went upstate to Woodstock and to his rambling farmhouse in Vermont. It was easier to be with him when he wasn't constantly teaching me something.

The day came when I needed to go see Andrew. He'd gone home for knee surgery and was recuperating at his mother's house in Scotland. We'd been writing back and forth. He'd write me poems I couldn't understand and God only knows what I'd been writing him. My heart ached for him. Whenever another mystic, psychic, or medium said he wasn't for me, I'd feel more drawn to him, but no one knew that but me.

The day before I left, Norman wrote me a tiny note and put it in a small box. I think he said it was for when I got back from Scotland. I opened it anyway.

It said simply, "Will you marry me?"

I didn't know what to think; this was a game-changer. It had been pounded into my head that I needed to be released from my marriage to break a curse. All of the mystics, psychics, and mediums agreed that a person's fate becomes sealed in their twenty-fifth year. Maybe I'd been talking to these people too much, but it made sense to me. I took it to mean that the twenty-fifth year becomes a blueprint for life.

I hadn't found the words to tell Andrew about the warlock thing or what had unfolded with Norman, but I had been sharing what I did have words for (I didn't want to keep secrets; we were married, after all). But was it even safe to talk to him? If Andrew really had dark powers, he could hurt Norman, and Norman was vulnerable—plus he seemed very jealous. Andrew didn't mind knowing that Norman was both my roommate and my confidant.

I flew to Scotland, and when I saw Andrew at the airport I fell in love again.

CHAPTER 16

✿ FALLING HARD ✿

He leaned on his crutch, staring at me like I was a work of art. He looked thicker and more tame but he looked good, very good. His eyes locked onto mine as he welcomed me into his arms. I hugged him from the side to avoid his banged-up knee, but my body melted into his as though a hot iron pressed us together. I knew it would be hard to guard myself against him. I was already beginning to drown in his beauty. Driving from the airport, I tried to remember all the dangerous things about him.

We got to his mother's home, and once inside I felt like a bent-over tall person in a short person's house. I didn't fit. We sat in a small, airless dining room with a lunch of hard-boiled eggs, a bowl of mayonnaise, and some scary-looking gelatinous fish. She never smiled or welcomed me. I think she thought I was fat. Andrew whispered, "I want to hold you," and again I melted.

The next day we took off on our honeymoon to Inverness. I hadn't expected that. We toured a castle, and I was amazed by the sheer size of everything in it. I had always dreamed of being a princess, and it seemed like I'd met my prince. We stayed in castles and made love in ancient places. We drove through hills covered with heather and drank warm beer from big mugs in small pubs in quaint villages.

Andrew was a good old boy in the pubs, a joy to travel with, and a great lover. My new husband was his mum's pride and joy and a warlock to those in the know. Each day I not only liked him more but was more convinced that I had to sever our ties. I was afraid that if evil overtook my life again, it would ruin everything.

A poet and scholar, Andrew sought adventure and I loved looking at the world through his eyes, feeling the excitement that life gave him. He also made me feel feminine, and his laughter came from deep within his belly. He didn't seem to care what people thought of him.

I wanted to find the whole situation with Norman absurd. I wanted to ride a horse over the Scottish hills. I wanted to live in a castle and do something amazing with my life. I wanted to lose a stone or two and cause Andrew's mama to love me. I wanted to, but I couldn't let myself. I had to tell him the news.

In his bedroom at his mum's place, I put a beautiful silk scarf over the lamp to soften the light. In the living room, preparations were underway for a mock wedding, one that the family could attend. And there I was, lying in bed with my husband, telling him he was a warlock. He was speechless. I felt like an idiot. The silk scarf grew too hot and started to burn.

I played the tape from that East Indian psychic, describing Andrew from an occult perspective. The sound of the man's voice grated on me. Words that made no sense came between us. The room filled with innuendo and false evidence, but Andrew didn't balk. He didn't defend himself or call it crazy; he just carefully removed the melting scarf from the lamp, opened the door, and went to tell his family that the mock wedding was off. I felt dead inside.

I flew home the next day. No one in the house talked to me. Andrew was courteous. His mother kept the door to her room firmly closed and I'm sure she was secretly delighted that I was out of the picture, no longer hers to consider. Andrew planned to fly to New York to file the divorce papers, and that was that.

I flew back into the loving arms that I hadn't let love or hold me. Norman waited at baggage claim, twitchy and nervous, shifting from one foot to the other.

We drove in to Manhattan in silence. Norman didn't ask me how it had gone or how I felt. He didn't make any attempt to console me. I'd done this for him as much as for myself, and he didn't care. I regretted everything. Everything. All the months I had rested my hands upon his aching head or held his hand vanished in a poof. Nothing mattered. I could tell he didn't love me.

I held my breath, curled my toes, and dreaded the rest of my life. I couldn't stand it. We dropped the van at his warehouse and I walked beside him, but he wasn't there. I must have done something wrong, I thought, and he wasn't telling me what it was, which tortured me.

Life became awkward and more uncomfortable than I could tolerate. The days passed quickly but not well. I was no longer the prize. Now I didn't have anybody. I had to get high. I needed money to buy cocaine. My life became about pain reduction. I would massage Norman's skull, neck, and boyish, slim shoulders for hours at a time. I would walk all the way to Herb's house to save a subway token and once there I would finagle and finesse my way to a few free lines, like getting enough gas to get home but not enough to go anywhere. Like a soldier in a foreign country, I reported for duty every day, and like a lonely child, I begged for crumbs of affection.

I don't remember how many days, weeks, or months passed before Andrew returned to New York to appear in court and sign the divorce papers. When I saw him I knew I'd made a mistake. He was everything a woman would want in a man. He was warm and treated me with respect but kept his distance. I had arranged for a small apartment in which he could stay during the few days he would be around, and we went there shortly after he got through Customs.

We went to the courthouse the next day. I had this other me pulling on my hand, trying to get me to stop, to reason, to reconsider. But I had to do this in order to please Norman and, I thought, to protect myself. I had to do this. We stood in the center of the gorgeous, marble-floored hall, and Andrew decided to admit to having committed adultery as our reason for divorcing. That seemed so heroic.

A few days later he flew home. I went back to Norman's, where I found nothing to sustain me. I gave every ounce of my energy to his well-being, but he didn't get well. My life meant nothing.

I still sometimes went to acting classes, and I still collected a small amount of money from the trust fund, which I promptly spent, doing drugs and then doing everything I could to undo them. I learned to cook macrobiotic food. I got colonics, I juiced, and I ran.

The woman who gave me colonics recommended the Ukrainian baths to steam and detoxify, just around the corner from her office, on East Tenth Street. I took her suggestion, arriving for the first time at the baths on Ladies' Day. I'd stepped into a new world.

Growing up in Minnesota, I'd never come across Eastern Europeans and was unfamiliar with people like those I met at the baths. I'd grown up taking saunas with my mom, but this was a whole different thing. I paid eight dollars and was given a locker and two towels and told to make myself at home.

Upstairs there were lockers and rows of twin beds for resting should you feel dizzy or tired. I saw a man at the far end of the room working on someone who was lying on a massage table. He used a lighter inside a shot glass and then placed the glass on the person's muscle. I looked away before he could see me studying him. A sign pointed to the basement for steam and sauna and I headed down.

I'd paid a few dollars extra for a peppermint scrub. I took off my clothes, wrapped myself in a towel, and walked into the sauna, which was the heart of this enterprise. When I opened the thick sauna door, a blast of heat tightened the skin on my face. This was a real sauna, a big sauna, full of women sitting beside little wooden buckets of water. Each of us was lost in our own world. It was too hot to talk.

I found a place to sit, unwrapped the towel from around me, and laid it down on the hot wooden slats. The other women sat until their bodies felt scalded and then poured the bucket of cold water over their heads. As they did so they would chatter in their native tongue. Within minutes it was too hot and I had to get out.

I looked for a lady named Agnes, who was supposed to do my peppermint scrub. I saw a big naked woman biting her nails. She had large, rounded features and her melon-like breasts hung to her waist. She walked toward me armed with Dr. Bronner's peppermint soap and a scrub brush and asked me to lie down on a long table. She squirted me with the soap and started scrubbing. It felt good but it hurt. Then she sprayed it all off with a high-pressure hose and started over again. She scrubbed me front and back as her breasts rolled along my body. It was oddly comforting.

My body tingled. I was more sensitive to the heat after Agnes had scrubbed off all my dead skin and I went upstairs to rest. There I met the man I'd seen earlier doing massages. His name was Jack Ben David. He told me how he used ancient practices handed down to him from his Israeli grandfather in Netanya. I lay down on his table and he applied warm, fragrant oil, his hands working deeply on my tense muscles. I relaxed for the first time in years.

A steam and massage became my weekly ritual, to undo the wrongs I had done and put me back on the path to right living. Jack became a person I could talk to and count on. He'd work the cups on me by first swabbing the shot glass with alcohol and then using a lighter, heating it to just the right temperature and then swirling it over a tight muscle. As the muscle would get sucked up into the cup, the spasm and the tension would simply melt away. We'd talk about things that had

I was eight years old when Daddy bought me my first pony, Pogo's Jubilee. We won so many ribbons.

Photo circa 1965.

shaped my body and my character. It fascinated him that I had grown up riding and showing horses and he longed to learn to ride.

I wanted to do something to thank him for his care, so I called Claremont Stables near Central Park and arranged to hire two horses for the following Sunday. They wanted proof I was a good rider, and this I could give them. I was well trained and gifted with horses and had names and dates and just enough moxie to get us two horses.

When I arrived I had to sign a thorough disclaimer, which I didn't take the time to read. I was weak from succumbing to a bout with cocaine the previous evening, but I didn't want to disappoint my friend or admit my weakness. We waited outside the stables on a cold January morning. They gave Jack Ben David a friendly old pinto, whose name I have forgotten, and me a frisky thoroughbred named Paramount.

Paramount essentially ignored me. Even at the stable I couldn't get him to listen. He was a tall and handsome thoroughbred, a young retired racehorse, wired in a way I'd never experienced. Even though

I'd grown up on a pony and later had a horse of my own that loved me, and I'd ridden plenty of horses that didn't listen, I'd never had one that completely disregarded me. The barn manager had warned me that Paramount had been off the track for a short time only and hadn't been ridden much. I knew he was telling me to pay attention, but I had longed for a horse just like him since I was a little girl: a big, impressive, powerful horse that could take six-foot jumps with ease.

Paramount was jumpy. I asked the barn manager if we could warm up in the ring so I could get him collected under me. However, a lesson was taking place in the indoor arena so we hit the street with Jack Ben David smiling his wide grin and me trying desperately to calm a nervous horse.

Out of the barn and clippety-clopping down the street, Paramount got all twitchy, tossing his head and giving short whinnies as if in pain. I looked over at Jack Ben David and he was smiling like a four-year-old, flapping the reins and lifting his legs up and down, saying, "Gitty up." I had to hush and subdue him so he wouldn't further startle the horses. I rounded in front of him, and on my skittering mount began our first riding lesson peppered with Jack saying, "Let's run" in between me saying, "We aren't going to run today. Today you are going to learn to walk and trot."

With Paramount fidgeting beneath me, I showed Jack the correct way to hold the reins and adjust his stirrups. It's only a few blocks from Eighty-ninth Street and Columbus Avenue to Central Park, where we headed over toward the bridle path. The moment we hit the soft earth, I felt Paramount connect with the ground. He didn't calm down, but he wasn't dancing on concrete anymore.

I whispered to him and stroked his neck, trying to find his spot, the one that would soothe him. When we passed under an old stone bridge somebody rang a bike bell and Paramount took the bit, lengthened his neck, compressed his spine, and ran.

My gloved hands lost their grip on the reins; my feet went through the irons far enough to make it awkward to get them back in the right place. I was in trouble and I knew there was a man behind me on a little pinto, a man whose wish to run had been granted and who had no clue how to survive it. Paramount had gone mad; he didn't know his way, which I imagine infuriated him, and he sped up to compensate for not knowing where he was going. Even in January, Central Park swarmed with people, and the trail he chose was littered with obstacles. The park benches in our way could have killed us, but, just as this horse was used to racing, I was used to jumping horses, and so we jumped. We jumped benches and strollers and bicycles and we zigzagged around people. At points in our mad dash my hands had no control, as I'd had to pull my gloves off with my teeth and lean too far forward to try to recoup the reins. I felt the strength drain out of me and I began to give up. I couldn't hold on anymore. I had to let go. I just had to.

Paramount returned us to where we had started and he intended to cross the street as cars streamed past. I just couldn't die that way! He was not calling the shots. I let go. As I flew more than fell off his back, I caught a glimpse of his shod feet sending up sparks as he galloped across the street. I didn't know where Jack Ben David was; nothing mattered to me anymore, and I floated up toward the sky before falling to the ground with a thud.

CHAPTER 17

☙ A Cabin in Woodstock ☙

I opened my eyes and over a dozen people surrounded me like caricatures, all distorted because of my position. My position. I was alive and on the hard, cold ground under a tree in Central Park right next to the road. It felt as though the people looking down at me were behind glass. They just stared. I tried to talk, surprised to find my voice.

"Is the horse okay?" No one answered. Maybe I didn't talk. Maybe I wasn't there. Maybe this didn't happen. Just then, a taxi screeched to a halt and the cabbie came running over saying he had called the police. He said he had clocked the horse going forty-seven miles per hour.

"I never seen anything like that in my life," he said. "That horse jumped a fuckin' car and almost lost it. You're some rider, kid. I never seen anyone ride like that. Are you a professional?"

I shut my eyes.

When I opened them the cab driver's face was so close to mine that I could smell cigarette smoke on his breath. The rest of the onlookers still encircled me, their faces contorted. The cab driver's words began to make sense when I heard him say, "The horse made it back to the barn." I closed my eyes in relief and felt a surge of anger rise up in me, and, right behind it, fear for my friend Jack Ben David. I opened my eyes again and saw him behind the maddening and thickening crowd trying to control his horse. I looked at the cab driver and asked him to help Jack Ben David get to the barn. He asked if there was anyone he could call.

I shut my eyes under the sheer weight of that question. Who was there to call besides Norman? Who in the world could help me but Norman? Who could I possibly call who would actually help me and not make me feel bad? I gave him Norman's number and wished I could explain how I met Norman and how I didn't know what was going on between us. I wished I could tell him how much I used to mean to people, but all those people were gone. Again, I shut my eyes, as a razor sharp pain cut through my body and I realized I couldn't feel my legs.

The paramedics didn't say a word, didn't say hello, didn't ask a single question until they had snapped a huge neck brace on me, rolled me on my side, and slid a backboard underneath me. The whole time they were working, the cab driver kept up a monologue about how fast the horse was running, how it looked when the horse jumped that little Japanese car, how many sparks flew, how many people fled, how many lives I may have saved. All this while I lay there knowing I had been the one who put everyone in danger in the first place. I had lost my strength over those months in New York City, and, lying there numb below my tailbone, I was terrified.

There were many firsts for me that day: it was the first time I didn't get back up and ride after a fall; it was the first time I'd ever run that fast for that long and not enjoyed it; it was the first time I'd ridden in an ambulance as a patient; and it was the first time I'd ever seen Harlem Emergency. They wheeled me into a very busy waiting room outside the ER, where I was immediately surrounded by doctors, nurses, and techs. They called out orders and talked about me as if I couldn't hear them.

An old black man saw the crowd around me and staggered over to us saying, "Help me, help me, I've been stabbed."

I couldn't see him until he got so close I could smell him, but there really was a knife sticking out of his chest. Oh my God, I thought, nearly passing out.

Because I didn't have any riding breeches, I had been wearing very tight cream-colored corduroys, and a few people tried to cut them off me. As if witnessing the scene from behind a gauzy veil, I thought I was still in the lobby but surrounded by doctors.

Norman showed up within an hour and placed some remedies under my tongue. He wasn't happy. He put his mouth near my ear and whispered that I had caused the accident to get attention. I what? I went from broken to destroyed. I didn't have health insurance and they discharged me. Numb from the waist down, I didn't care what happened. An orderly pushed my wheelchair to Norman's van and helped Norman lift me into it. There was no passenger seat, so they propped me up in the back with some cushions and rags.

Norman and I didn't talk. There was nothing more to say. He had told me that I'd caused the accident . . . to get attention. I had no one to take care of me, no one to feel sorry for me, and no one to rescue me. I figured he was right about the accident, but I had no idea what it all meant.

It hurt to sit. My tailbone throbbed with pain, but from there down I was numb. I hoisted myself up his four flights of stairs, wishing I had a different life, watching him take the stairs two at a time in front of me. He was in the apartment on the phone by the time I dragged myself through the door. Welcome to rehab.

&

Our life together was quiet. We didn't have robust discussions or interesting arguments. We were quiet until it was time for Norman to correct, instruct, or test me on whatever the lesson of that particular day might be. Was Norman helping me realize my dream of receiving my father's legacy of knowledge? As if we had no choice, the dynamic continued: he had to teach me everything, and I had everything to learn.

Norman would find things to improve upon no matter how thoroughly I applied myself to the task. If I massaged him, he would draw diagrams to correct whatever I had done wrong. He provided detailed instructions on how to do practically everything. Norman took great pains to help me become a better person, but in the process I felt worse and worse about myself. Eventually I could get around, but not easily. I had to focus hard to guide my legs, as if they'd fallen asleep and never awakened.

One day, after a rousing session of how I put too much tahini in the rice, I asked Norman if he would just take me somewhere, drop me off, and leave me there. Then we'd see if I got well or just died. I couldn't keep doing what we were doing. If I stayed in New York City another day, I believed, it would wipe out whatever remained okay about me.

I didn't know why or when Norman quit loving me, but he did. There were no more fun times; he didn't look young and happy anymore, and I was brokenhearted. He packed me up and drove me upstate with big pots of rice, rice cream, kudzu, and adzuki beans, and I moved into a rustic cabin in Woodstock, New York. It was April 7, 1982.

The cabin had wood heat, which I'd never dealt with, and was infested with mice, which totally grossed me out. There was no television or radio to keep me company. I could use the phone in the main house some distance away belonging to a guy who co-owned the house. He would be up in the summer and I figured that by then I would be well or gone. I was free to get my life together, or let it fall apart.

Thank God I was out of New York City and out from under Norman's microscope of critical analysis. The no-frills cabin was rough for the princess in me, but she had been starving to death for some time. Help did not come running; my legs still didn't work well, and I had absolutely zero self-confidence.

I did have a little stuffed monkey that Norman had won for me by swinging a sledgehammer the only time he took me to Coney Island. I had named him Irby because Norman had also won me a forty-five rpm recording called "Brotherly Love," by James Irby. I could hold Irby close; he had little arms and legs, a big red nose, and a smile made from thread. We would brave this new life together.

Norman helped me get everything set up. We had cooked my food ahead of time and he offered to bring me more every few weeks. It was just basic stuff, but I like basic stuff. Rice, rice cream, kudzu, beans, Baldwin Hill bread, almond butter, rice syrup, and a few other things. I had a mattress and a little couch, and at the big house there was a deck overlooking the mountains. It was quiet and beautiful, a welcome change from the noise and neediness of New York City, but I was not feeling so brave.

Norman couldn't wait to leave me there. It got dark soon after he left and I climbed into my little bed on the rough-cut loft and propped myself up on saggy pillows so I could read: an adventure book by Tristan Jones. As I read, I moved my hand to scratch an itch and found a mouse standing on my arm. There I was, alone on an elevated loft, unable to move my legs very well, with a mouse sitting on my arm. I screamed and flung the mouse. It landed on the wall as though we'd been working on our routine for years.

What a horrible, cheap, filthy, disgusting feeling to have a mouse on my arm! I lay there feeling all creepy, and heard the tap dance of what sounded like several mice on the other side of the drop ceiling over my head. The more I listened, the louder it became, until all I could hear was dancing mice. Too spooked to get up in the middle of the night and drag myself into the kitchen to rig something up to catch them, I tried to sleep, tried not to think about the mouse stuck to the wall, tried not to think about the way things were or the way things might have been. When I got up in the early morning light I was still tired, tired of everything.

One of Norman's friends, his man Friday, had built the cabin. It was solid but corners had been cut in its construction. My dad would've done a much better job. The place had an awful sense of neglect and emptiness about it, like a lake house that hadn't been lived in for years.

I searched for something in the cabin to use as a mousetrap and found an empty plastic gallon jug under the rusted sink. Then I came across a flat piece of metal about two feet long that I could use as a gangplank. I dropped some almond butter into the bottom of the jug for bait and set my gizmo up, pulling my heavy, numb legs around until I got some wood burning in the woodstove and some rice cream cooking. I returned to my book and slipped into an alternate world of adventure and hope.

Even though I had no one to talk to, I didn't feel as alone as I had at other times in my life. It would be worse, I thought, to be around people who don't understand you than to not have anyone around at all.

A loud scratching at the thick door pulled me from my book. I opened the door and there was a funny-looking little yellow dog. When he saw me he jumped around in a circle, barking and whining at the same time. It felt like a reunion in a Disney movie, except I'd never seen the cute little guy before. He finally quit spinning and yelping and began digging a hole just outside the cabin, then began running back forth between the hole and me. I named him Digger.

Digger became my personal guide on the road to joy. Unlike little Irby, Digger was alive and full of energy. The days he didn't show up were harder to get through. I cried a lot. I'd told myself that every time I cried it was an opportunity to cleanse my soul. I'd read that in a wise book somewhere.

That night, after I turned out the lights, I heard something plop, squeal, and frantically claw at the sides the plastic jug. I'd caught a mouse! It worked! I went into the kitchen, grabbed the jug, put a lid on it, and tossed it out the door. Yes! I went back to bed victorious, confident, and empowered.

Three hours later I sat bolt upright in bed. I'd forgotten to make air holes; the mouse was suffering, and I could sense it. I grabbed a sharp knife and somehow got myself outside to listen for any sound that might help me locate the jug. On that moonless night, I groped my way in the pitch black until I heard a faint sound. I felt around for the jug, found it, and carried it inside.

I peered in through the opaque plastic. The mouse was in a sauna: little eyes bulging out of its head, fur sopping wet and slicked against its body. I plunged the knife through the plastic to give the little guy some air and left the jug on the front step, trembling my way back to sleep.

Every day felt long; a day can last forever when there's nothing to distract you. I'd listen to nature, to the sound of the wind and the conversations of the birds. I'd fall into reveries of awe only to end up in pits of dark despair. One day Digger dug a hole under a rainspout, then looked up at me and started barking. It began to rain, and his barking got louder. I stood mystified until he came and took me to the muddy hole full of rainwater. I remembered how my mom used to have me sit in Brushy Creek when I had aches and pains, so I naturally pulled my pants off, at Digger's insistence, and sat down in the cool, muddy water. It actually felt good. Digger lay down beside me. I shut my eyes and turned my face up to the gently falling rain just as Digger did. Maybe that's when my body began to heal.

The days rolled over and into each other for months. Norman arrived every three weeks with more food and supplies, but even that didn't much matter. He came out of obligation, so there was little joy in his company. He just came and went. Digger never came around when he was there. The weird guy who co-owned the house showed up twice, and both times were uncomfortable. I felt like the broken girl in the forgotten cabin. When he wasn't there I felt as if I owned the place.

If I got really scared or lonely, I had the option of using the phone in the main house, but I'd end up staring at it trying to think of someone to call. I called Norman more than once, but mostly I remember the one time when he said he had a terrible confession to make. I held my breath and gripped the phone like it was the only thing holding me together.

"When you were in Scotland with Andrew, I was lying on the bed in that little room and I saw your journal. I missed you so much and I just wanted to be with you. I wanted to know all about you, so I read it." My heart raced as I tried to remember what my journal said.

"I loved you so much," he said. "I couldn't wait for you to come back to me so we could get married and start our life together. You were everything to me. When I got home from taking you to the airport I saw your journal and I told myself not to read it, but I did."

I wrapped the phone cord around my wrist and stared at the dirty stone fireplace in the living room while Norman spoke. Filled with guilt and dread, I tried desperately to remember what I'd written.

"It didn't stop there," he went on. "I read every journal I could find. I read about your teenage trip to Europe when you made love to that older man on the airplane next to your sleeping mother. That was disgusting," he said.

My body went numb, my heart on high alert.

"You wrote too much about sex. I couldn't deal with it. I couldn't stop reading, but I started to hate you." His voice cracked. "I couldn't tell you because I shouldn't have done it, and then you hurt yourself and I thought it was because of me, because I couldn't stand to be around you anymore."

As Norman said those final words, I found the strength to hang up the phone.

Now I truly was on my own. The illusion had ended. Norman hated me. I had nowhere to go. I had nothing. It was too much. I needed a cup of coffee and a cigarette. My months of rehab with Digger had strengthened me. I figured I could make it to town. I just had to find some money. I looked through the house for forgotten change in the cushions or along the baseboards. I found old quarters turned the color of pewter, pennies black with grime, dimes green with neglect. I put together quite a nice little pile: eleven dollars and three cents. I hadn't seen Digger for two weeks, and this too was heavy on my mind. I wanted to see him but hoped he wouldn't show up when I'd ventured down a mountain on numb legs.

The sensation of walking down the mountain from the cabin was breathtaking. I wondered if this was how a hibernating bear felt when it left its cave in the spring. My body was groggy but it wanted to do this; I wanted to do this. With my numb legs and my pile of change, I headed down Meads Mountain Road toward the hamlet of Woodstock. As I rounded the first bend in the road, an attractive man with a long braid was checking his mailbox. Alarmed to see a person, I stood still. I wasn't prepared to deal with anybody quite yet. He turned to go back into his house and I hustled by before he saw me. Next thing I knew, he was standing next to me, saying something. "*Women in Love* is playing at Tinker Street tonight; do you want to go?"

"I don't know what that means," I said.

"It's a Ken Russell film. I'll let you think about it and ask you again on my run home." And he was off running while I walked toward a small ravine beside the road. I stopped, pulled myself together, and smiled. I'd just gotten asked out.

As I walked the last stretch of Rock City Road into Woodstock, civilization had never looked so good. The walk had felt like miles, even though it was all downhill. It felt good to be out and about and free. My body was pumped from the exercise, and I didn't feel too scared. I rubbed my eyes to make sure I was seeing clearly when a guy with his toenails painted red and wearing a long peasant dress made eye contact with me and smiled. He had long hair and strings of bells hanging from somewhere under his Dr. Seuss hat. Then a woman wrapped from head to toe in thick layers of cream-colored fabric crossed the street in front of me. She reminded me of the Michelin man. A hyper-skinny guy came up and introduced himself as Rocky. He eyed me up and down while claiming to have been the lightweight boxing champion of somewhere.

Enough of all these characters. I needed a cigarette and some coffee. I spotted a little deli on the corner that I thought might satisfy both my cravings. But then I caught the aroma of fresh-ground coffee and followed the scent to Pleasures, where I ordered a large cup of rich, dark coffee with fresh cream.

Afterward I walked back up Tinker Street toward the corner deli, arguing back and forth with myself about buying cigarettes. According to the clock, it had taken me over two hours to make my mile-plus descent into Woodstock. I stared at the cigarette display. "You're new," the clerk said. "Never seen you before. Where do you hail from?"

"Minnesota."

"Well, hello, Minnesota. Welcome to beautiful Woodstock, New York. What can I get you?"

"Pack of Camels, please."

"Filtered or unfiltered?"

"I'll try the unfiltered, please, and I need some matches."

My legs wobbly and unsure and my balance questionable, I had my reward. I leaned against a brick wall in front of the shop, set my coffee cup on the ledge, and tapped the cigarette pack upside down, finding the red cellophane string and pulling it off. I lifted the corner of the silver paper and opened half the top, turned the pack over, and tapped one out. It felt good to do something I hadn't done in so long. I tapped my cigarette on the stone window ledge, making a one-eighth-of-an-inch cap of empty paper on the end. I struck my match, inhaled deeply, and nearly passed out.

I reached for my coffee, took a big sip, and promptly threw up.

Though it was probably a macrobiotic gag reflex to poison, I still didn't like doing it right there on the sidewalk. I took my nausea, my coffee, and my nineteen remaining cigarettes and went around to the back, where I hoped I would be able to smoke, faint, drink, and gag in a more relaxed and unguarded atmosphere. All these months of pure food and healing had left my system unprepared for such toxins.

I walked through a narrow alley and sat down on a stump behind Houst's hardware to smoke and drink my coffee. I wanted everything this tie-dyed little town had to offer. I wanted to be around people and I wanted to stay in hiding. I wanted to be free and healthy. I wanted to smoke cigarettes and drink coffee and get high.

Remembering I still had a steep mountain road to walk up, I finished my coffee, smoked another cigarette, and pushed my way to a standing position. I cut through a little alley between the tepee place and a locksmith, holding onto whatever I could find to steady myself, and was soon back on Tinker Street. By the time I got to Meads Mountain Road, the guy who had asked me out was running in place next to me.

Maybe he noticed the fear etched on my face or saw my awkward gait, because he quit running in place and eased to a walk. He introduced himself as Peter and cupped my elbow in his hand, giving me just enough support to make the long climb to my cabin.

It was strange to have someone touching my body, even if it was only my elbow. Every nerve fiber must collide at that marvelous joint, the elbow. You forget about so many things when all you can think about is what happened and why it happened, and what the hell you are going to do now that it did happen. As Peter held my elbow, I wondered when I had last shaved my legs.

As hard as it was to walk uphill, it set me free to think more kindly about myself. His sweaty white shirt began to dry as we walked very slowly up the steep hill. I kept my eyes on the road just to make sure I didn't put one foot down on the other—or, more truthfully, so I wouldn't be able to see whether Peter was looking at me in that way a man looks at a woman.

Instead of exploring the tedious world of my flaws and shortcomings, I was thinking only about shaving my legs. I tried to listen as Peter talked. He was from Michigan and was now a programmer for IBM. Everything about him seemed wholesome. I felt like a hairy, unkempt woman who'd made all the wrong choices. When I got a glimpse of his hand, it looked cared for, as though he had pushed back his cuticles. He was talking about some doctor he knew who might be able to help me. I just nodded and continued to lift one leg and then the other. I wanted to tell him all about myself, but as he kept talking my words went farther and farther away.

When we got to his home I became jealous. He had a real life, a big house, and a beautiful view of the Hudson Valley, much like my view at the cabin but I didn't own it. I was a squatter, not a land baron. Peter ushered me to an Adirondack chair and went inside to make coffee. Sitting in the unyielding wooden chair, I realized how knotted up I was, how tense and unaccustomed to civilized behavior. I had spent the last six months alone on a mountainside doing my best to survive my ego's unrelenting need to suffer the deep sadness in my heart. Peter returned with two large mugs of coffee and an article about Dr. John Mackinnon, a local chiropractor.

While sipping the deliciously strong coffee, silky with real cream, I read the article. Peter wanted to make me an appointment with the doctor, offering to drive me there and pay for it. I gratefully accepted. It felt as though something inside me opened up and I could see things from Peter's place. The view, the caffeine, and the new friend were good medicine for me. We got into his VW Beetle and he drove me to my cabin. Though it was just up the hill, it could've taken me well over an hour to get there if I'd walked.

When Peter dropped me off, there were a brief hug, a few words of thanks, and a promise to see each other soon. He had showered at his place while I'd rested in the embrace of the mountain view, and I could smell his shampoo. Such simple things: that fresh smell and the way my heart thumped hard against my chest when he reached across my lap to open my door for me. I started out of the car before coming to the sobering realization that I had to lift each leg up and put it down in order for it to move.

No Digger. I opened the cabin door and smelled mouse pee and mildew.

◦ IV ◦

REDEMPTION

The idea of redemption is always good news, even if it means sacrifice or some difficult times.

—Patti Smith

CHAPTER 18

◌ My Healing Begins ◌

When morning arrived, I came to life. I cleaned the cabin from front to back. When I opened the thick front door first thing to let the day in, I found a head of broccoli on my stoop—this, and a note from Peter telling me that he had made an appointment for me with the doctor the next day at noon. I held the note to my heart and picked up the broccoli. A green worm wriggled free from one of the florets. I screamed and threw the broccoli across the room.

I had been in seclusion for so long, preparing for my doctor's appointment was a big deal. I searched the main house for a razor so I could shave my legs, careful to let the slightly rusty blade glide over my numb flesh. I practiced putting my medical history into as few words as possible. I didn't believe it wise to overwhelm a ninety-two-year-old doctor with the warlock dilemma or the cocaine saga, but I wanted to tell him enough so that he could help me. I didn't have any makeup so I couldn't wear any, but I made sure I was wearing clean underwear.

I was a nervous wreck in the car. I wanted to chain smoke and to numb more than my legs. Instead, I fidgeted and fretted. Peter skillfully maneuvered the streets of historic Kingston, trying to find a parking space while giving me a mini-tour of the area. He drove as if he had a stiff neck, flipping his long hair over his shoulders repeatedly as in a shampoo commercial.

We stopped in front of an old colonial house. Having been brought up in Rochester, Minnesota, and going to the Mayo Clinic for the slightest of ailments, I have a certain distrust of doctors' offices that look like houses. The receptionist was warm and appeared organized. She listened to Peter first and then to me. When Peter left, she touched the top of my hand and said, "The doctor really is amazing."

Dr. Mackinnon came shuffling in wearing bedroom slippers. Oh, not a good thing, I thought. He had the thick-lidded eyes of a reptile. As a matter of fact, his facial skin looked so thick and heavy that he could have been half asleep or slightly uninterested. He asked me to sit on the edge of the old examining table in my thin paper gown and shuffled around behind me. He asked questions I couldn't quite understand unless I turned around to watch his mouth move. When I did turn around, I saw a Sharpie marker in his hand.

Joanne, the receptionist, walked into the room with a clipboard and took notes. The doctor mumbled while he used his marker on my spine. He told me to lie down on my stomach and placed some sort of wire across my feet. He probed around a bit more, pushing lightly here and there, when I heard him snap on a latex examination glove. I turned to see what he was doing and saw Joanne squirt lubricant on the glove's index finger. Without warning, he pushed his finger into my rectum. A hot searing pain sliced through my lower body as he lifted up on my coccyx and withdrew his finger. The pain took my breath away, as pure fire spread from my sternum to the soles of my feet. And just like that, I could feel my legs again.

I screamed. When my screaming stopped, so did some of my pain. I took a deep breath and looked in amazement at my shuffling savior. His face, which had been too heavy, too thick, and too sorrowful to raise itself into a smile, became radiant. Like a kid at Christmas who'd opened the best present under the tree, he looked at me and grinned. My body was covered in sweat, my legs were all pins and needles, and my ass hurt like hell. He left the room. I stood up, put my feet on the cold linoleum floor, and got dressed, feeling the sweep of my pants as I pulled them up over my legs.

Joanne was waiting for me with an expectant look on her face, and I nodded. She got it; she knew I'd been healed. It cost fifteen dollars to resurrect my legs. I was thrilled and slightly scared. My legs had gone numb in Central Park and had come back to life in the Catskills. I was twenty-six years old and I'd been given a second chance.

I asked Joanne where I might go to get my body back in shape now that I could feel my legs. She directed me to the YMCA on Broadway, not too far from where we were. I made another appointment for the following week, wanting also to thank the doctor. I had been broken and now I could walk without grabbing onto walls and chair backs, without each step reminding me what had gotten me into this mess.

I decided to walk to the Y to see how much it cost. I asked Joanne to tell Peter to pick me up there when he came back, but to be sure to look for me along the way. It would be my walk toward freedom.

I walked past people who had no idea of the hell I had just been pulled from. I figured that most of them were trying to find their way out of their own hells. I walked by prostitutes and bums and angry-looking men. I walked by a shady-looking motel that resembled a crack house. I walked down one hill and up another, until there it was, the YMCA, the place where I would put my body back in order, a sort of temple where I could find a way to thank God for healing me.

⊱⊰

I needed money to join the Y. I needed money to eat something other than the beige macrobiotic food that Norman had brought me. I needed money to find a place to live with no strings attached and with no mice in residence. The trouble was, the only person I could look to for money was Norman. The only way I knew about much of anything was through Norman.

Norman respected old healers, so it would be to my credit to have discovered Dr. Mackinnon. The fact that I could feel my legs again would be secondary to Norman. I don't think Norman believed I couldn't feel my legs in the first place.

The next time Norman came up, I told him about my healing. He seemed relieved and wanted to meet the doctor. I couldn't arrange it for that day, so we headed into town and found a flea market. As we walked around, I had a business idea: I would sell those same monkey puppets that I'd sold at Macy's. Norman felt sure we could find them in Brooklyn. He thought you could find anything in Brooklyn.

He made a few calls and did find the monkey puppets. A few days later I got cartons of the exact-same puppets that cost twenty-four and thirty-six dollars at Macy's. Norman paid four and six dollars for quantities of five hundred wholesale. My cabin became a jungle of stuffed animals, and my hopes hung on the walls with them.

I planned to go to town on the following Saturday, having paid to participate in the flea market. I figured I'd use the old junker in the driveway to take my stuffed friends and me down the mountain. Even though it didn't have insurance, it did have plates. I'd started it up a while back, thinking I could eventually use it, and it had screamed its way to life. This time, it didn't scream or even whine; it just clicked.

I maneuvered the huge carton out of the backseat of the hideous, useless car and wrangled it over to the side of the road. I had no choice but to hitchhike, but there was no traffic halfway up the mountain. A car had gone by while I was bending over my box without my thumb out. I went into the middle of the road and began jumping up and down and waving my arms to bring the driver back.

Most people wouldn't look in their rearview mirror while driving downhill around a curve on a steep mountain road, but Hannah Bonilla did. Apparently she couldn't quite figure out how to back up without killing the engine in her little Japanese car. She stopped and waited as I dragged my wide, heavy box down the road and into her car. I recognized her as the lady who'd sold me that cup of aromatic coffee on the first day I'd walked into Woodstock. We talked about all sorts of deep and interesting things, as though we'd been friends for years. Unlike Peter, she didn't scare me, or at least not as much. She drove me directly to the big field where all the vendors were setting up for the flea market.

I felt very tense. All the details of checking in and setting up were stressful. Plus, I hadn't brought a table, a tent, or a chair; I didn't have a receipt book, a bottle of water, or even a pen. However, I did have two different sizes of tender-eyed monkey puppets. I took two of them out of the box. I unfastened the strong Velcro patches at their hands and feet and wrapped them around my neck and waist. I stood shyly for a few moments until my need for this venture to be a success overwhelmed my insecurity and I set out to sell my monkeys. I sold twenty puppets for twenty dollars each. That was the most money I'd held in my hand since I'd borrowed the five hundred dollars from Gina to replace Andrew's stolen cash. Hannah came by after work and drove me back up the mountain.

That afternoon I caught another mouse in my gallon jug. I took the jug with the mouse to the dead car in the driveway. I asked nicely, got in, and it started right up. We careened down the mountain. I dared not ride the brakes, but it hurtled down much too fast for me. I got to the bottom of the hill where Meads Mountain Road becomes Rock City Road and took a left. Within a few hundred feet I came to a little road called Patricia Lane. I felt it suited my tiny companion and I turned the stiff steering wheel onto the gravel road. I took my mouse and set out to free her, but she held on like a cartoon character. When I turned the jug over, she clung to its edges, slipped down the side, and finally got stuck in the neck. I couldn't make her leave. I shook the jug, but the peanut butter from the bottom hit her in the head. Now I felt karma backing up on me. She looked terrified. I felt awful. I laid the jug down and she calmly walked out wearing the wad of peanut butter on her head.

I slid back behind the wheel of the idling, now smoking, car and turned around in time to see the little mouse slip into the bushes. I drove to the corner, stopped, took a deep breath, and rallied my courage to get back up the mountain in my temporarily magic automobile. When I looked up, a chubby-faced teenager stood in front of my car, crying. Wiping her tears when she realized I'd seen her, she smiled a big, gap-toothed smile. She approached the window. There was no window crank so I opened the door, which fell from its hinges and almost off the car. We both laughed. I told her to get in. We drove back up the mountain.

Sharon's face, though full in the cheeks, was flat like a Persian cat's and covered with acne, but she had a gorgeous, gap-toothed grin that seemed to pull light from the heavens. She was thick with no sharp edges. She told me that her parents had kicked her out and she'd been living in a teen residence run by Family of Woodstock, a human services agency in town. She'd recently given up her place there for a live-in job that had just fallen through.

She couldn't stop talking and didn't take her eyes off me while we chitty-bang-banged our way up the mountain. Her open admiration for me felt foreign and good at the same time. I offered her some coffee and we sat on the deck of the main house, where I'd never considered sitting before, and we talked about her troubles.

First on the list: she had no place to live. Second on the list: she had no money. Third on the list: she had burned every bridge she'd crossed to get here. She sounded exactly like me. I asked her about the job that had fallen through. She was supposed to be living with an elderly man named Copley Clarke. Her job would be to cook, clean, and drive him around. She'd just come from him when I met her. She begged me to help her talk some sense into him. I left her to sit and stare in wonder at the gorgeous Hudson Valley while I went into the main house and called the number she'd given me for Copley to see if he might change his mind. I invited myself over to his house, got directions, gathered up Sharon, and took one more dangerous trip down the mountain in a car that wasn't fit to be driven.

I dropped Sharon off in town and drove to Joy Road. Copley answered the door wearing baggy, dingy white long johns covered by a tattered yellow terrycloth bathrobe. He looked like a baby bird with his smooth pale skin and thatch of white hair. He was making toast when I arrived at five in the afternoon. There were four burnt slices on his gray Formica kitchen table, atop a stack of typewritten sheets and little books with titles like *Guideposts for Living* and *Oral Roberts Today*. I pulled one of the yellow vinyl chairs out from the table only to find more papers. I tried another chair, same situation there, so I moved that pile to the table and sat down.

"We have a problem," I suggested.

He said he was angry with Sharon and remained firm in his decision not to hire her. He gave myriad reasons why it wouldn't work out. Number one: she was only fifteen and she didn't have a driver's license. I nodded in agreement, looking around his cluttered living space while he rattled on. The living room had two red walls and one black wall. The fourth wall I couldn't see. Thin, disintegrating plastic curtains hung at the big, wood-framed windows, linoleum area rugs covered the wood floors, and there were booklets, papers, and pieces of toast everywhere. We talked for over an hour. He seemed sweet and smart, and was old, alone, and sick with some kind of cancer. I wondered if I should move in and help him. I went back into town to pick up Sharon and figure this whole thing out.

Copley reminded me of my dad when he was dying from cancer, except that Copley didn't have anyone to look after him. I had visions of making him happy and throwing out all of the stuff that he seemed to be drowning in. After making sure Sharon was okay with it, I called Copley and offered to move in and help by doing light chores and running errands. He loved the idea. Sharon found a place to live, and two days after that I moved into his upstairs bedroom. I stripped the walls of the Oral Roberts posters, the windows of their torn plastic curtains, and the bed of its dusty sheets.

At ninety-three years old, Copley still phoned the local radio station every day to add his voice to those on the call-in program. He wrote letters to the editor of the Kingston newspaper and had heated debates with whoever stopped by. Every day there was a fresh pile of burnt toast. I overheard him tell his neighbor Helen that an angel had sent me.

Copley asked me to take him to the post office in town in his old Ford Fairlane. I pulled open the heavy sliding garage door, got into the old white car, turned the key, and slid the shifter into reverse. My foot fell through the bottom of the vehicle. I looked down and saw the cement garage floor through the hole. Fred Flintstone would have had a field day with this one. I got out and hunted in the cluttered garage for something I could turn into a temporary floor. I found a thick square of plywood, which became both floor and floor mat for the old Ford. I loaded Copley in and we headed to Woodstock.

I'd always wanted an old house to explore, one with nooks and crannies and treasures forgotten in attics. I'd always hoped for a chance to find things that had gotten left behind. But this house on Joy Road held only an old man with cancer, stale toast and papers on every flat surface, and a damp basement. This house had old double-hung windows whose weights had long abandoned their posts. This house had broken appliances and linoleum flooring so old it had become brittle. This house was not full of treasures or secret places.

Deciding that for now I would take care of Copley and hope that Norman would one day want me back, I persevered. I called Norman regularly, trying to read the pauses in our talks, of which there were many—both talks and pauses. I would project myself through the phone line into his tiny, shriveled-up peach pit of a heart and search for my answers. I could only do this when we were on the phone. It didn't work in person. Maybe it didn't work at all.

CHAPTER 19

❧ FINDING JOY ROAD ❧

Throughout my life, when times were tough and I didn't know what to do, I would always end up taking care of someone worse off than me. It was my medicine. That's why I was a good fit for Copley. I cooked for him and cleaned up after him. I went to the gym every day and worked the flea markets on the weekends. I got by.

It ended the day that I had his little-old-man, baby-bird body sitting in the freshly scrubbed but still mineral-stained bathtub. I was washing the bowel movement off him when he squeezed and twisted my breast so hard that I yelped. He said he would pay me to have his baby and would give me his house. I dropped the green washcloth into the murky water and yanked him to his feet. I didn't say anything. I just dried him off and made sure his bony feet made it safely out of the tub and onto the rubber-backed bathmat. I gently held out his tattered yellow terrycloth robe, straightened out the belt, and closed the front of his robe, putting to rest the sight of his thin erect penis. I was done. It was over. I would have to move.

Over the next several weekends I sold the remainder of my five hundred monkey puppets. I made ten dollars per sale after I'd deducted what I owed Norman for buying them, and finally I had enough money to move. I moved into an apartment that was located over a working garage, where each morning two mechanics would show up to work on cars. Not a good fit.

I needed help. The phone rang and startled me out of my despair. It was Norman. He'd gotten a call from Copley's neighbor, Helen. Copley had fallen and broken his hip, and it had been determined that it was my fault for having abandoned him. I thought of the bathtub scene. I had been gone for a full month, and, even though I knew it wasn't my fault, the words stung. I wanted to run to the hospital or use my paltry funds to buy Copley a soft blanket or a new bathrobe. I hung up the phone and stared at the wall. The phone rang a second time. It was Norman again. "Buy the house," he said. And although I couldn't think of a house I would want less, as usual I did as I was told.

I called Marquette Savings and Trust in Rochester, Minnesota, and asked to speak to the person in charge of my father's estate. I felt I was letting my dad down. But he'd want me to have a house, wouldn't he? The man who came on the line hadn't known my dad, how he'd sweated and struggled for every dollar he had. He didn't know that most of the money Jack Evans had wanted to leave his daughters had been spent—gone on hospital bills. He told me there was a balance of nineteen thousand in the account and what I would need to submit in order to have it. As soon as it started, it seemed, the call was over. My hands trembled as I hung up the phone. It felt like the end of my daddy taking care of me.

ଚ୨

A few weeks later, with check in hand, Norman and I went to the closing, where together we would buy Copley's house for me to live in, fix up, sell for a profit, and repay Norman for his investment before we went our merry ways. I tried to imagine my daddy's face, but time had stolen the memory of both my parents' faces. I could no longer picture either one of them. I only had their photographs to remind me. This realization took them another step farther away from me.

At the closing, I found myself thinking back to a day a few years earlier when my kinfolk gathered to bury Aunt Lizzy down in Zena, Oklahoma. As everyone had stood in their family huddles, I unknowingly stood on my parents' graves, the heels of my pumps sinking into the earth that covered their caskets.

The lawyer at the closing cleared his throat, pulling me back to the present, and Norman handed me a pen to sign the document to take possession of Copley's house. My eyes filled with tears when I saw the house listed as "s/b/l 18.0036.41, Zena, New York." My parents were buried in their Zena, and I would now come to life in a different Zena, a fact that gave me some comfort and hope.

Norman sat across the table from me fiddling with the pen in his hand. The beauty of his long, pale fingers mesmerized me. A shudder passed through my body. We weren't buying our first home; we were merely reluctant partners in the purchase of a house where I could live so I would no longer be in his way. I looked up through his smallish spectacles into his blue eyes, and our eyes connected for a split second. I did love him: how very sad.

It was March 23, 1983, a cold and dreary day. We drove to the ugly house clad in graying asbestos shingles with peeling black trim. No fancy touches, no gingerbread trim, no flair, nothing Victorian, a simple cross between the Cape Cod and Craftsman styles. Over the front and back doors hung flimsy white-and-red metal awnings. The steps were made from large, hand-chiseled squares of thick bluestone; the doors were simple, unadorned pine; and the windows were made of old, wavy glass.

Standing in my new kitchen and looking out at the driveway, I saw an open field where a gigantic black walnut tree had just begun to bud and two large willow trees were rather bare of their weeping. Three crabapple trees would dress up the yard with their blossoms in a few short months. The scrubby-looking lot, bordered by roads on its west and south sides, and with its gravel and its tangle of bushes, couldn't have been more ordinary.

The front yard, also to the west, bordered a gorgeous rock-strewn stream called the Sawkill; however, a blacktop road with a guardrail and an ugly chain-link fence and some scraggly bushes took up most of the stream frontage. I was glad to see there were some ducks in the stream.

Behind the house, beyond a row of scraggly bushes and a few small trees, there was a barren-looking playground buffering my property and the Zena Elementary School. The school resembled every other school built in the 1960s—terracotta-colored brick with institutional light-blue trim. A majestic pine tree stood sentinel over a rusted propane tank and a detached two-car garage filled with old-man junk, its old-fashioned sliding door wide open while Norman unloaded carton after carton from his blue Chevy van.

About to fall apart, I saw the piles of toast and boxes of *Guideposts for Living* on the kitchen table. I picked up a piece of toast preserved by virtue of the burnt outer crust and took a bite, sat down on one of the cracked yellow vinyl kitchen chairs, and picked up an issue of *Guideposts* dated September 1980. The toast was somehow delicious. I read a daily meditation about a young man who had left home, squandered his inheritance, and returned broken to his house, where a feast was prepared in his honor. I looked at the old toast in my hand and started to cry.

I put the toast and the *Guideposts* down and looked around. The kitchen had long since seen its best days. The ancient stove was missing a firewall and only two of the four burners worked. The stained ceramic sink was stuck inconveniently in a corner, far from the windows and the light fixture; the faucets were mottled and rusted. The fridge was shorter than I was and rocked forward each time I opened it. Much to my horror, Norman had bought me all the contents of the house so I wouldn't have to worry about buying anything.

I tried to open one of the heavily painted kitchen cabinets by turning its small, elongated metal knob, but the knob wouldn't turn and the door wouldn't open. I got an old spatula out of the sticky-faced drawer and stuck its thin head between the cabinet door and the cabinet, and when I jiggled it the spatula fell apart in my hand. I tried a butter knife but that didn't work either. Finally I got the damn door open with a heavily rusted putty knife that I found under the sink. The modest treasure in the cabinet included ancient cylinders of Quaker Oats and several cans of green beans. Oh, goody.

As I walked into the large master bedroom where Copley had slept, his urine-stained mattress lay stark in the daylight streaming through the open-curtained window. I'd never really looked around this room. I found a half-melted light-blue plastic laundry basket that had stupidly been set down on the large metal heater grate in the hallway. I had been living in the house when it melted, filling the air with the toxic, acrid smell of burning plastic. I couldn't believe I owned all of this crap. I wanted to throw it all away. I wanted to get rid of everything, including the house. That was the plan. We would fix it up, "flip" it, and make enough money for me to return Norman's twenty-one thousand. He said I could keep the remainder as a nest egg for my new life. That was the plan.

A few things happened on my way to becoming a real estate maven. It turned out that I had no gift for renovating houses. I found taping and painting extremely difficult. I had no interest in reading how-to books and had no real design ideas, whereas Norman was on fire with jobs for me to complete. He wanted me to not only fix up the house but also make the venture a success. I didn't have the energy to aspire to a single thing he recommended.

Norman would call daily from the city to get the latest progress report. I would pretend to be making headway, or I'd think up intelligent-sounding questions to keep him on the phone. He sent letters filled with diagrams of how I should build things and blueprints for how to redefine the rooms. Each suggestion left me no choice but to pursue the one avenue that I had open to me, the one area where I had tremendous experience and where I hoped to get some relief. Cocaine.

I called my friend Peter, who promised to introduce me to a guy named Greg who had a connection.

ဢ

Before copping, the anticipation is ninety percent of the equation, and I could think of nothing else. My waiting spawned a cleaning, organizing, dump-run frenzy. In the three days it took Greg to get back to me, I made over forty floor-less Ford Fairlane dump runs; broke and stacked into neat movable piles all the squares of faux-Persian-rug linoleum that had covered almost every floor in the house; emptied every kitchen cupboard; scrubbed all three sinks, one bathtub, and two toilets a dozen times or more; WD-40'd the garage door; thought about but abandoned the idea of emptying the garage of all its crappy tools and dried-out paint cans; and even cleaned the dead mouse and squirrel parts out of the rancid, gag-inducing sump-pump hole in the basement.

Greg didn't just call; he took me to pick it up. After making sure, sure, sure that I had the right amount of money, he recited the rules. Don't ever say anything over the phone (duh, yes, of course, go on), don't ever tell anyone the dealer's name or where she lives (yep, yep, yep), don't call after nine o'clock at night, and never, ever before noon (yeah, yeah, yeah), park your car in the Grand Union parking lot, and never, ever say anything to her if you see her in public. Fine. Of course. An addict will agree to everything, every time, and never hear a word that has been said.

We pulled into the Grand Union parking lot, then walked across the street and down three doors. It was a simple nothing of a house, but still valuable because it was located in Woodstock, the town where the concert didn't really happen. My heart was pounding. I felt alive, excited, and terrified. The woman opened the door and immediately walked away from us and into the house. Greg pushed me in, shut the door quickly, and locked it. My mouth went dry. I smiled at her but she wasn't looking and my lips got stuck above my front teeth. I licked them and that is when she looked at me and saw me licking my lips. I felt like a maniac.

She never smiled. We didn't look into one another's eyes. She asked how many grams I wanted and I couldn't really tell her because I wanted all of them but could scarcely afford the two I planned to get. It was more money than I had spent on anything, other than the house, in over a year and a half.

I want everything, I thought to myself. I want new furniture, a new car, clothes, running shoes, a new refrigerator, Norman to love me, and another second chance to live a good life. I want out of here, I want this mean-looking woman to be my best friend. I want, I want.

"I want three," I said, spending every dollar I had on me. She sold me an eight ball, three and a half grams for the price of three. Ah, the joys and pitfalls of buying in bulk. When she handed me the small plastic bag, instead of three wax-papered rectangles, my artful fingers played the plastic bag like an instrument. I instinctively searched among the powdery substance for rocks, usually indicating unstepped-on cocaine.

The decent thing would be to give a line or two to Greg for setting the whole thing up, but I really hated that idea. As Greg and I got into the car, I wished that I was alone and could just stick a neat, tightly rolled hundred-dollar bill or a clean, four-inch section of a fresh drinking straw into the bag in my hand and pull what I loved deeply into my heart, my mind, my essence. I longed for that feeling of burn, that searing pain of snorting something into my body. I wanted to feel that clot of cocaine hit the back of my sinuses, to make that awful who-cares-who's-listening snort that could pull it into the emptiest part of me. But I didn't. Instead, I looked around Greg's car for something I could fashion into the kind of tiny envelope that I had made thousands of times before. I needed somewhat glossy paper. I was a master at this. And I knew that, hours later, when all the rest had been consumed, I would be very sorry that I had given even this tiny ungenerous amount away.

CHAPTER 20

❧ MOUNTAIN PONY ❧

Life happens too fast. One decision and the reins had slipped out of my hands. I had hoped to use the cocaine to help me get stuff done, to accomplish even the things I didn't know how to do. I planned on really getting it together, which is why I used another chunk of my building allowance to get just one more quarter ounce of cocaine.

This time I didn't need Greg, I didn't tell anyone, and I didn't mince my words. I didn't say anything over the phone and I didn't have enough money to go out, so I never saw her in public. I did park at the Grand Union, and I planned it better this time. Again, the anticipation had helped immensely, and I had done some more dump runs and washed the filthy, wavy-glassed, impossible-to-clean windows, and I'd made a list. I'd gotten a phone call from Greg asking me if I knew anyone who had a pony that he and his wife could borrow for their kid's birthday the next Saturday. I told him I'd try to think of someone, saying whatever was necessary to get him off the phone. It was only Tuesday and plenty of time remained to find a pony.

I snorted the lines I'd prepared, loaded the car with more linoleum squares, old silverware, rusted cast-iron skillets, old shovels, and cans partially filled with congealed paint before heading to the Woodstock landfill. When I pulled in, there was a man rifling through the metal

She was called Mountain Pony when she galloped into my life and decided I was worth saving.

Photo taken January 1995.

pile, and when he saw me he came over and began unloading my car and putting my stuff into his van, including my crappy silverware. He was wearing rust-colored Carhartt pants, a thin sweatshirt, and a huge smile. He was handsome and chain smoking. I liked him immediately. His name was Johnny Muth. I asked him about the pony thing and he told me to go to the diner in Bradley Meadows at around nine in the morning and ask some of the locals.

All the times I'd been to the dump I'd never really looked around and seen how much great stuff was there. I found a bunch of things that would come in handy if I ever found chimpanzees in need of rescuing. I'd dreamed of that since I first saw the movie *Born Free*. I wanted to save chimps from zoos and research and take care of them until I could get them back to Africa.

I loaded my car with a cute white crib, a bassinet, and a five-foot-tall stuffed doll dressed in clothes like my mother used to wear. Fueled with purpose, I drove my dream-filled car to the local diner and walked up to a table filled with local-looking guys, and the youngest, most handsome, immediately took to my cause to find a pony. He tried to pull me onto his lap, but, being familiar with salty dogs and horny men, I held out my hand instead. He took my hand and brought it to his lips, then wrote down the number of a woman named Risa who lived out past Lake Hill. She had a couple of ponies.

When I contacted the woman, she told me that I could have the pony on Saturday, but warned me that it was hard to catch and didn't like kids. Perfect for a little boy's birthday party, I thought. It both pleased and bothered me that a woman would give me a pony without meeting me, but I'd satisfied an important request and that's what seemed, at the time, to matter more.

I'd been feeling okay, not terribly wired or tired or scared—at least not until Norman called to tell me he would be coming up on Friday and wanted an accounting of what had been done. I began to nibble on my cuticles and jump from one pile of regret to another. I'd made over twenty dump runs; I'd made a friend named Johnny at the dump; I'd found a diner full of handymen; I'd found a coke dealer; I'd found a pony; and I'd thrown away bad paint, the burnt toast, the *Guideposts*, and, so far, about eight hundred dollars.

I may have been a needy, broken, nervous wreck, but that could be remedied, I said to myself, by doing some big, thick lines and grabbing the bull by the horns. I went upstairs and opened the little cardboard box full of single-edge razor blades. I took a blade out of its box and pulled the gray strip of cardboard from its edge. I took out the little mirror, the tightly rolled dollar bill, and the little brown glass vial that I would use to carefully smash the rocks. I took the two largest chunks out of the custom-made baggie and placed the largest one in the center of the mirror, holding it reverently in place with my thumb and forefinger. I picked up the blade and placed it in the center of the chunk, working it through the crystal. Oh, it was beautiful, pure like the Peruvian mother-of-pearl cocaine I'd done too much of before I'd broken my back. I sliced it up, as if it was the finest beef tenderloin and I was creating little filets mignons. I then pulverized each slice, chopping it up until the piles of brilliant white shone like hills of virgin snow.

It took a while to release myself from the mirror, the bill, and the cigarettes. It took even longer to determine if I looked normal enough to get into the car and go somewhere. It took so long to decide where I should go and what I might be able to do that I decided to just go find the pony. High as a kite and feeling very alive, I hopped into Copley's old car with its missing driver-side floor. The road whizzing by under my feet kept catching my eye, but I forced myself to look directly at the road, even though my hands were shaking. I drove through Woodstock very slowly, my eyes looking straight ahead, my hands on the wheel at ten o'clock and two o'clock, and a casual I'm-just-fine smile on my face. No one seemed to notice; everything was going well, but I realized I needed carrots or apples for the pony.

Stopping at the Woodstock Meat Market to buy a bag of carrots and a pack of Camels used up some of my momentum, so I decided to slightly recharge. I opened the tiny envelope of coke that I'd cleverly brought with me and leaned over as if looking for something on the floor of the car. I inhaled swiftly and deeply and sat up, put the car in reverse, checked around me like a jungle animal looking for predators, and tucked the refolded coke envelope into my sock. I pressed my fingers into my cheek and inhaled again to get the coke out of my nose and into my bloodstream. I turned right onto Mill Hill Road. I figured it would take about fifteen minutes to find the road that would lead me to the pony known only as Mountain Pony.

The unnamed road at the right fork out of town that I'd been instructed to follow ended at an unnamed farm. I parked near the house where Risa had told me I would find a halter and a lead rope.

It was a sprawling place, and very isolated. I spotted a white swayback horse and a wild-looking pony far out in an immense green pasture. Near a little lean-to by the fence, I climbed through the barbless wire to meet my little friend. I hadn't been near a horse since that fateful day in Central Park when Paramount and I had parted company.

I hesitated, wondering if this had been a good idea, and felt weak in the knees. The pony looked at me and whinnied, pulled her ears back, and started galloping towards me, farting, bucking, and carrying on. The old white horse lifted his heavy head from his grazing and put it back down again. Within moments the pony galloped into the lean-to.

I was shaking. I went to meet Mountain Pony where she stood. I noticed dangerous broken floorboards in her little shelter. Her hooves were overgrown and cracked, her long black mane was tangled into a giant knot and her bony ribs showed through her matted coat.

"Hello, hello, little girl, you are so beautiful. I'm Julie," I cooed, slowly extending my hand toward her muzzle for her to smell. Her soft nose came into my palm and she licked the salt from my skin. I pulled the carrots out of my back pocket and offered her one. She ate it as if she hadn't seen a good carrot in a long time.

As she took the carrot I petted her face and let my hand search under her matted forelock for the soft, foal-like hair that hid beneath it. She had burrs in her forelock, mane, and tail, and there was a salty residue on her back from a hard sweat where a saddle had been. One of her legs was scabbed and another was bleeding from a little cut where a broken board in the lean-to had just punctured her. I coaxed her out of the shelter, put the halter over her ears, and secured it under her cheek. She pushed at my shoulder with her head as I led her over to my car and tied her lead rope to the door handle.

I went looking for a brush or a comb, neither of which I could find, so I detangled and combed her mane, tail, and forelock with my fingers, carefully removing the burrs while she greedily ate the carrots.

When I put my open hand on her muscular neck, it felt warm, strong, and solid, unsullied by life, and something moved through me. When I pressed the heel of my hand solidly against her, some kind of energy, some force of balance, some longed for connection moved from my hand into my heart, down to the base of my spine, and on to my feet. I flashed to myself as a little eight-year-old riding my first pony, and then as an eleven-year-old galloping bareback through a cornfield on my very own horse—clear images of a young girl loved by these beautiful creatures. When Mountain Pony turned to look at me, I was embarrassed that I was high on coke.

I couldn't find any sweet feed or grain anywhere in the shed, so I gave her all the carrots except one, which I thought should go to the old white horse. I walked Mountain Pony around a bit to see how she moved. She was small, maybe eleven hands tall at the whither. As we walked, she pushed my back hard with her head, which I took to mean that she liked me.

But after I'd walked her back to the rickety gate and leaned toward her to unclasp her halter, she bit me. I let her go and held out half the carrot to the now curious and closer white horse, giving Mountain Pony the other half. She turned on her heels, bit him too, and ran like the wind to the far side of the pasture. I drove toward home with the sticky grime and wholesome smell of horse dust on my hands, stopping at the local diner to see if I could get the number of a farrier to trim her hooves. A fierce desire to be as free as that wild pony surged through my heart.

Wednesday came and went and Thursday threatened to do the same, but meeting the pony had done something to me. I had gotten a farrier to agree to meet me at the unnamed farm, found some pretty decent scrub brushes and a comb that would do the job, and bought a box of Raisin Bran to give her as a treat. I called Risa to make sure it was okay to take care of the pony. She easily agreed to anything I wanted to do and I headed over to see my little friend and get her hooves trimmed.

The pony came running to meet me, but she went right by me when I tried unsuccessfully to prevent her from charging into the shed with the splintered floor. She stopped short, her leg bleeding and her head nodding. The white horse was gone; Risa had said his owners had come to get him, so now Mountain Pony was alone. The farrier pulled up and I led the pony into the driveway, holding her tight, as he grumbled and complained about how some people should not be allowed to have horses if they aren't going to take care of them. I agreed and silently decided that I would rescue her. He left. I brushed her and put hoof conditioner on her newly cared-for-feet, hoping that the shape of her deformed hooves could be corrected. I saw a hose by the side of the house and decided to bathe her.

I needed some shampoo, and Risa had told me to feel free to go into the house if I needed anything. When I opened the door, the smell of rotting flesh assaulted me. I'd smelled that odor countless times on the cancer ward years ago, but this came from a little spaniel whose back end was festering with sores and squirming with maggots. I'd never seen such a sight. I ran outside to get some fresh air and to think for a minute. I put the pony back in the pasture, got into the car, and went home. I sat in the car, holding onto the steering wheel and staring straight ahead for a very long time. I got out, called Risa, and told her I would be drawing up papers to buy the pony from her for one dollar. I told her that she had to get her dog to the vet and that she had no choice in the matter because, if she didn't agree, I would have her arrested for cruelty to animals. She kept muttering how sorry she was. I knew I had won.

Problem: I had just rescued a pony but had no barn. Another problem: Norman would be arriving the next day. I called to tell him the news. He thought it was wonderful, amazing even, but he wasn't coming. I was relieved, pissed, and relieved again.

I called my friend Cary, a woman I had met at the YMCA during one of my healing steam baths. She came right over. The first thing we did was take the hideous awnings off the house and fashion them into a shed roof. Then we gathered saplings and made what we would come to refer to as the O.K. Corral in the side yard under the shade of a black walnut tree. Cary knew how to build, and she had brought along some intense plastic cable fasteners to tie the saplings together. Within a few hours we had the makings of a somewhat solid outdoor stable.

I called around and found someone with a truck, a trailer, and the time to help me. We went together to retrieve my pony. I had Risa sign a paper selling me the pony, had my friend sign as a witness, and handed her a dollar. I loaded my stubborn, nippy, frightened little friend onto the trailer and we wended our way along the curvy country roads. I could feel the weight of her compact body being thrust from side to side and I could hardly endure it. When we finally arrived home, the paddock seemed inadequate and precarious, as if all she had to do was lean on it and the whole thing would come tumbling down. But to my surprise, when I undid the lead rope she went directly to her little lean-to, where I had hung a bucket of sweet feed and a bucket of water. She took a long, deep drink and kept her head buried in the other bucket until she'd consumed every morsel.

Satisfied that she was safe for the moment, I went into the house and began calling lumberyards for prices on posts and boards, while simultaneously laying out a few thick lines of coke. I inhaled all three within the time it took to say oh my God, then went to the window and stared out at the pony.

Impulsively, I decided to tear the horrible carpet off each step of the stairs. I carried the nasty carpet out the front door, set it down, and went around the back of the house, surprising the pony, who jerked her head up and nickered when she saw me. I gave her a pat and went back into the house. The rooms seemed so small and boxy. Opening the door between the living room and the kitchen, I remembered watching my dad slide doors on and off their hinges. From my collection of inherited tools on the front porch, I grabbed a hammer and a chisel and removed the unnecessary door. Next I took a flat crowbar and slid it behind the doorframe, loosening it quickly and easily. Feeling endowed with power and skill, I pried it off on both sides, neatly stacking the boards near the front door.

I went back to the window and stared out at the pony. I felt capable and brave. I picked up a heavy-headed mallet that I had found in the garage and began to knock away the plasterboard to the right side of the doorframe where I'd removed the door. First I smashed a hole in the wall and then I meticulously removed all of the pieces until I was down to the bare two by fours. I could see through to the living room. It looked amazingly better, everything seeming bigger.

I ripped all the disgusting, deteriorating plastic curtains off all the windows, wadded them into balls, and stuffed them into the trash. I took down the cheap, hollow, brass-like curtain rods and tied them all together with a piece of twine I'd removed from the bale of hay I'd bought for the pony. When I carried them out to the garage, the pony nickered again and bobbed her head.

For three days I oscillated between the mirror, the pony, and the demolition of my house. I removed all the wood between the living room and the kitchen by kicking it, finessing it, or, when necessary, prying it loose. I also got rid of most of the furniture and all of the cocaine.

Danny, the guy who'd helped me bring the pony home, stopped by one afternoon to check on how she was doing. Not finding me around and seeing I had torn down a wall, he wrote me a note in marker pen on the kitchen wall that said, Julie Do Not Tear Down This Wall.

When he walked around to the back to see the pony, he found me. He was furious and told me I didn't have a header and that the house could collapse! I had no clue what he meant. He could tell that I was wired and said he would come back the next day. I was exhausted but satisfied. After checking on and feeding the pony, I took the phone off the hook and slept for two days.

I woke up with Norman leaning in over me. I sat bolt upright and thanked God I'd had the presence of mind to put away every scrap of evidence that I'd been doing cocaine since he last saw me.

I stretched my long, slender arms over my head in that movie star caught-off-guard way and said casually, "I must have dozed off."

He said he'd been trying to call me for two days and that the operator said the phone was off the hook.

I feigned surprise and said, "Really? Oh, I'm so sorry. I didn't realize it. I've been working nonstop and taking care of the pony. It must have gotten knocked off the hook."

At that point I frantically tried to figure out what day it was and if the pony was still here, alive but starving. I gestured for Norman to back up to give me room to rise. I went to the bathroom and took a quick glance out the window. The pony was there but I still didn't know what day it was.

Trotting down the steps and grabbing some apples and carrots, I very casually suggested that Norman come meet the pony. I looked to my right, and true to form my friend Danny must have shown up, because there was a big, thick, impressive-looking piece of wood running from the saved wall to the chimney. I had been rescued, just like the pony.

The writing on the wall still said, Julie Do Not Tear Down This Wall, but now there was a smiley face and a heart. I turned to see Norman rounding the corner, and he didn't look happy. My mind raced to remember if there was anything he could have seen or read or sensed as he walked toward me. I braced myself and he grabbed me by the shoulders and pulled me into his arms.

Grateful. I felt grateful that maybe this time things would work out. I'd always thought they would, but then they never had. I didn't imagine our embrace would last long; it never did with Norman. I willed the seconds to seem like hours, and the four or five breaths we took together did seem like hundreds. I broke the embrace so *he* wouldn't get to, or have to, or want to, and I took him by his glorious sensitive hand and led him out to meet the pony. She trotted around the perimeter of the corral like a show pony, her long mane glossy in the sunlight, the wind ruffling through it as if on a *National Geographic* cover. She looked at Norman and whinnied, arched her neck, raised her tail, and snorted. Uncomfortable with much emotion, Norman smiled and turned to butter.

He decided that we had to build Mountain Pony a better home. We went to the lumberyard and filled his van with one-inch-by-six-inch-by-ten-foot boards to fashion a real paddock for her. The lumbermen told us where to get cedar posts, and on our second run we filled the van with those. We bought galvanized fence nails in town and, precariously close to the coke dealer's house, I found myself hoping beyond hope that the "if you see me in public" rule went both ways.

Norman had brought some tools along and I had saved Copley's two old posthole diggers, several shovels, and a heavy metal tool I named "the digging bar." We set up a circular saw connected by a good eighth of a mile of extension cord and placed it on a worktable made of two crooked sawhorses and that door I'd removed between the kitchen and the living room. Then we got down to the business of putting up a fence.

Norman measured, sawed, and stacked while I awkwardly raised the old posthole digger and came down hard on the rock and clay soil, drilling into the most unwilling ground I'd ever encountered. It took three days to measure it out, mark the places where the posts would be, cut over a hundred boards, and put up fewer than half the posts we would need. It was hard, horrible, backbreaking work, and some of the most fun I'd ever had.

Norman shone like a star while I felt flung around like a dishrag, first by a posthole digger, then by a digging bar, and always by my insecurities. We slept in the same bed but didn't touch. We cooked together but didn't talk during our meals. We would walk, drive, sit, and stare, but we never really crossed the great divide that time had put between us.

As soon as Norman left I called the dealer to get some cocaine.

ᔕ

Given the precise instructions Norman had left on how I was to finish the job, I knew I needed help. On many a morning I headed over to the diner and spoke to any carpenter I could find. A fellow named John Kellogg helped me design and begin to build a modest two-stall barn beside the garage. I did the work as he guided me, corrected me, and took over when I could no longer swing a hammer. I loved being able to fix things, and I knew my daddy would have been proud of me. It thrilled me to walk out on my roof, replace a shingle, climb a ladder with a tool belt on, and balance perfectly as I drove a nail into the wood with three clean strikes of the hammer.

Almost every day I lifted weights at the YMCA and worked out on the Nautilus machines. I took long, luxurious steam baths using sea salt to scrub my body, putting rosemary oil in my hair, and using pumice on my feet. I continued to live for Norman's approval, and every day I fell more and more in love with my pony. Sometimes I thought I might be truly healing, but then I'd throw away my precious money and my precious self to buy more cocaine.

Eager to finish the fence, I enlisted the devoted help of a sexy, blue-eyed teenager named Tony who'd survived a chained-to-the-stove horror of a childhood. I hadn't had a lover since Andrew and I was ready for some rough-and-tumble sex. Tony loved it. On the rare occasions when Norman came up, Tony took to the hills or slept at a friend's house.

Tony and I worked tirelessly to finish the fence and the barn. I rode the pony every day, but I could tell she longed to gallop on her own as she had when I first met her. I'd made her long lead lines and she would graze near me wherever I worked. If I sunbathed in the yard, I'd tie her long line to a tree and she'd come over and tickle my legs with her lips as if she were eating grass. When I worked on the fence I'd tie her nearby, but not where she could pick up a nail in her hoof or, worse, get hit by a car.

I wanted the barn done, once and for all, to shelter her from the elements and the coyotes. The day we finished the barn the crabapple trees bloomed. I led my pony into the field and unsnapped her halter, and she took off like a shot. She galloped back and forth, each time as if she might plow right through the boards. But then she'd stop dead, grunt with satisfaction, realign her stance, and suddenly turn and gallop full-speed in the opposite direction. I worried about roots and rocks and boards and cars and nails and woodchuck holes and broken legs. She didn't seem to worry about a thing.

After she'd gone back and forth over a dozen times, traffic on Sawkill Road came to an appreciative standstill. As if making a final bow, she took to the fence line and began a brilliant, petulant trot around the field's perimeter, working the crowd. Finally she ran full-speed toward me and stopped. I threw my arms around her as car horns honked their approval of her finale. Watching her freedom, real freedom, helped me imagine my own.

With the fence in place and the pony enjoying her new life, I felt better about myself. I'd gotten a good job as a personal trainer at a new gym nearby, and I wanted Tony to move on, to find someone younger and kinder than me. He resisted, hooked, it seemed, on having someone tell him what to do, just like I'd been hooked on Norman. After he finally did leave, he returned in the night and stole some meaningful things.

CHAPTER 21

❦ WHITE MAGIC ❦

A beautiful little wisp of a girl showed up on Joy Road one day and asked if she could give the pony some grass. Somewhat allergic to unannounced company, I hesitated, but I liked her gentle enthusiasm and walked with her to offer my pony some grass.

"What's her name?" she asked.

"She doesn't really have one. They called her Mountain Pony."

I reached over the fence and the pony licked my hand, and the little girl, named Nadia, said, "I think she thinks you're her mommy. Maybe you should name her Baby." Upon hearing her name, the pony ran along the side of the paddock whinnying like a maniac and carrying on like a fool.

"I guess she likes it, so Baby it is," I said.

Nadia ran along the outside of the fence trying to keep up with a very proud and extremely fast little pony. Her mom had opened an upscale Italian restaurant next door to the stylish little health club where I worked as a personal trainer, aerobic instructor, and masseuse. I had become a masseuse largely inspired by Cary but mostly informed by a life of laying hands on people to bring them some relief.

Norman had given me an old massage table I could use at home, but I usually worked on people at the health club. It came naturally to me; I'd always been intrigued by the connection between bodies, hearts, and minds. For instance, I'll want to know why an old man on the corner has a drooping eyelid, or a limp, or how the body compensates for a missing finger. I've learned that most people don't know how they got to be the way they are, but the body carries its own memory. I've always had an ability to hear and understand what a body is saying.

At the health club I gave massages on a used mortician's table in a small room with a swinging door at either end. The men would come in from their steam room and the women from theirs. I like getting to know someone by giving them a massage. People seem more honest when they're lying in a dimly lit room without any clothes on. I enjoy hearing their stories and relieving their pain.

Tony got arrested and put in jail, Norman was deep into a health crisis and stuck in New York City, and I felt free. I joined a softball team and met a woman named Liz who would become a benefactor and a great friend to me. She had worked in investment banking, came from a wealthy family, and was older and more logical than I was.

At the gym I'd found a serious workout partner, and slowly but surely I became an amateur body builder. At home I worked hard to turn my house into a kind of sanctuary, a beautiful place where I belonged.

When I enlisted the local radio station to help me make a mixed-music tape for my exercise class, I met a guy named Richard. We had chemistry the moment we met. He took my music selections and my phone number and invited me to lunch the next day. When I got to his cabin, a big white dog trotted out to meet me. He was gorgeous and polite. As I approached Richard's front door, the dog got ahead of me and pulled on a leather strap to open the door. My heart melted.

While Richard made lunch, the Samoyed he called White Dog lay next to me on a daybed. At six o'clock the next morning, White Dog appeared at my front door. On each of the following days, he would travel the two miles to my house and we'd spend the day together. At

The first time I met White Dog, he held open a door for me and I fell in love with him.
Photo of Magic, 1993.

night I'd give him a ride home. After about two weeks of this, Richard brought him to me.

"He certainly knows where he wants to live," Richard said a bit sadly. "I'm honored that he's lived with me for the last three years, but now he wants you, and I don't blame him." And with that the dog jumped out of Richard's little blue convertible, bounded over to nudge me, and then peed on a bush, marking his new territory. Later that day when I took off his collar to bathe him, I read on his dog tag his rightful name, White Magic.

When I spoke his name aloud, Magic howled like a wolf. He had belonged to Stevie Wonder's lawyer before he was given to Richard, but now he was mine. He had benevolent brown eyes and was tall and muscular with dazzlingly white fur. Samoyeds have lanolin in their fur, so if they get covered in slime—for example, in an algae pond—they can come out and shake most of it off. My friend Liz had given me the use of an old Ford pickup truck, and Magic insisted on waiting in the truck for me when I went to work. When I worked at home, he lay under the massage table.

Magic seemed to feel perfectly at home with me, and Baby liked him too. She let him come into the barn and they'd touch noses. After I'd had Magic for a few months, I worried about the pony being alone at night. I'd mentioned my concern to a new client, and one day she showed up unannounced with a tiny goat she'd rescued from a slaughterhouse. He had long legs, long ears, and big eyes. I didn't want another animal, but the moment he clambered into my lap he climbed into my heart.

Later that day I realized he was ill, with constant diarrhea. Since he was too small to live in the barn, I had to tackle the job of cleaning out the garage, still filled with Copley's old junk. Dump runs were easier now that I had a truck, and I must have made fifty of them. When all the crap was gone it became a beautiful space.

As I prepared a place for the little goat, I could think of only one name that would suit him, a name I'd saved in case I had a kid. Well, here he was, a kid. I'd seen the name on a small tombstone in Zena, Oklahoma, where my parents and their families are buried. Willi-Belle Hampton had been only two when she died.

When I was home I always left my truck door open so Magic could get in and out. Willi-Belle would jump into the truck with him and they'd hang out there for hours. I looked forward to the day when he was old enough to live in the barn with Baby. When the two of them spent time together, Willi-Belle was the lovesick boy and Baby the uninterested starlet. I'd rescued him for Baby, but he'd become my friend too. I gathered willow branches and pine boughs, which he and Baby both loved to eat, and I hung them from the rafters in the garage, making his space an exotic goat jungle. I turned over old wooden toolboxes, creating launching pads for him to have hours of fun. I put an old radio out in the garage with him, and he would buck around doing his own kind of dance depending on the song.

Not long after Willi-Belle arrived, a small yellow chicken appeared in my front yard and continued to come every morning when I fed Baby and Willi-Belle. But I fretted over her safety at night when I'd hear coyotes in the distance. I wanted to get her into the garage. Each day I'd create trails of bread or corn leading into the barn, but then she just disappeared. I feared the worst.

Mallards and Canada geese waddled up to my house from the stream. Birds appeared. Chipmunks dashed across the driveway. The once silent property had come to life.

One day I looked out the window and saw that Baby was crazy with excitement over a homely-looking pony trotting by pulling a little carriage. Baby went mad. She made sounds I'd never heard before and started weaving her head back and forth like an overmedicated racehorse. I ran into the garage to get her little bridle and quickly slipped it over her head and behind her ears, fastening the chin strap and pulling the braided leather reins over her head so I could pop up onto her back as I had done a thousand times. But before I could mount her she started running, and I had no choice but to run along beside her until I could get her to stop.

She was anxious and unruly, even trying to bite me a few times. Finally, I jerked hard on her reins and told her to stop it so I could get on. I swung onto her back. She took off with me pulling on the reins. She sped her way down Joy Road and took a right onto Purdy Hollow, and there he was, a pony the color of mud, standing in a little pen next to a pig, staring at Baby as if she were a movie star.

I dismounted and led Baby to her new friend's humble little paddock. The big pig came grunting up to us and stuck its stiff-haired, dirty snout on my leg as Baby and the mud-colored pony wrapped their heads around one another's necks. After five minutes of this—with us being on someone else's property, not to mention having a drug addict's wariness of people—I could sense a stirring behind the curtains. I gathered up my smitten girl and off we walked, me leading her like a proud 4H-er while she strained to look back at her new love.

We came to the corner of Purdy Hollow just in time to see a gray squirrel struggling to pull itself across Joy Road. Its back end must have been run over by a car. It looked at me with panic when another squirrel came dashing out into the road, trying to pull its friend to safety, but the injured squirrel's squished legs made this impossible. I had to tie Baby somewhere so I could help. Taking my eyes off the squirrels, I tied the reins around a stop sign. Then a car whipped around the corner and ran over both squirrels, their eyes popping out of their skulls like swollen blueberries. I was devastated.

Using a broken No Trespassing sign that I found in the ditch, I scraped up the warm, lifeless bodies. With the reverence of a pallbearer, I lifted these little beings from the scene and carried them into the ravine at the side of the road. Heartbroken, I led my pony home. She continually turned back to smell, see, and remember her new boyfriend. That day, I committed to moving dead animals from the road as often as I could.

After I put Baby in the barn, I went to hang her bridle in the garage and I caught a glimpse of the yellow chicken. She was up in the rafters. She did not look good. Her feathers seemed greasy and her eyes glazed. I climbed one of my old-man rickety ladders to try to reach her. She pecked at me so I left her alone.

I didn't have any close friends who had chickens, but Liz gave me the phone number of an animal psychic she knew. I called Kay Cornish to ask about my chicken.

"Yours wants babies," she told me. "Get her some fertile eggs to sit on and she'll be fine."

We talked a bit about the other animals as well, and essentially she said everything would be fine. Easy for her to say, I thought, realizing I had some eggs to find. I knew of a farm down Joy Road she might have come from, and figured they could help me. My neighbor was friendly and I returned home from the farm with four warm, light blue, fertile—I hoped—eggs. I tucked first some hay and then the eggs under the little yellow chicken. I placed a bowl of water in her nesting box, as well as a plate with cornbread, lettuce, and a scoop of cat food to strengthen her. After taking care of my new charge, I went into the house and did a thick line of coke and smoked a cigarette, even though I was trying to quit both habits.

Only twelve days later, Peaches and Cream were born. Peaches, the first to hatch, fell from the box up in the rafters onto the hard concrete floor. She looked like a stunned cartoon character, wobbling about with her head bobbing. I caught Cream but nearly stepped on Mama Petunia in the process. I set him down and he scurried underneath his mama's wing to hide. I stood there in sheer amazement at the miracle of nature, proud of myself for caring so. Nici, an animal rehabilitator I'd consulted, instructed me to buy chick-cracked corn and to hard-boil some eggs, then to feed the yolks to the chicks for that extra protein babies need.

Life was good for about twenty-two hours and then it all fell apart again. I didn't know that chickens can't see in the dark; I didn't know that chickens have to be put in at night so a menacing raccoon, skunk, or weasel won't eat them.

Petunia was frantic the next morning when I went to find her, because her babies were missing. She hadn't been able to get them up into the rafters and out of harm's way. Still wearing my pajamas, I got into my pickup and returned to the farm to ask for four more fertile eggs.

The pony, the goat, and the chicken were only the beginning of the safe haven for animals and birds that my little house on Joy Road became. Quite by accident I had become an animal rescuer, and my home a healing sanctuary.

ဆ

Animals, birds, and my clients responded to my sane part. The rest of me was a crapshoot. At night I'd often be bent over a small mirror with a pile of cocaine and a straightedge razor blade. The next day I could be bent over a tiny baby bird and carefully balling up wet cat food, gently prying its fragile beak open and tipping its head back to place the wad of food as far back as I could, ever so cautiously pushing it down its throat with a moistened Q-tip. Or I could be tenderly holding a sightless little baby squirrel in the palm of my hand and encouraging it to drink kitty-cat formula from an itsy-bitsy baby bottle.

I had a lot of baby squirrels. They were often delivered to me in their original nests, as many as twelve arriving at a time. Nici would see a dead squirrel on the road and pull over to inspect the carcass. Whereas I would gently move such a smashed squirrel, she would deftly turn it over to see if it was a lactating mother. If it was, she would use her high-powered binoculars to search for the nest and then call a friend with a cherry picker to come get it out of the tree. She was brilliant, and her heart for wildlife was like no other. It would take months of warmth and care to ready a nest of these little creatures for release back into the wild.

CHAPTER 22

✠ ANIMAL SANCTUARY ✠

Norman didn't visit Woodstock much, but I felt his scrutiny and wanted desperately to get my life together. The one night he did show up, I'd been doing so much cocaine that I imagined evil shadow men surrounding the house, hiding behind the trees in the paddock, and planning to cause me harm. Since Tony had pried it open, my front door had never worked quite right, so on this particular evening I had barred the broken door shut with a chair and a broomstick.

Norman burst through the bizarre barricade like it was a joke, came directly upstairs, no doubt saw my paraphernalia, and ordered me to pack some clothes and get into his van. I was heading to detox in Manhattan, Norman-style. I did what he said, grabbing all the drugs and cigarettes I could locate in two minutes and some clothes I'd borrowed from a new friend. Before I knew what had happened, I was sitting in the stripped-down van with no real passenger seat, no heat, and a very angry man. Tony, just released from jail, was there that night and I asked him to take care of the animals.

Like my father, who knew all the wrong I'd done but never mentioned it until some fateful day when all my shit would hit the fan, Norman seemed to know all about my dysfunction. He warned me that I would lose my house if I didn't straighten up. I was about to experience the method of the doctor he knew whose life's work was to help addicts get clean.

I got acupuncture needles stuck in my ears and feet, drank olive oil and lemon to detox my liver, and spent hours locked in the all too familiar tiny bedroom with a cardboard box for a table and a mattress on the floor. It must have been God who took care of me, because Norman was so angry and disappointed, so shut down and freaked out, that he didn't do much more than let me out of my room to eat and to pee.

I followed Norman's orders and saw his acupuncturist friend and took the supplements given to me by his crazy healer in Jersey City. I ate macrobiotic food again and slowly began to lose my hold on life. I ran out of cigarettes, pot, coke, and Valium. I ran out of my own mind, screaming as if the place was on fire, but in reality I just stayed shut up in my little room in Norman's cluttered apartment. What ugly walls those were, what ugly thoughts I had, and how horrible I felt. I wanted to rip myself apart to get rid of all the pain.

A month or so after he'd ordered me into his van, Norman allowed me to go home—home to a house empty of spirit. It was just an old man's house that I'd torn apart but didn't know how to fix, a house that Jack hadn't built, and a house that almost got huffed and puffed and blown to the ground.

When I arrived, thanks to Tony the barns were surprisingly clean and the animals were fine for the most part. My momentum fully returned as Baby let out a deep-throated whinny when she saw me. Apparently, the sound of my voice was like music to the barnyard. It seemed every animal and bird perked up when they heard me bustling about, and that became my lifeline. They needed and loved me, and that made things bearable, much better for my bloodstream than the old alternative. It empowered me to move forward out of what had become a pit of hell.

I was off to the market for carrots, apples, lettuce, and whatever small things I might need; off to Adams Fairacre Farms for speckled pears, pink lady apples, and almonds; and off to drive by the coke dealer's house three times until I finally talked myself out of it.

This was my first day of a new way of living. I had to get my act together or I could lose everything that mattered to me. I felt superstitious about this first day, the first day to speak life into things I had nearly killed, the first day I had to make meaning and purpose out of my life. It foretold the many that followed. I spent it stocking up, cleaning, making amends, feeling grateful, and looking over my shoulder. Shaky as though I'd just recovered from the flu, scared as though I were in a witness protection program, I couldn't have been more tired. Norman, of course, had been right to haul me away and demand that I stop doing coke.

I had caused severe damage to my life and I had to get serious about different things, things that mattered. I had lost my old workout partner when she saw me doing a line of coke in a bar. Stout, muscular, and determined, she'd gone on to become a world champion bench presser. I found a new partner, a sweet guy whom I'd met in the weight room at the Y. He was in training to be a cop.

I never thought I'd survive my mother's death when I was sixteen, and I felt I had died along with my dad when I was eighteen. At nineteen I found my husband nearly dead, and at twenty-one I felt half dead myself when my husband abandoned me. Then, at twenty-five I messed up my second marriage. After all this, I didn't hold out much hope of surviving twenty-seven. I had no game plan, no dream, no degree, no clue, no chance in hell of catching up with myself.

Soon after I returned home, I reconnected with Liz when I rejoined the Woodstock Women's Softball League. She asked me to go to North Carolina with her to buy another pickup truck and to stay at a spiritual retreat center. We took off only days later. I got to see the wild horses of Chincoteague Island on the way and rescued a little lilac point Siamese cat named Nina.

Bringing Nina home drew out the little girl in me. She was a baby doll come to life. After initially panicking about being somewhere new and hiding inside the wall, she blossomed. I'd sleep with her wrapped in my arm under the blankets and would let my arm go numb rather than disturb her. She talked to me in her near-human Siamese voice. With Magic at the foot of my bed, Nina cuddled next to me, and Willi-Belle and Baby thrilled the moment I headed in their direction, my life became too precious for words.

Motivated by all that love and finally free from cocaine, I bought a datebook to plan things and to book people for massages. I did massage every day, including Sunday. I woke up every morning to Magic's cold, moist nose pressing against my cheek; I'd draw the covers back from Nina's sleeping body and slowly pull my arm out from under her.

Baby and Willi-Belle, circa 1995.

Whenever I took Baby for a ride Willi-Belle would trot along beside us and I always wished someone could see how beautiful we were.

Magic was always ready for chores. I'd developed a great habit of preparing all the feed buckets the night before. I'd chop carrots and apples for Willi-Belle and Baby. I'd measure out their sweet feed and have their little buckets all set on the back porch. They'd get a few Wheat Thins or Triscuits on top of their parfait of sweet feed, carrots, and apples. This guaranteed that they'd eat their meals. The wild critters (I'd released a few nests of squirrels, patched up a bunch of ducks and geese, and developed a devotion to songbirds) had their own buckets of seed, cornbread, chopped-up lettuce, almonds, and peanuts.

I usually did the early morning chores in my pajamas. I'd let Magic out and go around the back to collect first the goat food and then the pony food. I'd open the barn door to Baby's whinnying and Willi-Belle's butting his head against the door. I'd right their feed buckets, fill them up, refresh their water, and grab a pitchfork to bring the thick bedding of pine shavings back to pristine. I had little twin beds in their barn with old comforters tucked into them so they could really be comfortable. Wingsy, a chicken, lived with them along with her newly acquired companion and guardian, a gorgeous khaki-colored mallard named Darling. Magic would stick his head in to check on my progress.

Next, I would open the garage to feed the doves, chickens, roosters, and ducks that couldn't fly for one reason or another. Some animals might be in a kennel for protection or might be on medication. By this time my repertoire had expanded and I had raccoons, skunks (very polite about not spraying as long as you don't startle them), opossums, swans, various songbirds with a variety of injuries, chipmunks (hard to give medicine to!), rabbits, sometimes deer, occasionally a hawk, and once even an eagle. I had ducks with deformed bills that I named Kit and Caboodle. When I watched my menagerie eat or play or sleep, I did so with a sense of wonder and sheer awe.

I bought some beautiful birdfeeder stations that looked like little farms or log cabins and held five to ten pounds of black oil sunflower seeds. I put piles of almonds and nuts on the ground and spread my cornbread, lettuce, and cat food feast on wooden platters for the one-legged or one-winged ducks and geese that lived in the stream and awaited my morning ministrations. My squirrels, squirrels that were raised by hand, played so much more than wild squirrels. I figured that they didn't worry about the food running out so didn't care if others got some. I wanted to provide abundance in their world.

I had every kind of chicken, all rescued, and they all liked having babies. I adore baby chicks. I collected the eggs most of the time but once in a while I'd let a nest hatch. That's why I had forty chickens and forty roosters—which is way too many roosters.

One morning I heard my little black chicken Trilly screaming bloody murder. I pulled open the garage door to find a thick, six-foot black snake eating her tiny babies. I grabbed that snake right behind its head, forced its jaws open, and got three little babies back. I roughed up that snake. Even though I am terrified of snakes, the only thing on my mind at that moment was rescuing those babies. That's when I saw another snake—thin, long, and dangerous—staring at me from the baseboard that runs along the far wall of the garage. This one was lying in wait, ready to attack a little chick balancing on that same baseboard.

I saw a dandelion picker, a metal fork on the end of a broomstick, and moved toward the snake in one fluid motion, grabbing the picker just as the snake moved to attack. I brought the fork down over it, pinning it to the baseboard, a split second away from its devouring the stunned little chick. Bedlam had erupted everywhere. The chickens had no idea I was a hero, the snakes couldn't have cared less about me, and the chicks ran under lawn tools and into old stereo equipment, freaking out. Broken eggs lay all over the floor, their nearly ready contents exposed.

I reached for the snake with my free hand and immediately it twined around my arm. I screamed. Feathers flew. Its grip tightened. I wanted to somehow remove my arm. That not being an option, I edged toward an empty plastic garbage can. I kicked off the lid with my foot, slid the can toward me, and pulled with all my might on the snake's tail. Its grip tightened again. I screamed again. I slowly pulled it off me, dropped it into the garbage can, and secured the lid with nearby bungee cords.

I threw a sheet over the fatter snake while it stared, apparently mystified by my antics. I picked up the heavy critter and dropped it in with the other snake, which I assumed to be the Bonnie to his Clyde. I secured the lid with four more strong bungee cords, put the garbage can in the back of my pickup, and, still in my pajamas, headed out to release them. I drove to a site five miles away where I thought they would thrive. I climbed into the back and opened the lid; I was stunned to find that the plastic bin was empty. On the slow drive home, I remembered my first chicken massacre, back when I had just left Kenny.

I was twenty years old and feeling sad because it was my first holiday season without family. I called Kenny. He sounded fine, which made me feel even worse. He didn't say, "Come to East Hampton—I can't live without you." He told me he had a New Year's Eve gig at some club and had to get going, so I went to a party at Gary Powell's house.

Gary had been a close friend of my sister's and I think he felt sorry for me. We both worked at the Masonic Hospital. When I entered his gorgeous home he welcomed me warmly and it was nice to be around people. A woman there was reading tarot cards, which I had never seen or heard of at the time. When she read my cards, I remember making myself quit listening when she drew the Death card. I just sat there staring at that stupid card, willing it to shut up and leave me alone.

Gary and his lover were gay, which was another first for me. They were funny, feminine, and charming. We toasted the new year at midnight with champagne, smoked pot, and laughed. I tried to act as if these were my people, but they really weren't. They were my sister Cyndi's people, all about four or five years older than me. But they were kind company and they seemed to know I was a lost soul. I think it was Gary's lover, Marty, who offered me a few hits of mild speed. I gladly took it. I wanted to stay awake because I'd decided to drive back to the horse farm where I was living.

It was about an hour later, maybe three in the morning, when I found myself driving to the farm in Mendota Heights, where I lived with Laura and Stan. I didn't remember leaving the party and was confused. I stopped at a phone booth to call Kenny and told him I was scared. He told me not to be afraid, that our breakup had been the best thing for us. He said, "Happy New Year," and I wanted to cry. At Mendota Heights I parked my Dodge on the ice-covered driveway close enough to the extension cord to plug it into the dipstick warmer so my engine wouldn't freeze. I went into the empty house and there was a strange man sitting in the kitchen chair. I froze.

He stood up and said that the owners had called him and asked him to come and fix the stove. In the middle of the night? On New Year's Eve? I couldn't gather my senses. I asked him to leave and called to my pretend husband to come downstairs. The guy came to the door where I stood and said, "I know there isn't anyone here." My blood thickened in my veins and I couldn't understand why it felt like I was tripping, unable to handle this situation.

And then it dawned on me: what Marty thought was speed must have been acid. Finally, I got the guy out the door, locked it, and kept my hand pressed against it. I didn't dare go upstairs. I heard the sound of a snowmobile and watched for several long and scary minutes as its headlights circled the house and then the barn. When the sound of his engine finally faded I found a flashlight and walked out to the barn to sit with the horses until daybreak. I had to be around the warmth of living beings.

When I opened the heavy barn door the horses seemed agitated. I made my way through the chicken coop into the horse stalls and then turned and aimed my flashlight back over the floor. The barn was littered with dead chickens. Every single one of them had been decapitated. It was easily twenty below zero, so whatever had happened to these beautiful creatures had happened before I got there. I hunkered down in the corner of a horse stall, brought my knees up to my chest, made myself as small and quiet as I could, and waited for the sun to rise.

ॐ

This new chicken massacre was much sadder for me, because these chickens were my friends and my babies. I had rescued them and nervously awaited their hatchings. Trilly was some sort of miniature breed and her babies were small enough to sit in a teaspoon. They were a warm golden color with black spots. Knowing they were scared, on my watch, and some even eaten by a big black snake, was just too much to bear.

Once back from my attempt to release the murderous snakes, I had my work cut out for me. I searched the garage for survivors. There were more than thirty babies born to about six different mamas. Some of the little critters had run, terrified, into various machine parts or into crevices in the cement floor. I spent the better part of the day attempting to find them, free them, and soothe them.

CHAPTER 23

❧ BECOMING WHOLE ❧

Whatever my life was now, if it wasn't about helping the helpless or mending the broken it stopped mattering much. I was no longer thinking constantly about Norman and how to please him, and I wasn't interested at all in getting him to love me again. It's true I still felt on trial at times, or at least on alert for Norman's scrutiny. But as the animals started coming, his grip on me loosened. After the chicken incident I insisted that he sort through, disperse, and discard all the stuff he'd schlepped up from the city: crates of rare books upstairs, old ammunition downstairs, old telephones, dated stereo parts. Plus, he'd spread into the junk drawers as though he lived there. It all had to go. Not since the very beginning of our relationship, when I was somewhat authentic, had I actually told Norman what to do. And he did it. He came up, sorted through his stuff, went on dump runs with me, and loaded half of it back into his van. I felt relieved to be rid of his crap.

With all the birds and chickens living in the garage and my feeding them in there, I hadn't realized that I was also feeding rats that must have arrived in Norman's crates of stuff. We found stinky rats' nests in his boxes, and I began to notice that the walls moved when I opened the garage doors in the morning, and that the musky, dirty smell was real.

It turned out that the rat population had multiplied to over fifty in the walls of my critter sanctuary. These rats weren't fuzzy, warm-eyed, tame rats that we might see in a pet store; these were rough-and-tumble, greaser, Mafia rats. Even the nests of newborns were unappealing—raw, pink, and squirmy. The first time I found a fresh nest I ran into the house to get my thick hawk gloves so I could move them, but by the time I got back the very protective mother rat had already taken her young to safety.

When Norman brought me two Havahart traps, I caught and released thirty-seven rats in just one week. But they quickly outpaced me. They were as prolific as rabbits, and every morning the walls were alive with rats. I wanted to get rid of them immediately. They were not only filthy but a danger to the young chicks and detrimental to my business.

I once walked a very wealthy client down the driveway and a sick rat slunk around the side of the house well within our view. Knowing that I rescued animals, my client wanted to stop and admire the cute little critter, but I diverted her attention to the pony galloping in the paddock. Later, I picked up the sweating rat with my hawk gloves and tried to drown it in a bucket of water. It looked up at me with sad eyes and I reached in and rescued it from my own murderous intent. I cannot drown a rat.

After that I quit feeding in the garage and moved almost all the feeding stations to the stream. I had fourteen feeding areas at that time and well over two hundred animals or birds in my care at any given moment. The rats persisted.

I hired an Indian shaman to rid my property of them. He came and set himself up in the garage. I left him to his metaphysical techniques and went upstairs to pray and to wait and hope, while visualizing a world without rats. Standing at the window in my writing room, I could see that the shaman had left the garage door open. I watched in horror as this supposedly spiritual man poured Coleman fuel over the rat he held in his hands. He then lit it on fire and released it onto the ground. I stormed down the steps and grabbed that shaman, screaming in his face. I told him to take his torture somewhere else. I had become Julie, defender of the rat. I nearly kicked him in the rear, I was so mad. He said that the burned rat would go back to the nest and alert the other rats to the fire and they would leave. Bullshit. The rat turned into toast before it got to the wall.

I couldn't use rat poison because of the many other animals, and on principle I couldn't use killer traps. I also couldn't live with rats, so my humane approach wore thin. I couldn't stand the smell or the knowledge that rats had overtaken my farm. I couldn't feed the crippled animals in their pens, since the rats followed the food wherever I put it. I couldn't blame them but I also couldn't stand them.

I hired Jimmy, my friend the feed man, to shoot them. He would bring his lawn chair and a cigar, sit down with his pistol, and wait for them to slither along the foundation. He killed six or seven rats this way. But this means to an end, lying in wait and shooting, created the wrong vibe for a sanctuary. Seeing Jimmy walk away holding the rats by their tails, blood dripping from wherever the bullet entered, was too much, too mean, and too horrible.

Looking back, I see that I used these rats as a platform to get rid of the insidious demons in my life. Number one: all of Norman's stuff had to go. Number two: I got rid of all the cocaine mirrors and old straws. I unwound three one-dollar bills and two one-hundred-dollar bills from their cocoons as drug paraphernalia without inhaling the thick, yellowed coating from any of them. It had taken a lot of energy to cover up my wrongdoing. I had my own rats to deal with. I'd had to veneer my life, and it had been exhausting. No one should keep people in their lives who think so little of them, and no one should avoid growing just because it's uncomfortable.

Julie with Red, 1989.

Red, a rescued Rhode Island Red who loved being in the house and getting pampered. She was one of the many animals that saved me.

The animals were the pitch to mend the leaks in my ark, to make it seaworthy—even the tough cases like the opossums, the rabid raccoons, and the bats trapped in people's houses where I had to wear a motorcycle helmet and carry a fishing net to catch them. Even the gigantic swan with the broken wing that lived on my front porch for six weeks, and the chipmunk that sank its razor-sharp teeth into my index finger and wouldn't let go. And the little squirrel I raised from a newborn that ripped open a client's face while trying to protect me. And the hawk that wouldn't fly to freedom but instead took up residence in a nearby pine tree. And the pony that always tried to bite me, the cat that lived in the secret wall for a month before deciding to love me, and especially the one-legged rooster that would jump up on the overturned water trough and bongo to its heart's content. These animals prepared me for and ushered me into a holy life of love and service and attention to detail. These animals were my ministers—each of them gave me back a piece of myself that would one day make me whole.

I hadn't had much abundance for as long as I'd been on my own. Not real abundance. So it wasn't that much of a sacrifice to live without things so my animal friends could have what they needed. They ate carrots and apples and so did I. I had cases of almonds around for the squirrels that were raised in Copley's old bedroom, which I fashioned into a sort of physical therapy and whole foods emporium. Little guys would come here with a busted-up leg or a smashed-in face and somehow I'd find a way to get them eating, drinking, and strong again.

I never felt alone, even though much of the time I was. I always knew what to do or whom to call. I seemed always to have what I needed even before I knew I needed it. When Baby put her head between the fence boards and strained that extra little bit to get that unreachable blade of grass, I'd hear the rough-cut pine board crack and she'd take off like a light down Sawkill Road, leading the traffic or making it bend to her will.

Being sensitive to the sounds of my yard, I'd be close behind her, running in bare feet and whatever I happened to be wearing, having heard the crack or having spied her the moment when the board broke. I'd do whatever I could to get her off the road and into the playground behind the house, where she'd kick and fuss and gallop until she ran out of steam and let me catch her. I became a maxed-out, adrenaline-enriched version of myself at least once a day, and more often than not I felt that I needed to be hospitalized once I'd put her back in the paddock.

All that, and I also had to fix the fence. I was never in boots with a hammer. No, that would have been too dreamlike. Nope, I was usually barefoot, shaking, and empty-handed. I trusted that whatever I needed would be right there within reach as it always had been.

CHAPTER 24

❧ FAST FORWARD TO ANDY ❧

I saw the squirrel on my way to town and kept going until my conscience got the better of me and I turned the truck around. Pulling over behind the body, I turned on my flashers, then left my door open while I gently slipped my hands under the warm squirrel. One eye had popped out of its head. As I scooped it up, I felt a heartbeat. I stuck it inside my T-shirt, zipped up my sweatshirt to cradle it, and drove home with the flashers on. I kept saying to myself, he's alive, he's alive! I took him inside and laid him down carefully on a fresh towel. I had some liquid Arnica on hand and I washed it over his eye, its socket, a little gash on his head, and his limp, lifeless leg. I sprinkled him with Vita Fons powder, and kept up what seemed a relentless monologue with God. I prepared a soft, safe, warm place for him to rest and heal.

The day had its own momentum but I kept checking on my squirrel. I kept his eyeball moist and reapplied different remedies, but I couldn't feed him, give him water, or pick him up. I could only wait and see.

I ached for a cigarette but resisted its pull. When I woke up the next day dreading the awful discovery that he had died alone, I found him alert and calm and the eye returned to its socket. Now, how did that happen? Such mystery. I named him Rocky. He had an injured leg, so I fashioned a little gizmo out of the metal wire from a small spiral notebook into a piece of exercise equipment to see if we could get it working again. I fastened his leg to it with a tiny rubber band and we did physical therapy. Within days he had the full use of his leg.

When the day came to let him go free, I was a nervous wreck but he was fine. For a few days he came only when called, then he became wild again.

Every animal, and every challenge I was presented with, brought out the best in me. I became the girl who could whisper hope to the wounded and peace to the terrified; the girl who knew what to do by knowing next to nothing at all; the hoper and dreamer and doer of things others wouldn't think of doing because they weren't the right thing. Caring for injured creatures was both inspiring and terrifying. I don't know how people do it. I started smoking way too many cigarettes.

ɞ

Ten, eleven, twelve years went by with me caring for animals and people. Both devotions consumed my life. I fed on the good things I tried to do. I had systems in place. Buckets of food got distributed every day, which is a glamorous way of saying I was a slave to wildlife. The hundreds of squirrels and birds that got well and were released on my farm were also fed here. There was such a volume of feed consumed daily that I bought almonds by the case, speckle pears and apples by the bushel, twenty-five-pound bags of carrots, and cases of cat food. I even had twenty-nine loaves of Meredith's fresh-baked cornbread delivered every week. It cost too much, and not just in money. Every time an animal died I'd tell myself I couldn't do it anymore. I hurt so much. Every time I lit a cigarette to distance myself from my agony I'd think of my dad, his lungs, his sorrow. It deeply disturbed me that I couldn't, or didn't, just quit. It felt so stupid.

This brings me to Andy. I met him in 1995 at Jeanette's outdoor pagan wedding. Andy seemed very interested in me, although he sat

Tinkerbelle with headbutting toy and house she climbed on, 1996.

*After Baby died, Willi-Belle was lonely until we rescued Tinkerbelle—
who was pregnant with Mickey McBelle, who died much too soon
from a spider bite. Then along came Alexander Graham Belle to cheer
us up. Was I caring for them or were they caring for me?*

on a small, worn-out peach-colored blanket with a woman who had a
fresh-looking black eye. He got up and followed me into the cramped
Rosendale kitchen as I searched for an open place in the small, packed
refrigerator to stash a few Rolling Rocks. Andy was the only one in the
circle who knew how divine was the sticky-bud grass that I had expertly
rolled into quick joints. Andy walked me to my red pickup truck as I left
the gathering well within the one hour I'd allotted myself for social affairs
such as this. Andy called Jeanette while she was on her honeymoon to
ask for my number.

He told me, when he called, that the woman with the black eye
was just a friend and that I was the woman he had always dreamed
of. Yet I couldn't even remember what he looked like. We waited three
weeks to have our first date. He was scheduled to come over on July
third at three in the afternoon, and I was so nervous that I went out to

the barn and sat with the goat and the pony. When I heard him pull up, I stole a peek through the propped-open barn window. He was totally hot—slender, muscular, tan, and tall, with long, dark wavy hair that fell in tendrils to his shoulders. I rounded the side of the barn and our eyes met. He looked down at his crotch and up at me. I looked at the brown stain covering his crotch as I walked toward him. He explained that he had spilled his coffee on his lap when he'd turned into the driveway.

My heart thudded in my chest. I wished Magic were still alive so he could give me his character-read on this man, but I was pretty much on my own. The pony didn't usually like anyone right away and tried to bite just about everyone, but she didn't bite Andy. Willi-Belle considered everyone a saint and a friend and Andy was immediately in good standing with him. After we'd toured the kennels, the barn, and the yard, I asked him if he wanted to go to a quarry I had access to.

We got into his Blazer where I spied a pack of Marlboros on the console, so at least I wouldn't have to pretend not to smoke. I couldn't resist, so I leaned over and played with his long, soft hair and I kissed him. His lips were a little less plump than I'd hoped, but when my kiss caused him to lose control of his vehicle, I found it charming. When we got to the quarry I could tell he was spellbound by the beauty of the place, but we didn't swim right away. I remember just lying on the warm hood of his truck and watching the clouds.

My life seemed even more interesting when Andy was around to witness part of it. Thankfully, I didn't use coke anymore. He smoked cigs and pot and drank beer, so I relaxed about all that stuff. We spent hours in search of one another's satisfaction. Sometimes we spent long, hot summer evenings on the phone, he in his mountain cabin doing an internship for environmental studies and me in my king-sized bed after a long day of work. He won Baby's heart when his hand instinctively found her sweet spot behind her right ear. He loved to cook, he cleaned, he made the bed perfectly, and he was a phenomenal gardener. Andy had become a more succulent-lipped kisser and a wonderful lover. He also loved to drink beer every day.

Andy had an eleven-year-old son and an eight-year-old daughter who lived with their mom in New Paltz, so he kept a room in a funky boarding house on Main Street where he had moved when he got divorced. He and his kids spent weekends there together. I worked weekends, which seemed easier on everyone. Still, when he spent weekends in that room in New Paltz, he would completely disconnect from me. This went on for three years. It drove me crazy so I started checking up on him.

I copied his keys and went to his apartment and sat there stunned in front of his computer. I had never seen porn sites before and I hope I never do again. His computer was loaded with them, and if that wasn't bad enough there were also letters to women he had met on dating sites. He'd written many of these letters during the four years he and I had been together—happy together, gardening together, planning our future together. I'd been wrong again, and I knew it was my own damn fault.

I'd thought he might be the right guy for me, but I broke up with him that same day. I knew how addictive it would be to continue going to his apartment and finding all the ways he was betraying me, so I taped a note to his computer monitor that asked, "HOW COULD YOU?" and locked the set of keys I'd copied inside his apartment. I drove away feeling poisoned.

He must have arrived home, seen my note, popped open a beer, and surfed the Web, because he didn't call me. I waited three long weeks before I broke down and called him. He sounded drunk and said I was too good for him.

We got back together. I had gotten into the habit of drinking beer with him every night and thought it would be smart if I quit drinking entirely. I joined Al-Anon and went to meetings with a friend. When I was eleven years old the counselor on the detox ward where my mom was going through a painful withdrawal from alcohol invited me to sit in on some meetings for kids with alcoholic parents, but I hated it. I didn't want an alcoholic mama back then, but as a forty-year-old I could appreciate the brave and hopeful company of fellow sufferers.

As I got clearer, things fell apart with Andy. I couldn't help but notice how he staggered more and lied harder. Something inside me was changing.

After we broke up for the last time I couldn't stop myself from looking for the faded green trout sticker on the back of every black Blazer on the road. I scoured the world in search of Andy's vehicle. It was dangerous—I even went off the road a few times. I had to stop, stop looking for Andy, stop smoking cigarettes, and stop freaking out all the time. I was beginning to wheeze.

Finally Andy took a job out of town. He came by to tell me. He looked terribly thin and had cut off all his gorgeous tendrils. He had bluish bags under his eyes. We sat in the yard near all the phenomenal gardens he had created over the years. He was drunk. I was devastated but this part of my nightmare was over.

We sat and smoked a cigarette together. He still smoked his Marlboros but I, trying to reduce the impact of cigarettes, chose an organic American Spirit instead. We were both shaky. He was leaving the next day for Jacksonville, Florida—leaving my grasp, leaving my nest. When we kissed goodbye it felt the same as that first, hard, thin-lipped kiss over four years before.

When he left my driveway I turned into a zombie. My problems weren't going to Jacksonville, Florida—they stayed right where I lived.

My phone rang later that day.

CHAPTER 25

❧ A Prayer to Quit Smoking ☙

A man who had been given a gift certificate for one of my massages called. I thought he wanted to schedule an appointment. His name was John and he was the chauffeur and "gofer" for an eccentric Hollywood screenwriter who had once been a client of mine. After introducing himself, he began an evangelical rant about how he had come to know Jesus. I didn't know John, I didn't know Jesus, and I didn't know how to get off the phone without being rude. Because he had that gift certificate I felt compelled to listen until there was a pause in his breathless monologue.

Before John finished he mentioned that the preacher who'd led him to the Lord had prayed over his pack of smokes, and since then he hadn't touched a single cigarette. John now had my interest and I asked him to repeat that part.

"Jesus set me free, sister. I haven't smoked since. No side effects. No withdrawal. I am free."

"How? What kind of prayer?" I asked. I desperately wanted to quit smoking. He didn't answer my question but he did ask me if I wanted to know Jesus. I knew God, but not having been raised in the church I thought the Catholics had just made Jesus up.

"No, John. I'm good, I've got my own God, but thank you anyway."

I put down the phone. Maybe I do need to find a preacher to pray over my pack of cigarettes, I thought. I'd seen how cigarettes squeezed the breath out of my daddy, and I lived in fear of dying the same death. I had tried to quit a hundred times. How could I call myself a healer and yet smoke cigarettes?

The next day I got into my truck and drove toward the Ashokan Reservoir, a route Andy and I had travelled countless times to park and watch the sunset over the beautiful water. I knew there was a little cinderblock church on that road. I found it and drove by slowly and read its sign: The Living Word Chapel. I turned around in its big empty parking lot and went home to look up the phone number. I wanted to schedule a quit-smoking, pray-over-my-pack-of-cigarettes appointment with the preacher by phone.

Christina, the secretary, sounded pleasant enough but she didn't understand what I was calling about.

"I need an appointment to see the preacher who can pray over my pack of cigarettes," I said.

"I'm sorry, I don't understand. Do you want to know the power of God's love?" she asked.

"I know the power of God's love. I just need some help with quitting smoking."

"Oh, so you need deliverance. Are you saved?"

"Am I what?"

"Saved. You know, like, are you a believer? Do you know God?"

"Of course I know God. Can't you just give me an appointment with the guy in charge who will pray over my cigarettes?" I asked for the third time.

"Pastor Don doesn't pray over cigarettes, at least not that I have ever seen. I've been his secretary a long time and . . . and I don't know," she said. "Maybe you want to be healed. I could make an appointment for that."

"Listen, Christina, I have been healed. I came to Woodstock with a broken back and was a mess. I know God healed me. Can't I just get an appointment so the preacher and I can work it out?"

"Pastor," she corrected me, "not preacher. And yes. How is Friday at ten in the morning?"

"You mean tomorrow Friday?" I asked, not so sure I was ready to quit smoking as soon as that.

"Yes, tomorrow at ten.

I went to the gas station and bought a fresh pack of American Spirit cigarettes, which I intended to be my last pack. I turned it upside down and firmly smacked the pack into the heel of my open palm, just like my daddy used to do. I turned the pack right side up, located the cellophane tab, and watched my hand skillfully do what it had done for so many years, on so many brands, in so many different circumstances. The cellophane off, I took out a cigarette, tapped it firmly on the dashboard, and lit up.

I spent a fitful day trying to come to terms with my upcoming prayer meeting. I think most of my ancestors smoked. Not just the peace pipe, which, by the way, we had never smoked, but cigarettes. Dad smoked, Mom smoked, and I was told that even Grandma Susie and Grandpa Paw Paw smoked. Bev didn't smoke but Cyndi smoked and I smoked. The day passed quickly, night became morning, and before I knew it the clock said half past nine. Thirty minutes of smoking left.

I didn't want to go through with it, but I figured it wouldn't be a good idea to cancel an appointment that had been so hard to make. Maybe I'd be okay. Maybe it would work out for me. I'd quit worse things. I went upstairs to the bathroom and brushed my teeth. I looked in the mirror and noticed how nervous I appeared. I went downstairs and smoked another cigarette. I'd be fine.

I drove to the church very slowly, so I noticed everything. The road crosses a gorgeous bridge called Dyke Road above an overflow of water for the reservoir, surrounded by a range of beautiful mountains in the distance. With no radio on to distract me, I thought about how my dad used to sit at the kitchen table and smoke his Salem while watching the sky through the big picture window. I thought about Mom and her Winston and her big mug of coffee.

Everything suddenly smelled like cigarettes. I sniffed my fingers and realized I'd forgotten to wash my hands after the last smoke. I put a piece of Juicy Fruit in my mouth after first rubbing it along my lips and the inside of my index and middle fingers to make them smell better. I glanced in the rearview mirror to see how I looked and noticed a car very close behind me. Peering at the speedometer, I realized how slowly I was moving, only ten miles per hour. I sped up to forty and the church appeared all too quickly.

Pulling into the church parking lot with three minutes to spare, I took a deep breath. Did I really want to quit smoking? Yes. Yes, I did. I headed toward the wide cement stairs, climbed them very slowly, and pulled open the door.

One stairway went down and the other went up. I hesitated but decided to go up. On the last step I heard a deep voice.

"Evans, get in here. Now, what the hell is it that you want?"

It must be the pastor, I thought, with a smile, a pastor saying "hell." I followed the voice through a lobby, up a few stairs, and into a small office. At first his back was to me, but when I entered he swiveled around in his squeaky blue chair. He didn't rise to meet me; he didn't reach for my hand or bother to stand. I handed him the pack of cigarettes when I sat in the other squeaky swivel chair, sinking so far down I almost toppled over backwards.

"I want to quit smoking," I said with conviction.

We looked at one another. His eyes and his skin were a warm chocolate brown and he wasn't much older than me. I'd had no idea he would be a black man, not that it made any difference.

"I'm Don Moore," he said. "My secretary told me she had trouble understanding what you wanted. So you want to quit smoking . . . well, that's good. What else? Who is Julie Evans?"

I looked around his office, searching for an answer. He looked at the pack of cigarettes.

"It's pretty amazing that they can get away with this stuff," he said.

I didn't really know what he meant but I let him go on.

"I mean, American Spirit."

He held up the pack to remind me of the brand. Suddenly, I felt embarrassed that I was a smoker. He changed the subject to Indians. I told him I was part Cherokee and part Cheyenne, sounding stupid to myself.

He looked at me and smiled. I decided I liked him and that I was ready to quit smoking. I had cleared my throat to say something when his phone rang. He picked it up and had a ten-minute discussion with a pastor in Africa who had troubles. I liked what I heard him telling the guy, but thought maybe I should just get up and leave. Maybe he was too busy; maybe I would quit smoking tomorrow.

Christina came in with coffee for both of us. She needed to ask him some questions about the church bulletin. He hung up the phone, took a sip of coffee, and asked her about her husband. Was he still "pissed off" about what some of the church members were saying about him? I was pretty sure I should leave. I felt invisible. I guzzled my coffee as they talked and he took a huge swallow of his. He told Christina to go, looked at me, and said, "Let's pray," reaching out both his hands.

I dragged my chair closer to his while looking at his hands. He had long fingers, well-manicured cuticles and nails. He wore a simple gold wedding band and a cheap watch. He shut his eyes. I shut mine too but kept them open enough to see him through my eyelashes.

He held my hands and didn't say a word. Long minutes went by. I got tired of holding hands and wondered what he was doing. I saw him crack open one of his eyes so I squeezed mine shut.

Neither one of us said a word, but some sort of energy passed through my hands. I wondered what it was, and out of nowhere I started to cry. He tightened his hold on my hands. I could hardly catch my breath between each huge, convulsive sob. It went on and on. I had no idea what was happening. Why was I crying so hard? Not knowing why made me sob even more.

Just as suddenly, I was flooded with relief. It felt good to have someone to hold onto. For the briefest moment I stopped hurting, almost like getting high, but my nose ran fiercely.

The pastor soon released his grip and placed a T-shirt in my hand.

"Blow your nose in this; I can't find any tissues," he said.

He put his hands on my legs and looked me in the eye.

"Evans, you've got a beautiful pool inside you but there's lots of crap in it. Smoking is the least of your problems. Keep smoking but keep coming back." He pressed the intercom button for Christina.

"Put Evans in for next Friday at the same time."

I wondered if it could be. Had I found someone who could help me, who could teach me and show me what I longed to know? Would I be able to quit smoking?

☙ SALVATION ☙

I was determined to quit smoking, so I kept showing up at The Living Word Chapel. Pastor Don's permission to smoke and his ability to see my beautiful pool (even if there was crap in it) enticed me, so I met with him every Friday morning at ten o'clock. And thus began the pouring out of my story. Friday after Friday, week after week, month after month, the pastor and I talked. I wanted more than just a smoke-free life. I wanted this kindhearted pastor to teach me everything he knew about God, healing, and living a grace-filled life. Pastor Don and I talked about everything. Every time we met he'd take phone calls, proofread Sunday's bulletin, press the intercom countless times when he thought of something to tell his secretary, eat the bagel or piece of pound cake I'd brought along, sip tea or coffee, and still, somehow, he listened to me, only me.

After a few months, I had a revelation that I'd been buried beneath the rubble of my life and that these simple meetings with a multitasking man were supernatural reconnaissance missions to rescue me.

During one of our meetings, Pastor Don asked me if I wanted to know Jesus. I simply said, "Sure."

He buzzed Christina on the intercom and she met us in the chapel. The pastor prayed over me and I kept my eyes open enough to see what he was doing. Christina stood right beside me. She handed him a small vial of oil. Pastor Don tipped the vial over and let the oil cover his middle and index fingers. He asked me if I wanted Jesus to come into my heart. With my heart pounding in my chest I said, "Yes, I do."

He placed his oiled fingers on my forehead. I shut my eyes and just let go, let go of all of it, all the muck in my pool. I felt lighter than air and I fell backward into Christina's arms. She placed me gently onto the carpeted sanctuary floor at the foot of the altar. My body vibrated with something new and pure. I cracked open an eye and saw the pastor with his arms raised, a radiant field of light surrounding him. I shut my eyes and lay there as long as they let me.

I felt free and I felt found. I felt empowered. I still smoked, but that didn't seem to bother God as much as it did me. I wanted to win this battle but there was obviously more going on here than I knew.

I came in with stories and questions about life and healing. I still wasn't too keen on going to church, but at the pastor's suggestion I started sticking my foot in the chapel for an hour or so on Sundays. The Bible was tough for me to read and understand, but Pastor could teach from one verse for a whole hour. He turned words on a page into a story that I could relate to. I was finding wisdom in the Bible that I'd never come across before.

The idea that we are all created in God's image never meant much to me until I had the realization that when God spoke things were created. So, when I speak, do I create things? Can we speak ourselves whole and wise and well? These were the things I wanted to know so I could share them with my little tribe of people who lack so much.

As Pastor would sermonize on a verse or a parable, revealing its meaning, it would swirl around in my heart and brain and then I'd sit down with it the next day and write about it in a way that made sense to me. My poems. I don't know how I thought these words made poems, but I liked writing in short phrases and just letting them string themselves together. Once the poem was written I would turn from my computer and face the rising sun and read it aloud. That is when the faith came, that is when the understanding rushed in, that is when I cried with joy, when I said the words out loud.

One Day Saved

I see now that no matter who you are, what you've done or who you know, when you are born again, you become a new creature. Old things pass away. I've watched faith-filled and awestruck as the many things I clung to or relied upon melted away in this newfound fire of belief.

There is no confusion. All that serves faith is strengthened and all that serves fear is washed away. It's amazing to witness my life so effortlessly transformed. I felt and saw it immediately. I am filled as my life is emptied, humbled as my life, as I once knew it, is stripped away.

What a revelation those weekly reading assignments, mentoring sessions, and poems were. I would write little notes to myself during the week so I could remember the things I wanted to talk about. I came each week hungry to know and ready to learn. As though I were experimenting with a remedy, I'd put the concepts and ideas that we discussed to work. Was what he told me true? Well, all I had to do was try it. Nobody knew what I was doing anyway. I'd been flying by the seat of my pants for so long it had become natural to lean on my instincts and impulses, but now something was saying, "Wait, watch, listen, question, protect yourself, and then act." I loved it. Pastor named it "discernment." Interesting.

He warned me not to witness to people who came for massages or counseling; he said it wasn't fair or right to put them in that position.

"Nobody needs a zealot." He explained that when people were on my table they were vulnerable and I should respect that. He suggested that, instead, I simply live a good life and tell them my story if they asked. "Just be an inspiration," he added.

Pastor Don invited different pastors, preachers, and prophets to come to the church to teach, and they all prayed over me to stop smoking. A radio evangelist told me to "Go get that pack of cigarettes, wrap it up in duct tape, and write on it with a black marker that you have been delivered." I did that. I bought packs of cigarettes, took two out, and threw the rest out the truck window; I drowned cigarettes; I borrowed four cigarettes at a time from the Pakistani guy at the Mobil station every other day; I sat by the stream thinking of my dad smoking his Salems; I sneaked around to smoke when I was with church people; I brushed my teeth a dozen or more times a day to keep fresh breath; I forgave everyone who ever hurt me and prayed that they'd forgiven me; I pictured myself not smoking; I smoked organic tobacco; I quit every day for four years until finally, on October 30, 2003, I was done.

Pastor Don was right about me having a lot of crap in that beautiful pool of mine. And much of that crap was old, and dredging it up and out of that pool was some of the hardest work I've ever done, much harder than quitting cigarettes. And the work is not done. It's taking its own sweet time.

❧ Coda ❧

The Eagle and Julie Evans

A breeze brushes over me. I look up, and three feet above me is an eagle in flight. Awestruck, I arch backward and open my arms to this powerful being. It circles back and flies over me again. It feels as though we've found one another. I hear someone yelling at me. But I'm lost in a reverie and I can't make sense of the words.

"Get the hell out of the way," someone says.

I look around and there is my neighbor Steve. My communication with the eagle shudders to a stop. I lower my arms. I look up and see the eagle flying across Joy Road and circling through the cornfield. I glare at Steve. He points accusingly at my feet. I look down and see a bloody rabbit lying in front of me. I say nothing but get into my truck and drive away.

When I return home a few hours later I think about phoning Steve to tell him that the Cherokee blood running through my veins reveres eagles, and that I'd once rescued an eagle with a broken wing and taken care of him until he could fly again, and that maybe this was the same eagle.

But I don't bother to call and tell him that, or how I teach Native American studies, or that my cousin has just given me an eagle feather.

Instead, he calls me. "I see how much that eagle meant to you and it seemed like it really was talking to you. I just wanted to say I'm sorry I disturbed your time together," he says.

A few months later I get an e-mail message from one of my students who knows my neighbor. Attached is a photo of a large painting of a bald eagle flying over my driveway carrying a young woman in his talons with two onlookers: my neighbor, who is also the artist and paints himself as a bear wearing rain boots, and a very happy rabbit. And I'm smiling as the eagle, with a glint in its eye, carries me away.

I bought the painting and it hangs in my massage room. Steve named it *Endangered Species* and he told me that the name was as much about me as it was about the eagle.

Endangered Species, by Steve Sax, 2012.

This painting inspires me as I massage clients in my home studio.

☙ Book Club Questions ❧

1. What sort of upbringing did Julie Evans have?

2. Were Julie's mother and dad traditional parents?

3. Julie seemed to find "love" in a succession of relationships. Choose three of the boyfriends and discuss what each imparted to her journey.

4. Did Tanya's flamboyant lifestyle encourage Julie to expand her outlook on life?

5. Julie lived her life on two tracks: one was in a "fact-based" dimension and the other was in a parallel or spiritual universe. Was Julie successful in integrating the two tracks?

6. Julie's life was intercut with addictions to alcohol, drugs, and cigarettes. How did these impact her life and her journey?

7. Discuss why Norman suggested that Julie divorce Andrew.

8. Julie's road to recovery began with animal therapy. Discuss the ways in which her animal friends empowered her sense of responsibility for others—and for herself.

9. Julie met many memorable personalities on her journey. Which ones particularly appeal/speak to you, and why?

10. Discuss the pivotal steps that allowed Julie to break free of her addictions and live a clean life.

ↄ Acknowledgments ↄ

This is where I attempt to thank those who have graced the pages of my life. First and forever I thank God for being real and taking me by the hand and walking through this terrifying and gorgeous life with me. I thank my mom for being vulnerable and for coming every time I called; I thank my dad for inspiring me to trust what I had on hand to fix what lay broken before me; I thank the Zena Hamptons for holding onto me; I thank Pastor Don Moore for introducing me to Jesus and encouraging me to finish what I started; and I thank Steve Lewis for showing me what it takes to teach, to write, and to get through the breaking waves and into the healing waters. Thanks go to my writer friends Joanna Fitzpatrick, Ed McCann, Tom Nolan, Mihai Grunfield, Kathy Curto, Jeanne Marie Fleming, and Larry and Helise Winters for being good, honest writers and helping me craft my stories. I thank the good people of Woodstock, New York, for making this stop on my journey a place I can call home. I thank the animals that have loved and guided me throughout my life: Heather, Pogo, Omar, Happy, Spirit, Nina, Magic, Baby, Willi-Belle, Tinker, Alex, Mickey, Wingsy, Darlin, Gorgeous, Rocky—along with all the birds and dolphins, chipmunks and squirrels—and especially my darlings, Chickpea and Marietta. Thanks go to my first husband, Kenny, who had an opportunity to read this manuscript before he passed away. His words made the writing of it all worthwhile: "I had no idea, Babe." Thanks go to my second husband, Andrew, who went on to help people around the world. I give thanks to all those who have prayed for me and helped me live a good life: Libby Tomforde, Ron Lasner, Susan, Cary Kittner, Jackie Nau, Gloria Variale, Cheri and Barry SweetJackson, Maggie Landis, Linda Bergenn, Sank, and Regina Kassler. I thank Lisa Ceryanek, who gave me my first word processor, and Annette Clarke-Jervoise, who blew my mind when she gave me my first computer. To my coach, Rusty Bergen, thank you for everything. I thank Catharine Clarke and her team at Soul Garden Press for putting together the first edition of this book, and Steve Sax for the incredible eagle painting. And a triumphant blast of praise to my husband, Tommy Porto: thank you, sweetheart, for holding a space for me to tell this story.

❧

And now it's time to thank two extraordinary people, Julia and Weston Blelock, of WoodstockArts, for choosing to publish my memoir. Julia, you are a constellation of gifts and merits with your poise, bright mind, and deep spirit. And Weston, you are the star-maker with your keen insight and abundant imagination; thank you for finding me. It has been a joy to work with you and with Jane Broderick and Abigail Sturges to bring this hard-won memoir to life.

ℭ About the Author ℬ

The author at home
on Joy Road, 2017.

*Photo courtesy of
Dion Ogust.*

Julie Evans, MA, is a licensed massage therapist, ordained deacon, healer, and freelance writer. With her mission to help people transform their wellness into a way of life, Julie takes personal pain, loss, and disease in hand, assisting others to interpret what their bodies and minds are telling them. Julie is a writer and columnist for *Healthy You* magazine. Her work has also appeared in numerous other media, including *Pulse* magazine (Voices from the Heart of Medicine), *Fictionique*, NPR's *The Roundtable*, the *Woodstock Times*, and Writers Read Online. With her upcoming writing projects—"Truly Julie: The Naked Truth" and "Visits with Vera"—Julie will offer recipes for hope and healing.

Julie grew up in Rochester, Minnesota, home to the world-renowned Mayo Clinic. Today she lives in Woodstock, New York, with her husband, Tommy Porto, and their cat, Marietta.

www.wordsbyjulieevans.com
www.voicebyjulieevans.com
www.massagebyjulieevans.com